Neil C.

# *A VILLAGE IN TIME*

# 1660 – 1990

### Discovering American History in a
### Small Virginia Quaker Village

# Neil C. Hughes

*To*
*Ellen,*
*Best Wishes*
*Neil Hughes*

**Library of Congress Cataloging-in-Publication Data**

Names: Hughes, Neil C., 1936- author.
Title: A village in time, 1660-1990 : discovering American history in a small Virginia Quaker village / Neil C. Hughes.
Other titles: Discovering American history in a small Virginia Quaker village
Description: Wellesley, MA : Branden Books, [2017] | Includes bibliographical references and index.
Identifiers: LCCN 2017036397 (print) | LCCN 2017037116 (ebook) ISBN 9780828326681 (E-Book) | ISBN 9780828326674 (pbk. : alk. paper)
Subjects: LCSH: Waterford (Va.)--History. | Historic buildings--Virginia--Waterford.
Classification: LCC F234.W266 (ebook) | LCC F234.W266 H84 2017 (print) | DDC
   975.5/28--dc23
LC record available at https://lccn.loc.gov/2017036397

ISBN 9780828326674 Paperback
ISBN 9780828326681 E-Book

Branden Books
PO Box 812094
Wellesley, MA 02482

Book orders:   *branden@brandenbooks.com*
               *Amazon.com*

Dedicated to
The People of Waterford, Virginia
Past and Present, and,
to
Kathleen

# CONTENTS

# PREFACE

I discovered American history on my own doorstep after a long career working in twenty-five countries as an international finance specialist with the World Bank. For the past 30 years, I have lived in an 1819 house in the National Historic Landmark village of Waterford Virginia, a beautiful old town just 45 miles from Washington, D.C. in northern Loudoun County, miraculously preserved in time.

*A Village in Time, 1660-1990,* grew out of my research into the people who built and lived in my own house and village. I discovered that, historic persons I "met" from Waterford, knew someone more famous outside the village. In 1744, John Hough, the grandfather of Samuel Hough, who later built my house, left Bucks County, Pennsylvania and settled in what would become the town of Waterford. As a senior surveyor for Lord Fairfax, John Hough befriended and mentored young surveyor George Washington, who then forged his military career in the French and Indian War, particularly in the battle of Braddock Heights about twenty miles from Waterford. Both Washington and Hough were visionaries who became partners in attempting to develop water access to the Midwest through their Patowmack Canal Co.

As I wrote about these people, the book became much more than the story of a house. It grew into the story of how one ordinary Virginia town, Waterford, came into being and got caught up in the extraordinary events that both divided and defined America from the mid-17th to the late-20th century—300 years of American history.

One of the first buildings built in Waterford was a grist mill. Early mechanization and soil-enriching techniques enabled the local Quakers to produce the world's finest flour, "American Super Fine," and become exporters to Europe, the West Indies, and South America. Yet these prosperous wheat farmers were as affected as the rest of America during the "Panic of 1819," America's first boom-and-bust business cycle, when the price of flour tumbled 60 percent over three years.

President Thomas Jefferson—whose library included Loudoun County farmer John Binn's *Treatise on Practical Farming,* which extolled local Quakers' revolutionary agricultural methods––defined a national consensus that "agriculture, manufactures, commerce, and navigation, the four pillars of our prosperity, are the most thriving when left most free to individual enterprise." Looking back, I question whether this pursuit of "individual enterprise" has led to a belief in "individual entitlement," and distrust of any government regulation that hinders the pursuit of self-interest, that persists today.

Before the Civil War, as slavery was banned by the Society of Friends, but not the country, some Waterford Quakers became part of a Great Migration from the East to the Midwest, and then on to the far West. The town itself became a haven for freed slaves who feared being kidnapped and "sold south," as well as a nest of "damned abolitionists" according to its slave-holding neighbors. Their anger turned to hatred during the Civil War, when the U.S. Government commissioned Waterford's Independent Loudoun Rangers as the only Union Army unit mustered in Virginia. Waterford also became a favorite target for John Mosby and his partisan rangers.

After the war, like much of rural America, Waterford was left behind by the rise of cities, where money and political power became concentrated. Cheaper mass produced goods shipped by railroad from the cities meant the end of local industry. Cyclical financial "panics" periodically brought Waterford's economy to its knees; and in the Great Depression, the town was bankrupt and lost its charter.

Because Waterford is nestled in the foothills of the Catoctin Mountains, neither railroad nor major highway passed through it. Many of its historic structures fell into decay. It was a forgotten rural enclave, and this ironically preserved it in time.

In the 1940s, paved highways, and the family car brought a new generation of settlers eager to restore and preserve their new historic village. Their grassroots efforts in the formation of the Waterford Foundation in 1943 led to the U.S. Department of the Interior's 1970 designation of the 1,420-acre Waterford National Historic Landmark, the nation's highest designation for historic property. Rapid growth in Loudoun County, Virginia, still threatens Historic Waterford, but residents of the village, stewards of their own historic homes, and the Waterford Foundation and its supporters work hard to preserve it.

After reading *A Village in Time,* I hope you will discover how small towns like Waterford are, in author Bill Bryson's words, "where history ends up," and join other preservationists in helping keep history alive in these charming old streets and buildings where so much of American history can still be found.

# Chapter 1
# A Simple Quaker House

**"Houses are where history ends up"—Bill Bryson, author of**
*At Home: A Short History of Private Life"*

Like Bill Bryson, I believed that by discovering how my old house came into being, I would come to know its builder, Samuel Hough. My interest in the architecture of the house, led me to the archives of the Loudoun County Courthouse and the Waterford Foundation, as well as records at Leesburg's John Balch Library and other sources, to discover more. I found that he was born in 1779, the son of John Hough Jr. and Lydia Hollingsworth, who were married at Waterford's Fairfax Quaker Meeting House in 1772. Little is known of his early life, except that his father, John Jr., who died suddenly when Samuel was 13 years old, left no will. When his wealthy grandfather, John Hough Sr. died in 1797 at age 77, he left his grandson Samuel 50 pounds to be paid on his twenty-first birthday.

In 1819, when Samuel built my house for his mother, Lydia, he had become a successful landowner and mill owner. However, he was about to suffer financially in the "Panic of 1819," which is considered to be the first boom-and-bust business cycle in American history. It affected everyone, from wealthy banker and landowner, to the most humble trader and holder of a mortgage on a log cabin. Samuel Hough sold this house to his mother in 1820, and she paid him the incredible sum of $3,500—neighboring houses would sell for one-half that amount.

What Lydia did was provide Samuel with money he undoubtedly needed because the Panic had seriously impacted his many entrepreneurial activities. The speculative fever in land and investments, in new production, especially cotton, which had been going on for decades, was brought to a sudden halt by a fall in cotton prices of 60 percent between 1818-19, when British investors shifted to Indian cotton. The price per barrel of American Superfine Flour produced by Samuel Hough's Beaverdam Mill near Waterford, fell 65 percent.

Lydia had grown up in Winchester, Virginia, and Samuel made sure the house reflected Winchester architectural styles of that period. The hall is the most important room in the house, and runs the entire length of the original house, making it appear bigger than it is. I sent photographs of the house to Calder Loth, who was Virginia's Senior Architectural Historian. He wrote to me that "the woodwork is quite remarkable; much more elaborate than one would expect in an otherwise simple village house." The stair spandrel with its large radiating panels is "unique and very striking" and "a real display of design ingenuity and craftsmanship." He also singled out the band of ovals and diamonds accented by punches, which frame the panels as "unique in my experience," and the sunburst frieze wainscot below the stair windows as "a rarely seen and very fine extra effort at decoration."

Loth identified the fireplace mantels as typical of the Federal period, yet "quite sophisticated, with the cornice and frieze breaking above the pilasters and central panel." He says the sharp moldings under the top cornice are based on Greek Doric columns, similar to those at the Parthenon. Loth believed these decorative concepts came to Waterford from the Winchester, Virginia area, and he suggested the interior woodwork "may well have been executed by a Winchester Joiner."

Lydia Hollingsworth Hough was a well-liked member of the Women's Meeting, and was very active in its affairs. She was often selected to represent the Fairfax Meeting at Quarterly Meetings in Baltimore. She served on nominating committees to find good candidates for the positions of Elder, Overseer, and Clerk. She helped determine if any impediments existed to marriages expected to take place at Meeting, and to reason with young women who married non-Quakers to "return to discipline." Unfortunately, she was unable to prevent her own children from marrying "out of unity" and being separated from the Quaker faith.

Although he was a member of Waterford's Fairfax Quaker Meeting, Samuel Hough seemed quite willing to challenge Quaker orthodoxy and discipline if it interfered with his ambitions. In 1817, he violated Quaker discipline by marrying a non-Quaker, Jane Gray Edwards, who was much younger than he was. In 1818, he violated Quaker Discipline again by becoming a justice of the peace. He was charged with "accepting the office of magistrate in the exercise of which he had administered oaths" and "accomplishing his marriage contrary to discipline with a woman not in membership with friends," and was finally disowned in 1819 after four months of unsuccessful "friendly persuasion."

Most of Samuel's siblings were as rebellious as he. Brother Isaac continued to be "the black sheep of the family," and was disowned for "attending places of diversion, being guilty of fornication, being charged by a woman as the father of her illegitimate child, which he does not deny." Sister Sarah was disowned in 1803 for "having become the mother of an illegitimate child (a daughter)." In 1820, she "united herself to the Methodist Society." Sister Elizabeth Hough Donaldson was disowned in 1815 "for accomplishing her marriage contrary to the discipline with a man not in membership with us, she being removed with her husband to the state of Ohio." Sister Rachel was disowned in 1798 for "unchaste company," and for marrying Levi James "out of unity." Rachel joined the Evangelical Reformed Church. Their sons John and David were born before they moved to Cincinnati, Ohio in 1816. Levi James became one of the first entrepreneurs to build and operate steamboats on the Ohio River going from Cincinnati to New Orleans and back. Only sister Mary never married and apparently never transgressed.

In 1816, Samuel's mother, sisters, and brother-in-law lent Samuel a total of $9,000, which enabled him to buy from his mother180 acres of the Hollingsworth Farm which her father Isaac had purchased from George William Fairfax in 1757 and left to her in 1759. On the following day, Samuel sold the land to two trustees, who were instructed to sell the land to the highest bidder on March 1, 1823 if Samuel had not repaid the $9,000 by September

1, 1822. The land was held in trust for Samuel until he was able to pay these debts or defaulted on them, enabling him to operate the farm and mill for four years without having title or having to pay his debts.

There are no known likenesses of either Samuel or Lydia Hough. Two sisters who have been frequent visitors to the house, and who indicate they both have the gift of "seeing" what others do not, say they have glimpsed a woman in a long, high-collared blue dress, with her hair pulled tightly back, standing on the main staircase landing. Unfortunately, she cannot be Lydia, who, according to custom, would have been wearing a plain white Quaker bonnet, and would never wear a blue dress. Quaker women avoided the color blue because it was derived from dye produced by slave labor used in harvesting the indigo plant.

During 1816-1828 Samuel Hough corresponded with his nephew, John Hough James, who lived in Cincinnati, Ohio. Letters written in 1816-1819 reveal that Samuel's behavior in the acquisition of the Hollingsworth family farm had caused a major break with his Ohio siblings and their spouses. In the letter dated December 10, 1816, Samuel wrote:

> I understand there is a good deal of displeasure expressed by some of my Cincinnati relation on the part which I have acted in relation to this property [Beaverdam Mills]—none of them seem disposed to write even in answer to my writing—But if I have acted an unjustifiable part I have never as yet been convinced of it neither do I ever expect to be, yet I am open to correction, time will explain my motives.

Samuel wrote again to John Hough James on February 14, 1818, insisting that "I can convince any unprejudiced mind of the *correctness* of my conduct...I can lay my hand upon my breast and say, in the presence of the Most High God, that I believe that I was governed by no other motive than that of justice towards every member of the family."

A year later, Samuel's unhappiness had become an obsession. He complained bitterly to his nephew, "I have felt anxious to receive a letter from *you* as the *rest a*re I believe sworn foes to writing to me," and "I fear the Devil has taken possession so far of some of my dearly beloved relations there." He goes on, quoting Shakespeare's Brutus on "ambition" in *Julius Caesar*; stating that "I have been falsely accused," and concluding "it is impossible for us all to think alike concerning certain of our pecuniary affairs." He acknowledged that "I should write to your dear mother this time but that I expect you can answer my letter with less inconvenience than she could—I know not how it is indeed that I have never written her since I left there...for she continues as she ever has been my favorite sister." In 1820, Samuel Hough paid back his sisters and brother-in-law the $1,000 he owed each of them.

Samuel Hough graphically described in an 1821 letter to John Hough James what appears to have been the first major epidemic to strike Waterford:

> ...the most melancholy season on acc't of disease that we have ever experienced in this country...the prevailing epidemic of the neighborhood [was] Bilious fever [typhoid]... scarcely ½ doz. persons have escaped the disease and the country around has not been much if any more favour'd.

What seems shocking today is the multiple deaths in individual families mentioned in the letter:

> David Janney and his wife both died and left a family of children 5 or 6 in number...our cousin Phoebe Steer & her child, Mrs. John Lacey and Lacey's sister Ann...Wm Wright, his wife and their son Wm...Mr. Low, his wife and child...three of Obed Cooksey's boys were buried in one grave...Two or three out of a family was no uncommon loss.

Samuel Hough and his own family escaped death but were very ill:

> Your Aunt Jane (Samuel's wife) has had several attacks as also our little son. As for myself, I have become accustom'd to the Bilious fever...within 15 months I have been bedfast or in a convalescent state in all about 6 mos...my actual confinement within this time is about 100 days...I have had 5 relapses but with the all sustaining hand of Divine Providence we are once more restored to health.

Typhoid fever is caused by various strains of the *baccillum salmonella typhi.* Humans ingested the disease though food and drink. In the early 19th century, most physicians treated the disease using the "allopathic system," based on blood-letting and ingesting "calomel," a mercury-based medicine. Although many patients died of mercury poisoning, the vast majority of the medical profession believed large doses of a powerful metal like mercury could cure most ailments. The medical profession seemed little improved since the end of the 16th century, when British naturalist Sir Francis Bacon complained that "the remedy is worse than the disease." During the Civil War, typhoid fever accounted for almost as many deaths as battle wounds.

From 1816 to 1832, Samuel and Jane Hough lived on the original Hollingsworth Mill Farm, renamed Beaverdam Mills Farm, after the creek three miles north of Waterford upon which his property was located. He moved his Catoctin Woolen Manufactory to his Beaverdam property, and renamed it Beaverdam Woolen Manufactory. He advertised it in Leesburg's *Genius of Liberty* as the best in receiving "wool to be manufactured or carded, or country cloth to be fulled and finished...with dispatch, and in the best manner," offering customers who had come some distance to simply wait for their product, rather than having to return again. He emphasized the efficiency of his plant in avoiding "delays and disappointments, incident to the dry season" because his two large (15 feet in diameter) overshot water wheels were backed up by "a tread wheel of the best construction, by means of which the power of eight horses or oxen can be applied in cooperation with the water."

He claimed his manufactory was a fully integrated operation, in which he "embraced the manufacturing of cloths, casinetts, fulled linsey, women's do. [domestic] blankets full or half width, carpeting, etc., etc." Since most women made clothing for their families, his mill provided services such as "wool carding, weaving, fulling and dying...in the neatest manner and with the greatest dispatch." In the absence of cash, payment could be made in "soap, lard and wool." The customer also had to provide "one pound of lard, or a pint of oil," for every eight pounds of wool they brought to be carded."

Samuel described his flour mill as "a strong framed building, with two runs of French burr mill stones with [Oliver] Evans's machinery complete quality"—indicating his mill was a fully mechanized merchant mill capable of producing American Super Fine flour for export. Mahlon Janney's Old Mill in Waterford and Israel Janney's mill on Goose Creek near Lincoln were also producing American Superfine Flour for export. Waterford and neighboring farmers and mill owners were at the forefront of America's agricultural and industrial revolution.

The Samuel Hough House stayed in the family when Lydia Hough sold it to daughters Mary and Sarah in 1830 for a dollar. Lydia died shortly thereafter. The census of 1830 lists five slaves as Samuel Hough's property, evidence he violated another basic tenet of his Quaker origins. In 1832-33, Samuel and Jane sold all 180 acres of the Beaverdam Mill Farm to Andrew Graham for $8,191. Samuel Hough also put up for auction his 450 acre Edwards Ferry tract north of Leesburg, 165 acres adjacent to and north of Waterford, and several lots in town. Two of the properties did not sell, and were once again up for sale in 1835, when Samuel informed the public he was "intending to move to the West." In 1836, Samuel Hough put up for sale his "Leesburg house and goods, first rate riding horses, an excellent milch cow, and unless otherwise disposed of, a family of NEGROES." "Unless otherwise disposed of," were code words for willingness to break up the family if it could not be sold as a unit. Unfortunately, we do not know the fate of this family. Slave-owner Samuel Hough had strayed far from his Quaker roots.

In 1837, Samuel Hough, his wife Jane, their teenage son, sisters Mary and Sarah, and Sarah's daughter Pleasant, became part of the great East-West movement, which was spurred by the creation of the non-slave Northwest Territory, a transportation revolution, a flood of new immigrants, and government sale of millions of acres of western land after the subjugation and forced removal of American Indians from their ancestral lands. Samuel Hough must have reconciled himself with his Ohio relatives, and it is likely Cincinnati was his destination.

My heartfelt thanks to Bronwen and John Souders, who shared with me an unpublished historic document, *Descendents of John Hough Jr.,* and a copy of *Samuel Hough, Letters 1816-1828 to John Hough James,* Walter Havighurst Special Collection, Miami University Libraries, Oxford Ohio.

# Chapter 2
# A Litany of Transgressions

**"I have not been able to get from [the Carters] a list of the land they hold"**
**—Thomas, Sixth Lord Fairfax**

The story of Waterford begins on land in the Sixth Lord Fairfax's Northern Neck Proprietary after the Treaty of Albany in 1722 forced the Native Americans living there to move west of the Blue Ridge Mountains.

In 1728, Thomas, Sixth Lord Fairfax, who had been ignored by his father and mistrusted by his mother, was finally able to assume full control and management of the Fairfax estate in Virginia. In 1724, his mother's agent, Robert Carter, had acquired 41,660 acres of the Bull Run Tract. In 1727, Carter's son, Robert Jr., had acquired the 11,375 acre "Goose Creek" tract, spanning both sides of today's Route 15 south of Leesburg. Lord Fairfax decided to keep employing Robert Carter.

In 1731, two of Robert Carter's other sons, Landon and George Carter, acquired 13,278 acres of Northern Neck land. Although Landon (20 years old) and George (13 years old) were minors, and not legally competent to purchase the land, it made no difference to their father. The grand total of these Carter family acquisitions of Northern Neck Proprietary land in what is now Loudoun County, was an astonishing 66,313 acres. Yet Carter family land acquisitions in other parts of the Proprietary, especially the Shenandoah Valley, were far greater.

Carter had a problem, however. His tenants claimed the north branch of the Rappahannock River was the southern boundary of the Northern Neck Proprietary, and not the south branch. Tenants who lived in between the two branches refused to pay their quit rents. These settlers were supported by William Gooch, who became Virginia's Lieutenant Governor in 1727.

Lieutenant Governor William Gooch was proving to be a difficult adversary. He argued that the Colony of Virginia, not Lord Fairfax, owned the Shenandoah Valley. Nine hundred square miles of excellent land was at stake, and the "Valley" had become a grand prize being sought after by Lord Baltimore, the sons of William Penn, the Sixth Lord Fairfax, and the Colony of Virginia. All their claims were based upon which branches of the Potomac and Rappahannock Rivers defined the Northern Neck Proprietary. The recurring theme in all these disputes was that no adequate survey or map existed which could settle these claims.

Procedures for acquiring land consumed both time and money. A buyer would have to apply for a *warrant* (for Northern Neck Proprietary lands owned by Lord Fairfax), or an *order in council* (for other Virginia lands owned by the King); pay for a survey, plat, and other fees; present proof that the land was settled; and then pay *annual quit rents* of ten shillings per 100 acres. Ten shillings was one-half a pound and a lot of money. Many settlers in the wilderness of the Proprietary had never seen ten shillings. These included the victims of Britain's Civil War (first Cavaliers, then Puritans); Ulster "Scotch-Irish" who left the Emerald Isle for religious or economic reasons; Scottish Highlanders forced to leave their homeland after the abortive Jacobite Revolts of 1715 and 1745; as well as debtors and persons convicted of certain felonies, who were condemned to "transportation" to the Colonies, where they served a seven year term as indentured servants. After their indenture, they took any job available, living day-to-day in abject poverty. Farmers who did not have the funds to purchase the land outright could lease it for a lifetime, provided they built a "patent" or "lease" house measuring 16 by 20 feet with a masonry chimney. They were also required to plant an apple orchard of 100 trees.

The Episcopal or Anglican Church was the only established religion of colonial Virginia until 1698, when the English Parliament passed the Act of Toleration, and Virginia followed suit in

1699. Victims from Europe's religious wars of the Reformation and religious dissenters of all kinds headed for America. British Quakers, French Huguenots, German Lutherans, and followers of John Hus from Moravia (part of today's Czech Republic), who were bound together by strong religious and cultural ties and supported each other in their own communities, were much more successful in establishing themselves on Virginia's wild frontier. They were also encouraged to do so by Virginia's colonial government, which was promoting frontier settlements as a buffer against possible Indian attacks against the settled eastern part of the state, as well as providing a barrier to stop slaves hoping to escape into the wilderness.

All these new immigrants were clamoring for land. In 1730-31, Virginia's Colonial Council issued orders in council for 270,000 acres of land to the north and south of the forks of the Shenandoah River. Robert Carter, representing Lord Fairfax, vigorously opposed the Council's actions because the land involved was located within the Northern Neck Proprietary. The still unresolved question was who held the King's patent? It all seemed a huge gamble, because no one knew how Britain's Privy Council would rule.

In 1732, while turning the pages of *The Gentleman's Magazine* at his club in London, Lord Fairfax was astonished to read that Robert Carter had died after accumulating 300,000 acres of Northern Neck Proprietary land, 1,000 slaves and 1,000 pounds in cash. At the time, Lord Fairfax was unaware that Carter's relatives had also acquired thousands of acres more. Fairfax had two close relatives in America's Colonial Customs. One was his former guardian Bryan Fairfax, who was a Commissioner of the Customs, and the other his first cousin and boyhood friend, William Fairfax, who was a Collector of Customs in Massachusetts. William agreed to act as Lord Fairfax's agent, and Bryan had William transferred to the South Potomac District Customs Office, which was responsible for the Northern Neck Proprietary. Unlike Robert Carter, William Fairfax was not given the authority to sell land. His job was to collect the monies due the Proprietary, and restore its financial viability.

William Fairfax proved to be a wise selection. His letters to Lord Fairfax revealed a litany of transgressions committed by Robert Carter: falsified and unreliable accounts; "exorbitant land grants and unpaid loans" to Carter's relatives; "very imperfect rent rolls" reflecting nonpayment of quit rents; land grant documents signed by Carter and left blank for later insertions; "warrants of survey" issued by Carter to favored brokers who would then seek out buyers and split the profits with Carter, whose relatives did not pay quit rents, in violation of the grant's conditions.

Further speculation was forestalled by Lord Fairfax's stopping *all* Northern Neck Proprietary land sales. The selling of Proprietary land would not begin again until new surveys and maps established the true boundaries of the Proprietary, and they were accepted by Britain's Privy Council. In February 1735, Fairfax was able to "kiss his Majesty's hand," and sail for Virginia on the appropriately named ship *George*.

Lord Fairfax was a plain man, in both looks and clothes. This attribute was reflected in the wardrobe he took with him, which was limited to a silk coat, waistcoat, and breeches, a cloth waistcoat, a ruffle waistcoat, a drab coat and breeches, two pairs of everlasting breeches, a horseman's coat, twelve each of shirts, stocks (close fitting bands or cravats worn around the neck), nightcaps and handkerchiefs, six pairs each of thread, worsted and silk stockings, two pairs of Doncaster stockings, a dozen gloves, six thin silk caps, two bob periwigs, and a piece of black ribbon.

When Fairfax arrived in Virginia, he found thousands of acres set aside by planters for their own future use, and thousands more held by greedy speculators. But Fairfax was in no position to antagonize the Carters, arguably the most prominent and powerful family in Virginia at the time, or members of Virginia's other "First Families," many of whom had acquired large grants of land from Carter.

His other adversary was Lieutenant Governor Gooch, who had issued patents for 300,000 acres of land in the Proprietary. The same families who had benefited from Carter's agency dominated Virginia's Colonial Council. Fairfax's strength lay in his close relationship to the British Crown, but he was out of favor of Parliament, which was dominated by his enemy Sir Robert Walpole.

Lord Fairfax set out to win supporters to his cause. He was determined, but mild-mannered, and had great personal charm. He insisted his argument was not with the settlers, but with the colonial government, because it questioned the validity of his royal grant. He named a son of Robert Carter and an important Northern Neck land speculator as two of his three commissioners. In 1736, he had his lawyer draft a bill for the Virginia General Assembly making all and every grant of the "Proprietary" binding by law. This ruling recognized the land grants made by the State of Virginia, and satisfied both speculators and settlers.

Virginia's Council promptly approved the bill and sent it to England, recommending approval by the Privy Council. Ironically, after Britain's Privy Council reaffirmed Lord Fairfax's royal title to the Northern Neck Proprietary in 1745, he changed his mind and sued Northern Neck landowners who had been granted land by the State.

England's Privy Council forbade Virginia Governor Gooch from issuing any patents until the boundary disputes were resolved. The survey of the Northern Neck Proprietary was finally completed in 1736. The surveyors had to climb the Catoctin, Blue Ridge, and Allegheny mountains to reach the headwaters of the Potomac River. They struggled through thick forests and treacherous swamps—home to bear, wildcat, panther, buffalo, elk, deer, wild turkey, grouse, quail, beaver, fox, diamond-backed rattlesnake, copperhead, and cottonmouth moccasin. There were no roads. They traveled by canoe when possible, but most of the time, had to follow their compass bearings overland, either by Indian and buffalo trails—which were simply openings through dense vegetation and around or over natural barriers—or by breaking trail themselves.

The pack horses suffered more than the surveyors. One party even abandoned their horses, which were exhausted and unable to continue. Men and horses suffered injuries, some of them serious. They often ran out of food, and had to live off the land. The occasional deer or small game was not enough, and they became so hungry they would eat their food half-cooked. While crossing swamps, they had to prevent their hungry horses from eating poisonous laurel leaves.

Colonel William Byrd II, president of the County Council and an explorer in his own right, remarked after reading their reports that they were "almost reduced to cutting up the most useless person among them to support and save the lives of the rest." Similar problems were encountered in the Rappahannock survey. Nevertheless, new maps for both rivers were completed in 1737.

Lord Fairfax still had to convince the British Parliament to accept the boundaries and re-affirm his royal grant. He sailed for England in 1737, and would not return to Virginia until 1747. Fairfax's petition to the Privy Council made little progress so long as Robert Walpole was prime minister. It was not until 1745, when Fairfax's representative met with the Privy Council and reminded those learned gentlemen that the King could do no wrong and the King's words in the royal patent explicitly stated that the boundaries of the Northern Neck Proprietary were the "first heads or springs" of the Potomac and Rappahannock.

The Privy Council agreed, and fixed the Proprietary boundaries at the "first springs" of both the Potomac's north branch, and the Rappahannock's south branch. It was a great victory for Lord Fairfax. In 1746, the north-south boundary, "Fairfax Line," between the two great rivers was established, completing the survey. The surveyors were led by Colonel Peter Jefferson, Thomas Jefferson's father. Colonel Jefferson had a stone marker erected and the initials "PJ" carved on beech trees on both sides of the head spring of the Potomac. They celebrated by killing and roasting a deer, and toasting King George.

Lord Fairfax established his home on the frontier, ten miles southeast of Winchester, where he first built a simple one-room log cabin, and then his wooden "mansion" house, Greenway Court, with four gables, two stone chimneys, and two wooden bell towers.

The house was near the Ashby Gap-Winchester road, and Fairfax erected a white post so visitors would know when to turn off. Since then, there have been many generations of white posts, and the current one marks the present village of the same name.

Fairfax was in many ways a solitary man, and lived with his nephew, Thomas Bryan Martin, who became his close companion and assistant. When he had visitors, he often slept apart in a log cabin. A housekeeper did the cooking and cleaning. Business required him to visit Williamsburg regularly, and he often visited "Bellvoir," his nephew William's plantation house on the Potomac, where he met 15-year-old George Washington in 1747. Fairfax was favorably impressed.

When George Washington qualified as a county surveyor for Culpeper County in 1749, Fairfax hired him to make extensive surveys along the Cacapon and Lost Rivers. Fairfax also invited young George to live at Greenway Court, where Washington stayed during the time he worked for Fairfax. Washington had access to Lord Fairfax's library, and made good use of it. Samuel Hough's grandfather, John Hough, who was a surveyor for Lord Fairfax, befriended young Washington, and became a close confidant of his for 50 years.

Although there is no record of any woman in Lord Fairfax's life, he was no celibate. Among his surviving papers is a receipt dated February 27, 1777, for "ten shilling on the Lordship account for bring a negro wench to bed." Fairfax was 83 years old. One woman who did become devoted to Fairfax was Mrs. Polly Ann Green, a very devout Methodist who nursed him through a series of illnesses. She was forever grateful to Fairfax because he had donated 10 acres to her congregation on which to build a church. While ministering to Fairfax, she once mentioned she had visited Hades, had seen him there, and would pray for him. Lord Fairfax died at Greenway Court in 1781.

# Chapter 3
# Settlers and Speculators

**"[My] acknowledgement of the said Jemima['s] right of Dower"—George the Second, By the Grace of God of Great Britain, France, and Ireland King, Defender of the Faith**

The French Enlightenment philosopher Voltaire appropriately likened the Society of Friends to the first Christians because they avoided sacraments, dogmas, temples, altars, and images of Jesus Christ. Friends and early Christians followed the Judaic and Muslim tradition that God was to be worshipped in spirit and truth and not represented in any way. Jesus was first represented in human form only when the Romans, who personified their numerous gods, included a likeness of Jesus in their pantheon.

Friends became known as "Quakers," after their founder, George Fox, was called a "Quaker" by an English judge, and Fox retorted by telling his honor he too should "tremble at the word of the Lord." When Quakers came together for worship or business, with men on one side and women on the other, they called their gatherings "meetings." Quakers believed God was a living presence, who did not dwell in temples made by human hands, but in people's hearts. Meetings for worship were silent, except when the Holy Spirit inspired an individual to share his or her thoughts with others. In England, the expression "Sunday Meeting" became a term of ridicule for all worship services dissenting from the Anglican faith.

In the 17th century, the Society of Friends had almost been destroyed by its enemies due to the excesses of some of its members, and George Fox felt the Society had no choice but to strictly regulate the behavior of its members under threat of disownment. Quaker "Christian testimony and discipline" was enforced through a system of annual, quarterly, and monthly meetings. Although the

Society of Friends continued to gain many followers, it lost many others who could not deal with the tensions arising from worship based on individual spiritual development, while adhering to a discipline that rigidly controlled individual behavior.

Quakers were not welcome in 17th century Virginia. The Virginia Assembly passed legislation that "made it [a crime] for any master of a vessel to bring a Quaker into the state; ordered those already here, and such as should come thereafter, to be imprisoned until they should abjure." In the early 18th century, they were allowed to practice their religion, and Amos Janney and his family were the first Quakers to settle in what would eventually become Waterford. (Author's Note: the land upon which the village of Waterford was established, was part of Stafford County until 1728, Prince William County to 1742, Fairfax County until 1759, and Loudoun County thereafter).

The Janneys would have needed a certificate from the Falls Meeting, to which they belonged in Bucks County, Pennsylvania, giving them permission to travel to Virginia. Once in Virginia, they had to present the certificate to the nearest Friends monthly meeting, which happened to be the East Nottingham Meeting in what is today Calvert, Maryland. The Janneys left the Falls Meeting in Bucks County, Pennsylvania, with a Certificate dated March 3, 1733. Amos' visit to the East Nottingham Meeting is confirmed in the minutes of the June 17th 1734 East Nottingham Meeting: "At our Moly Meeting of E. Nottingham held ye 17th day of ye 6th month 1734.Amos Janney produced a Certificate to this Meeting for ye ffals Moly Meeting in Bucks County, bearing date of ye 3rd Mo, 1733 for himself & Wife Recommending them to this Meeting as Members in Unity, they now living in Virginia."

The Register of Pennsylvania, vol. III, p.134, edited by Samuel Hazard in 1831, contained this account:

> About the year 1733, Amos Janney from Bucks County, and soon after divers other Friends, settled about 40 miles lower in Virginia than Opeckon [Opequan], who obtained leave to hold a meeting for worship on First Days, which

was held at the said Amos Janney's and other Friends houses till the year 1741, when a piece of land was purchased and a meeting house built, called Fairfax, where meetings are held twice a week.

Although the Great Philadelphia Wagon Road from the port of Philadelphia to Augusta, Georgia, was not completed until about 1750, it is likely the Janneys would have traveled the same route: southwest across the Susquehanna River; west through Lancaster and York, Pennsylvania; heading south across Antietam Creek, crossing the Potomac River at Harpers Ferry; then on to Opequan. Hopewell Meeting in Winchester gave Janney permission to settle in the Virginia piedmont and to establish a preparatory meeting. In 1744, Hopewell Meeting granted independent status to the newly-named Fairfax Monthly Meeting in the village named Janneys' Mill (now Waterford).

Meanwhile, land speculation fever in the Northern Neck Proprietary had reached what is now northwestern Loudoun County. Major speculators did not even live in the county. No one knew more about land transactions than Catesby Cocke, who was clerk of court successively for Stafford County (1728), Prince William County (1731) and Fairfax County (1742). In 1731, Catesby Cocke acquired 703 acres, which included the future Waterford. Cocke and partner John Mercer returned to the Waterford area during 1739-43, acquiring 7,473 acres east of Waterford, extending to Taylorstown in the north and almost to Leesburg in the southeast.

Between 1731-39, speculator John Colville acquired some 16,000 acres of land between the north and south forks of Catoctin Creek (the so-called "Kittocton Tract"), including 900 acres on the south side of Amos Janney's Waterford farm. Colville's land purchases in what is today northwestern Loudoun County eventually totaled some 46,000 acres.

Colville had made his money as a ship captain carrying indentured servants, slaves, and other goods. He was involved in the dark side of the international trade in human beings, and was known to carry passengers, both black and white, who had not come aboard voluntarily. To all appearances Colville was a pillar of the community. Legal documents described him as a "gentleman." He was a vestryman in the Presbyterian Church, a colonel in the Militia, and represented Prince William County in the Virginia House of Burgesses during 1744-47. He counted Lord Thomas Fairfax and his lordship's cousin, William Fairfax, among his friends.

Colville never married, but lived secretly with several women. In 1752, a grand jury found he had lived "in fornication" with Mary Carney. When he died land rich but cash poor in 1756, "he left a paper trail of personal faults and financial shortcomings." His will mentioned another woman living with him: his freed indentured servant Mary Foster, and their illegitimate daughter, Catherine. Colville was deeply indebted (and related by marriage) to Charles Bennett, Earl of Tankerville, whom he made executor of his estate. Colville's will convey to the earl some 15,000 acres of his "Kittocton Tract."

When Amos Janney actually purchased the property that included the future Waterford cannot be confirmed in any existing document. In 1733, Cocke sold the land to another speculator, John Meade, who divided the land into two parcels. The southern parcel of 400 acres, which would become Waterford and Talbot Farm, was sold to Amos Janney. (Author's note: Prince William County Deed Book C 1735-38, which would have listed this transaction, has been lost, although Amos Janney *is* mentioned as receiving title in a undated transaction listed as "Mead to Janney" in the Prince William County Deeds Abstracts 1740-1764 p.400-401). Amos Janney was a talented surveyor, and became a speculator, buying 4,720 acres of land for investment purposes during 1740-44.

Capt. John Minor's deed dated 5th of March, 1743 to Amos Janney, yeoman, for 1,373 acres on the south fork of "Kittockton"(near today's town of Round Hill) is of particular interest because it sheds light on the property rights of women during the early 18th century. Under English common law, a husband could sell land his wife brought to their marriage only after she had signed the deed, and declared in private she did so of her own free will.

Amos Janney's deed therefore contained an addendum entitled "Commission to Examine the Femme," in which Britain's king "GEORGE the second by the grace of God of Great Britain France and Ireland King defender of the faith" addressed four gentlemen from Loudoun County:

> Greeting, know ye that we trusting to your fidelity and provident circumspection in privately examining  Jemima the wife of John Minor gent apart from her said husband... And receiving the acknowledgement of the said Jemima of her right of Dower in the said land her Consent in manner aforesaid being first given and declared We therefore command you or any two of you that at a certain time or place you shall appoint you shall cause to come before you the said Jemima & her privately to examine touching the premises aforesaid and acknowledgment given.

Although today it seems remarkable that a reigning British sovereign would have any interest in the affairs of a land speculator and his wife on the frontier of America, it was all about the King's proprietary rights and responsibilities, which included making sure John Minor, who held the Royal Patent for the land, had not coerced his wife Jemima into approving the sale to Janney. King George II's likeness in profile on a British silver five shilling coin, shows him looking regal and crowned by laurel leaves. Beneath him is the word "Lima," indicating the coin was minted in Lima, Peru. The silver surely came from Potosi, the great "silver mountain" of the Andes, which in the early Spanish colonial era yielded an astonishing 50 percent silver ore.  Newly minted British silver coins such as this one would have paid for the exportation of American Superfine Flour from Virginia to Peru and other Latin American countries.

In colonial America, the property rights of women varied according to where they lived, because legislatures had been granted a great deal of leeway in establishing laws suitable to local conditions. Each colony had developed a legal system reflecting differing interpretations of British Common Law based upon the self-interest of the settlers, and the conditions they faced in trying to establish a law-abiding society.

Under Virginia colonial law, a widow's dower inheritance was valid only for her lifetime, while under British common law, it would have been hers to distribute to others after her death. A widow in Virginia was also limited to a "widow's third" of the estate's total value when more than two heirs were involved, although a childless widow had the right to one-half of her deceased husband's estate. Women also inherited the slaves that would be required to work the estate. But unlike men, women could not sell or bequeath slaves. This provision was deemed necessary by Virginia's all male Assembly: "to prevent the ruin which would otherwise soon happen to some of the best estates here, by widows marrying second husbands, and carrying with them a property in so many of their first husband slaves."

A 1705 Virginia colonial law defined "real property" as land and any other immovable property attached to it, including the slaves that were required to work the land. The law also mandated that land pass to one heir, usually the eldest son (primogeniture); and prevented future heirs from subdividing it (entail). In effect, the slaves were part of the land (i.e. real property), and could not be sold separately. Slave owners who wanted to sell only slaves claimed they *were* personal property, resulting in hundreds of lawsuits.

For white Virginians, 1776 meant a first blow for freedom from the yoke of British tyranny. For black Virginians, it meant the devastating breakup of their families, because when the 1705 law was finally repealed in 1776, slaves *did* become personal property, and could be sold separately from the land. Virginia had more slaves than any other state in the country, and in 1803, a "prime field hand" aged 20, sold for $600 in South Carolina and $400 in Virginia.

When the importation of slaves was barred in 1808, the deep South became even more dependent on Virginia slaves. To-day's Route 15, just 8 miles east of Waterford, was the Carolina Road upon which slaves who had been "sold south" began Virginia's own "trail of tears." In the 18th century, it was also known as "Rogues Road" due to the thieves and smugglers who patronized it. By 1860, the Virginia price of a "prime" 20-year-old male slave had soared to $1,400-$1,500.

In Loudoun County, talented surveyors like John Hough and Amos Janney who worked for Lord Fairfax, would have taken advantage of their inside knowledge of the best land in which to invest. There was nothing in the Quaker faith that forbade making money—so long as Quaker belief and discipline were not violated. John and Elizabeth Hough became members of The Society of Friends Fairfax Preparatory Meeting in Waterford, which had been established in 1741. Like Amos Janney, John Hough became a land speculator, purchasing a total of 4,082 acres of the Northern Neck Proprietary, mostly in the 1750s-60s. Both Hough and Janney also invested heavily in productive facilities, such as mills using water power to process agricultural and animal products into food and clothing.

John Hough became a leading figure in the new County of Loudoun. He carried out the survey for Leesburg, the county seat; and became a justice of the peace in the county court, which, along with the Anglican Church, amounted to local government in Virginia at the time. In Pennsylvania, Hough had grown up in a tradition of Quaker-led public service, and had no qualms about accepting such appointments in Virginia. Among Quakers, this attitude would soon change, because by the late 18th century, Quakers began removing themselves from positions of authority within civil government, because they believed such offices might require them to act in ways inconsistent with their religious principles.

In the mid-18th century, the county court *was* the local government. It exercised judicial, executive, and legislative powers, including preparing a county budget and levying taxes, and passing ordinances to implement and enforce the laws of the Virginia legislature. In those days, fornication, having an illegitimate child, and using vulgar and obscene language were crimes, and court order books were full of cases dealing with sexual improprieties and swearing in public. Women were fined for having an illegitimate child, and the father had to pay child support. An unwed mother who could not pay the fine, was hired out as an indentured servant to a man who could.

County courts were also responsible for establishing local infrastructure, and they frequently ordered new roads to be "cleared" or old ones "turned" from one mill to another. Many fines were paid in tobacco, which was considered currency and was much more plentiful than cash. The local parish was responsible for handling cases of profanity and sexual impropriety, and fines and other associated costs such as child support were paid to the parish. Quakers, as well as all other non-Anglicans, were required to pay a tithe to the Anglican Church, as the only recognized established church in Virginia. In 1785, the Statute of Religious Liberty became law, thus disestablishing the Anglican Church.

In 1750, John Hough completed construction of a "mansion house" one and one-half miles north of Waterford, which he called Corby Hall. Although greatly altered, it is still intact. Its bricks are reputed to have come from England as ballast, but most of the interior woodwork is late 19th century. Samuel Hough's father, John Hough Jr., was born there in 1751.

In 1759, John Hough surveyed and mapped a site plan for establishing the county seat at Leesburg. His town plan contained seventy lots with three streets going north and south, and four east and west. After vigorous lobbying by landowner Nicholas Minor, the Virginia General Assembly approved the site and the plan. The new county seat of Loudoun was strategically positioned where the Carolina Road (Route 15) and Georgetown & Alexandria Pike (Route 7) intersected. John Hough and Francis Hague of Waterford were selected as two of five new County Commissioners. John Hough bought several lots in the center of town, and became one of the first urban real estate investors in the county.

John Hough was also one of the county's leading entrepreneurs. Although he was a prominent Quaker, he had no qualms in 1762 about forming a partnership with a non-Quaker to obtain a license to keep a ferry and an ordinary (tavern and inn) on the lower side of Goose Creek. The name ordinary originated from the practice of serving "ordinary" meals often consisting of eggs, bacon, hoe cakes and peach brandy. Also in 1762, Hough joined other interested investors looking into the possibility of linking river travel on the Potomac to rivers further west. Hough's interest was far more than local. He would be involved very closely with George Washington for the next four decades in an effort to enhance the navigability of the Potomac and connect it with Ohio and the rest of the Northwest.

After George Washington became President, he dedicated himself to linking the Potomac River with the lands west of the Alleghenies. In 1785, he established the Potowmack Company to develop a water route to the Cumberland Gap in western Maryland, where it would link up with Braddock's Road heading west. John Hough was one of several Quakers who were among the first directors and investors in the company. In 1788, George Washington visited John Hough at Corby Hall, and did sleep there.

Washington had visited Great Falls, Virginia, the previous day. He wrote in his diary that he "was pleased to find...the Canal, banks and other operations...in such forwardness and so well executed." That night he "Dined at Leesburg and lodged at Mr. Jon. Hough's." The following day, Washington and Hough breakfasted before dawn and set off at five o'clock for Harper's Ferry, to check on progress made in constructing the head of the Potomac Canal.

> Piloted by Mr. Hough, thro' by Roads, over the Short hills, by the House and Mill of one Belt, and partly by a rugged Road" they reached their destination "at half after eight o'clock." Washington estimated they travelled 12 miles—which meant he took the shortest route crossing the Short Hill by buffalo/Indian trails—and was pleased by what he saw. The head of the Canal "appeared to be well walled on

both sides, and had a tow path on the Maryland side." Although there was much "yet to do...the supposition is...to open the navigation in the course of the summer." At Harper's Ferry, Washington and Hough had an early dinner, and left for "a Meeting of the Directors of the Potomack Company held at the Falls of Shenandoah."

Unfortunately, the names of the other attending directors are not mentioned, because they would have included several other prominent Virginia Quakers. In 1938, a large stone with a bronze plaque was erected in front of Corby Hall by the Daughters of the American Revolution to commemorate Washington's visit.

Washington's Potowmack Company was having a difficult time completing its canal to Harpers Ferry. It had become evident to the company's directors that white indentured servants hired for the back-breaking process of clearing the river of obstacles and debris, were having difficulty meeting the company's ambitious construction schedule. In 1786, the directors, including John Hough and other prominent Quakers on the Board, decided to hire Negro slaves, and until 1803, employed between 100 and 200 slaves annually. Director Thomas Johnson explained that "the labour of the Potomack Company is best performed by Negroe slaves," because overseers could exercise more control over them than "common white hirelings," and their services "could be depended on in all seasons of the year."

The Quaker directors who voted to hire slaves did not record their feelings, but must have had many a second thought and an uneasy night's sleep. Simply participating in northern Virginia's economy pushed Friends into moral compromises, because their economic welfare became reliant upon a system in which many of the goods produced and services required depended upon slave labor. Eventually, high construction costs—despite using slave labor—and design problems at Great Falls, Virginia, where five locks were required to raise and lower boat traffic, doomed the company. The sluices could not deal with high or low water extremes which restricted canal use to just one or two months a year.

The Potowmack Company went bankrupt in 1828 and was taken over by the Chesapeake and Ohio Canal Co.

# Chapter 4
# Abram's Delight

**"Abraham Hollingsworth absented himself from these parts Under Divers mean Circumstances...Disorderly behavior & Leaving Debts Unsettled"—East Nottingham Monthly Meeting Minutes 25th Day of the 10th mo 1734**

Abraham Hollingsworth, Samuel Hough's maternal grandfather, came to the Shenandoah Valley in 1732 with much the same motivation that brought John Hough to Loudoun Valley—to find rich soils and plentiful water. Abraham found Shawnee Indians camped by a beautiful spring. He declared it "a delight to behold," and the place was known thereafter as "Shawnee Spring."

According to family tradition, supported by documented fact, the Hollingsworth family bought the same 582 acre tract *three* times: first, about 1732 from the Shawnee, who asked for and received a cow, a calf, and a bolt of red cloth; second, in 1734 from Alexander Ross, a Quaker representing Virginia Governor Gooch in his capacity as Crown Agent for British King George I; and third, in 1754 from Lord Fairfax, who had begun legal proceedings against Hollingsworth and other landowners who had received land patents from Governor Gooch. Isaac Hollingsworth, Abraham's son, paid Lord Fairfax for the land to prevent a lawsuit.

Fairfax was not always the shrewd but amiable figure portrayed by biographer Stuart E. Brown, Jr. His pursuit of Isaac Hollingsworth and others who had bought Proprietary land from Virginia's colonial government, shows that once his ownership of the Northern Neck Proprietary was confirmed by the British government, he set out to reclaim all his land by suing its present owners, no matter how long it took.

Governor Gooch's agent, Alexander Ross, was of Scotch-Irish origin, and in 1693, at the age of eleven, travelled to America as the servant of Caleb Pusey, to whom he was bound by indenture to work until age twenty-one. As Virginia's population expanded in the 18th century, so did the demand for white, Protestant, young, indentured servants, who fetched the highest prices. Since there were so many destitute Scotch-Irish, the Emerald Isle became a favorite stopping place for ship captains in the indentured servant trade. They referred to their passengers as "kids." Since their passengers came on board unwillingly, the word "kidnapper" ("napper" was slang for thief) became commonly used in Virginia, quickly spreading to other colonies, and to English speakers everywhere.

The word "kidnapping" became widespread because the capture of white, English speaking children was widespread. Poor children living in the seaports of Scotland were also targeted: The years 1740-46 saw so many kidnappings in the Aberdeen area that parents were afraid to send their boys on errands for fear they would be carried off.

Ross was fortunate to have had a Quaker master, and became a Quaker himself. He was a founding member of the East Nottingham, Maryland, Monthly Meeting in 1730. In 1732, he moved to the Shenandoah Valley. Ross and fellow Quaker Morgan Bryan became agents for Virginia's colonial government, selling 100,000 acres on the west and north side of the River Opeckan. In 1734, Ross attended the third month East Nottingham Meeting, and "proposed on behalf of Friends at Opeckan that a Meeting for worship be settled amongst them." After a visit from East Nottingham elders, this request was forwarded to the Quarterly Meeting with the East Nottingham recommendation that it be approved. On "ye 15 Day 12 Mo 1734" the Opequan Quaker settlement became the Hopewell Monthly Meeting.

Hollingsworth was from an old yeoman Anglo-Saxon family from Macclesfield, in Cheshire County, England, where in 1022 they purchased an estate that came to be known as Hollingsworth Manor. The location and name of the manor are noted in William the Conqueror's *Doomsday Book* of 1086. The family name comes from the holly trees native to the area, and "worth," which meant farm. Henry and Catherine Hollingsworth left Macclesfield in the early 17th century, and settled in Belleniskcrannel, County Armagh, Ireland, according to the records of the Lugan Friends Meeting. Their son Valentine was born in 1632. Valentine left Ireland in 1682 with his family, probably because of religious persecution, and obtained a patent for 986 acres of land near Wilmington, Delaware, part of William Penn's Proprietary. Valentine Hollingsworth represented New Castle County in the first Assembly of Pennsylvania, was a justice of the peace, a signer of William Penn's Great Charter, a member of the provincial Council, and an elder in the New Ark Friends Meeting.

Abraham Hollingsworth was born in Newark (now part of Delaware) in 1686, the only child of Valentine's son Thomas Hollingsworth and his wife Margaret. In 1710, Abraham married Ann Robinson. Their first child, George, was born in 1712, and they joined the nearby East Nottingham Monthly Meeting in Calvert, Maryland. Abraham decided to move his family to the Shenandoah Valley in 1734. He left the East Nottingham Meeting under suspicion of conduct unbecoming a Quaker, as recorded in the Minutes of the Meeting dated "ye 18th Day of ye 3rd mo 1734:

> ...informs this meeting that Abraham Hollingsworth absented himself from these parts Under Divers mean Circumstances as to Disorderly walking or behavior & Leaving Debts Unsettled. Jas Johnson & John White are therefore appointed to write to him (he being now at Opeckan) to Come Speedily Back to answer to ye Same." One month later, Messrs. Johnson & White reported they had received Hollingsworth's answer stating that "he Intends to Come as Soon as he can & answer ye request of ye meeting.

Six months later, the Meeting minutes reported that Abraham Hollingsworth did return for the apparent purpose of "clearing himself," but Johnson & White "could not do it, he having given them but one day's warning before he left these parts, & then appointed them to meet him at Different Hours, so could not meet him at all,

& is Departed without Clearing himself." Johnson & White were told to write to him again, and tell him "the meeting will not be so put off and baffled...but if he comes not to Clear himself at ye time of, or before our meeting in ye 3$^{rd}$ month Next, Testimony may speedily go against him."

In September 1735, he showed up again and presented a paper condemning "those misbehaviors with which he was charged to the satisfaction of frds [friends] whch [which] John White is to read in a first day meeting at East Nottingham." Quaker understatement does not reveal how Hollingsworth answered the serious charges of "disorderly behavior and unsettled debts."

Abraham's father, Thomas, visited him at his new home, and they went hunting several miles north of Opeckan, where Thomas was killed by a wounded buffalo. Perhaps he had not encountered buffalo before and was unaware how fast and aggressive they are when threatened. It was a dangerous business hunting buffalo with a smooth bore musket that could fire a lead ball with reasonable accuracy perhaps 50 yards. Buffalo were well adapted to forested terrain as well as open fields or plain. Not only did they roam the great prairies of the west, but also the valley of the Shenandoah, and "the genesis of Loudoun's colonial roads were paths travelled by Indians and buffaloes." In his *Notes on the State of Virginia,* Thomas Jefferson refers to the average recorded weight of Virginia buffaloes as 1,800 pounds.

Abraham's son George, who was "living on the north side of the Opeckon," and Hannah McKay of the same place, decided to marry, and became the *first couple married* in the Shenandoah Valley. Quakers believed a lengthy—and tiresome—marriage process was fundamental in getting to know the potential marriage partners, ensure they would be faithful to Quaker doctrine and discipline, and would instill these virtues in their children. As required by Quaker custom, George and Hannah made two visits to the East Nottingham Meeting to convince its members to approve their marriage plans. Their marriage took place on the 19$^{th}$ day of December 1734 at the house of Isaac Parkins in Virginia. There were thirty-seven witnesses present at the wedding, including

George's father and mother, brother, and sisters Abraham Hollingsworth died in 1748, not long after he made his will. Eldest son George had left his dying father and moved to North Carolina with his family, and was not named as an executor in the will. Abraham's executors were his wife Ann, his son-in-law Louis Neill, and his second son Isaac. George did, however, receive 250 acres and "the sum of 7 pounds 10 shillings of Current money. What seems remarkable, given Quaker equality between men and women, was that Abraham did not bequeath his house or any land to his "well beloved wife Ann." Under Virginia law, she was entitled to a "widow's third." Ann was bequeathed only personal property: "one of my best feather beds with the furniture thereunto belonging...the household furniture...her riding horse and saddle."

Abraham's son Isaac became owner of the 582-acre original tract of land bought from the Shawnee, and all its "buildings and appurtenances. In 1748, Isaac married Rachel Parkins, daughter of miller Isaac Parkins. It is likely Isaac met Rachel at his brother George's wedding. By 1752, Isaac had built and was operating his own flour mill. He was a Quaker minister by the age of twenty-one, and was becoming quite prominent and travelling extensively on religious visits.

Isaac encouraged other Quakers to move to Winchester, and acquired additional land in the town to provide a place for them to settle. This time, Lord Fairfax was Isaac Hollingsworth's ally in petitioning the town to expand and allow more development. In 1754, stonemason Simon Taylor built the first native limestone house in Winchester for the Hollingsworth family, with walls two feet thick, which Isaac called "Abram's Delight," in honor of his father. A stone high on the east gable was incised with the initials "I" and "R" for Isaac and Rachel, and between the initials was a symbol representing their four children. The house was used for Quaker meetings, and Isaac had a wooden partition built between the dining room and parlor that could be swung up and attached to the ceiling, when meetings took place.

# Chapter 5
# The Forks of the Ohio

**"[They] turned and ran as sheep pursued by dogs."**
**—George Washington, Aide-de-Camp to General Braddock**

In the same year "Abram's Delight" was built, 22-year-old Winchester resident and newly promoted Lieutenant Colonel George
Washington, led 159 mostly "vagabonds and paupers who had
been coerced into service" to contest the French presence in the
valleys of the Allegheny, Monongahela, and Ohio rivers. Washington simply could not find able-bodied men who were willing to
serve in the militia. Farmers and artisans were reluctant to leave
their fields and workshops, and Isaac Hollingsworth, Samuel
Hough's maternal great grandfather, had tangled with Washington
over the refusal of young Quakers to serve on religious grounds.
Washington was wise enough to take with him Christopher Gist,
who knew Ohio Indians better than any other Virginian and could
speak their languages, and Tanagharisson, a Seneca Indian chief
and ally, who represented the Six Nation Iroquois Confederation,
the most powerful Indian tribal coalition in the northeast. Gist told
Washington that without the support of the Delaware and Shawnee
Indians, he could not accomplish his mission.

But Tanagharisson had lost influence with the Ohio tribes,
who were unwilling to commit to an alliance with the British, and
he was looking for a way to force the issue. Tanaghharisson had
also lost influence with the Iroquois Council, who had nicknamed
him the "Half-King."

The name must have stuck, because Washington only refers
to him as "Half-King" in his diary. He saw Washington's initiative
as a chance to restore his lost prestige, and told him the French had
occupied a fort begun by the British where the Allegheny and Monongahela Rivers meet to form the Ohio River. He urged Washing-

ton to retake the fort. This area was known as the "Forks of the Ohio," and was critical to controlling the entrance to the Ohio Valley and beyond. The French were enlarging the fort and named it Fort Duquesne (today's Pittsburgh). Washington and Tanaghrisson surprised a French patrol near the fort. After a brief exchange of volleys, the outnumbered French surrendered.

The wounded French commander, aristocrat Joseph Coulon de Villiers Sieur de Jumonville, tried to explain to Washington that he had not come as a soldier, but was only on a peace mission. Tanaghrisson, who understood French much better than Washington and wanted no peace between the British and French, said in French, "thou are not dead yet, my father," and split Jumonville's skull with his hatchet, pulled out his brain, and washed his hands in the blood and tissue. A horrified Washington watched as the other Indians scalped nine dead and wounded French soldiers. Washington's diary tells a somewhat different story: "We killed Mr. de Jumonville, the Commander of the party, as also nine others...the Indians scalped the dead and took away the greater part of their arms." By killing his French "father," Tanaghrisson hoped to reestablish his own stature and force the Iroquois to declare for the British, by sealing with blood an unbreakable covenant with Washington and the English king he represented.

Washington decided to return to a previous camp at a place known as Great Meadows, where he was joined by Tanaghrisson and his followers. Meanwhile, Gist had arranged for Washington to meet with the leaders of the Shawnee and Delaware tribes. Washington was unsuccessful in his appeal for their help in driving the French out of the Forks of the Ohio. He also failed to convince Tanaghrisson to stay with him until more British troops arrived. Tanaghrisson had only twelve warriors with him, and without the support of the Delaware and the Shawnee, he was certain Washington would be defeated by the French.

When 200 more British troops did arrive, Washington built a circular stockade fence, which he called Fort Necessity, to defend against a French attack. However, a forested hillside within musket range and with a clear view of the stockade, enabled a large French contingent, ironically led by Louis Coulon de Villers, brother of the dead Sieur de Jumonville, to take cover behind trees and fire at will at Washington's force. A hard rain had turned the stockade into a muddy morass, and his wet, cold, and frightened soldiers had broken into the rum supply. His men were slowly being killed or wounded as they huddled behind the stockade, but Washington held out until the French called for a ceasefire because they were running out of ammunition. Washington was allowed to surrender with "the honors of war," allowing him and his battered troops to keep their personal weapons and one cannon, and march away with drums beating and flags flying. Washington agreed and signed the surrender document.

Although Washington's honor was intact, his force had suffered a hundred casualties, while the French had only five killed or wounded. The surrender document he signed referred to the "assassination" of the French commander, whom the document also identified as a special envoy with diplomatic immunity." Washington's diary states that while the French soldiers he had taken prisoner referred to themselves as "Embassadors," who had been sent with a summons to order him to retire, he did not believe them. He wrote that their claim was simply "a plausible pretence to discover our camp and to obtain knowledge of our forces and our situation!"

If Washington's account was true, one wonders why he signed the surrender document. Its publication created a public furor and an international incident which greatly increased tensions between the British and the French. This was also the first armed clash in America between regular troops of the two countries, and Washington was credited by many with starting The French and Indian War. The credit, if any, should have gone to the HalfKing. It was not the only time a Seneca chief would affect George Washington's career.

The French and Indian War has been correctly called the "the war that made America" by historian Fred Anderson. Few Americans today understand or care about this war, which spread to the Caribbean, Europe, West Africa, the Philippines, and India. Winston Churchill called it "the first world war." It is a story of

America's first big step toward achieving its independence, and of the beginning of the systematic uprooting and destruction of the Native American way of life—although it took another 150 years for white Americans to finally subjugate their enemies. It is also a story of the beginning of America's march westward to find its "Manifest Destiny" among the nations of the world.

George Washington's first combat experience was a disaster, and he had many critics, but his bravery and aggressive spirit impressed others. Although he was inexperienced, he was universally admired for his "deportment," had enormous energy, ambition, dedication, and above all, self-confidence. He was also very fortunate. Gist had twice saved his life in his first reconnoitering expedition, and in the battle for Fort Necessity he seemed immune to musket balls and arrows aimed in his direction. Yet his tenacity in the face of a rapidly deteriorating situation, led to the death or wounding of many of his men.

He also had the support of the two most powerful men in Virginia. Lord Thomas Fairfax defended Washington's venture as a noble, if futile, effort to block a French invasion of Virginia's western borders. Virginia Lieutenant Governor Robert Dinwiddie was *de facto* governor, because the royal governor, the Earl of Albermarle, was a court figurehead in Britain who collected a huge annual salary (3,330pounds) while never setting foot in Virginia.

Dinwiddie was Washington's greatest supporter, but his *protégé's* relentless ambition wore even him down. Washington was not satisfied with being a major in command of Virginia's only militia regiment, and insisted that regimental command was a colonel's job. Dinwiddie eventually agreed, and in a letter dealing with many subjects, simply wrote "enclosed you have a commission for lieutenant Colonel, pay 12 shillings a day." However, the House of Burgesses would not vote new taxes to pursue a war with the French, and Washington's career languished until British Major General Edward Braddock became commander-in-chief of His Britannic Majesty's forces in America.

At a time when proper appearance and behavior were absolutely essential for an individual to be accepted into society, young

George Washington captivated almost everyone he met. Among his admirers were later presidents Thomas Jefferson and James Monroe. Jefferson wrote, "His stature was exactly what one would wish, his deportment easy, erect and noble." Monroe enthused, "A deportment, so firm, so dignified, but yet so modest and composed, I have never seen in any other person." These qualities endeared young Washington to eminent Virginians and explain in large part his success in gaining their support.

"Deportment" was the key word of praise for both Jefferson and Monroe. The word is not used today, but in the 18th century was an all-inclusive term for bearing, behavior, carriage, conduct, conversation, demeanor, and manner. Washington was just twenty-two years old, but to his admirers seemed mature far beyond his years. In today's world in which provocative speech and casual appearance are most admired, it is hard to comprehend the power of "deportment" some 250 years ago.

Any ambitious colonial military officer knew the only way to preferment and command lay in obtaining a commission in the British Army. But British Army regulations did not permit militia officers of the rank of major and above to be the equal of, or superior to any British regular army major. These regulations would have required Washington to accept a demotion from lieutenant colonel to captain if his militia regiment were to join the British Army.

Washington—like many Virginians—was enamored with Great Britain. When he sought successfully to become one of Braddock's aides-de-camp, he was overjoyed. Braddock arranged for Washington to be a volunteer aide-de-camp in the British regular army, performing the same duties as Braddock's two other aides, both regular British Army captains. He had an understanding with Braddock that if he did well, he would be granted a commission, hopefully as a major, in the regular British Army. Braddock must have been quite fond of Washington, because he gave him one of his pistols, which Washington treasured and carried with him in future campaigns.

Braddock built a fort at what is now Cumberland, Maryland, and held a council there with the chiefs of local Indian tribes who were supporting the British. When in answer to their question regarding Indian ownership of land, he replied, "No savage should inherit the land." All except a single chief left the meeting and went over to the French. Benjamin Franklin, who had come to Fort Cumberland to help procure horses and wagons for the army, met with Braddock, who told him, "Savages may indeed be a formidable enemy to your raw American militia; but upon the king's regular and disciplined troops, Sir, it is impossible they should make any impression."

In 1755, the British sent a much stronger force of 1,200 British regulars and Virginia militia and 250 noncombatants under Major General Braddock to drive the French from Fort Duquesne. Benjamin Franklin supplied the wagons, and Daniel Boone drove one of them. Braddock's soldiers hacked and blasted their way, creating a twelve-foot-wide path through the forest. An advance guard under Lieutenant Colonel Thomas Gage, entered a clearing in the forest near the fort, and confronted 900 French regulars, Canadian militia, and their Indian allies. The surprise was mutual. Gage and his men drove the French force back, but failed to occupy a key forested hill on their right. The French and Indians spread out behind trees. Gage withdrew his troops, colliding with the main British force, which had rushed forward upon hearing the sound of musket fire ahead.

Gage's regiment and the main force became hopelessly tangled along the narrow forest trail. Company officers were shot off their horses, and there was no one to give orders. The soldiers could not see the well-hidden enemy, and simply fired blindly into the woods or wherever they saw movement. As their comrades fell around them, and without most of their officers, the terrified British soldiers could not be brought to the charge. General Braddock himself ordered his British troops to advance, and a participant described what happened:

The Enemy kept behind Trees and Loggs of Wood, and cut down our Troops as fast as they cou'd advance. The Soldiers then insisted much to be allowed to take to the Trees, which the General denied and stormed much, calling them Cowards, and even went so far as to strike them with his own sword for attempting the Trees.

For more than two hours, the French fired into the mass of British troops, while Braddock had four horses shot from under him trying to rally his men to regroup and form a proper line. The Virginians, who had taken cover, "were contemptuous of this huddled mass of soldiers standing brutishly, allowing themselves to be slaughtered. The British, on the other hand, were amazed at the Colonials lack of discipline, and blamed it for making things worse." When the Virginians charged the enemy to oust them from their forest cover, many were shot by "friendly fire" from the British, for leaving formation.

Washington, who had two (some say three) horses killed under him and four musket ball holes in his coat and hat, and was the only aide-de-camp left unharmed, urged Braddock "that the men might be permitted to leave the ranks and shelter themselves, but the general turned a deaf ear." Braddock mounted a fifth horse, and "foaming with rage and indignation, he flew from rank to rank, with his own hands endeavoring to force his men into position."

It must have been incomprehensible to Braddock that British regulars would not form a line of battle, regardless of the circumstances. The blow to his pride was especially severe, because he had made his career in His Majesty's Coldstream Regiment of Foot Guards, who considered themselves the finest line regiment in the British Army.

"At last, when every aide but Washington was struck down, when the lives of the vast majority of his officers had been sacrificed with a reckless intrepidity, when scarce a third part of his army remained unscathed, at last, Braddock abandoned all hope of victory." When Braddock gave the order to retreat, his troops "turned and ran as sheep pursued by dogs, and it was impossible to rally them, despite all the efforts of the officers to the contrary," according to Washington. Braddock was shot through the right arm and lung and fell off his horse, while attempting to stop the panicked flight of his army. He was carried from the field in a cart, and then "placed in the folds of his large silken sash," whose ends were tied to two horses walking abreast.

Braddock knew he was dying and asked Washington to save his red sash, which had been worn by his father and represented 70 years service by father and son as officers in the Coldstream Guards. Braddock's force had been cutting a military road through the wilderness by enlarging and clearing an earlier Indian trail, and Washington had Braddock buried in the middle of the road. The departing troops marched over the grave to conceal its location from the Indians. Washington took the sash to Mount Vernon, and many years later gave it to a nephew for safe keeping, who then gave it to a friend. The scarlet sash was passed on, and on again, and a century after the battle, it came to U. S. President Zachary Taylor. He gave it to his daughter Betty Taylor Dandridge, living in Winchester, Virginia.

The British press found out and demanded the sash be returned. A delegation of senior Coldstream Guards officers came to America and visited Winchester, offering to buy the sash for the astounding sum of $3,000. Mrs. Dandridge politely declined the offer, and the sash passed to Mrs. Dandridge's niece, who eventually returned it to Mount Vernon, where it can be seen today.

Although he had confessed after the Battle of the Monongahela that "we have been scandalously beaten by a trifling body of men," it was for Washington one of those events which change a life. He emerged unscathed from the battle convinced that he had been chosen by Providence to achieve greatness. What happened that day stayed with him for the rest of his life. On July 9, 1776, when he ordered his Continental Army to assemble on parade to hear for the first time, the Declaration of Independence read by their battalion officers, he made a "grateful remembrance of [his] escape on the banks of the Monongahela, hoping that the same

Providence that protected us then, would make us happy instruments in restoring Peace & Liberty to this once favor'd, but now distressed Country."

The victorious French gave free reign to their Indian allies to raid British settlements, spreading havoc and terror along the frontier from Pennsylvania to the Carolinas. Fifteen hundred frontier settlers were killed and one thousand taken prisoner. Thousands more fled in panic, creating a flood of refugees that provincial governments were incapable of managing. In mid-September 1755 George Washington established his headquarters at Winchester, the largest settlement in the Shenandoah Valley, but he received no funds from the House of Burgesses to provide temporary shelter or food for the refugees. By mid-October 1755 so many were crossing the Blue Ridge Mountains to safety that one of Washington's subordinates reported "it was with great difficulty I passed the [Blue] Ridge for the Crowds of People who were flying as if every moment was death."

Lieutenant Colonel George Washington found people to be so confused, frightened, and desperate, he had no effective authority over them. Winchester was almost abandoned by its panic-stricken citizens, and when Washington tried to reason with fleeing refugees to stop running and defend themselves under the protection of the militia, some threatened "to blow out my brains." "No orders are obey'd," he reported, "but what a Party of Soldiers or my own drawn sword enforces." Washington could do little to alleviate the situation. In a letter to Governor Dinwiddie dated 22 April 1756 his frustration boiled over: "the supplicating tears of women, and moving petitions of men, melt me into such deadly sorrow, that I solemnly declare, if I know my own mind, I could offer myself a willing sacrifice to the butchering enemy."

Isaac and Rachel Hollingsworth decided to move their four children away from Winchester to safety east of the Blue Ridge Mountains after the raids began. Isaac Hollingsworth had much to lose by leaving Hopewell Meeting, where he was a highly respected elder and minister, and in abandoning "Abram's Delight." They chose Waterford because of their close connection to Waterford's Fairfax Meeting, and because it was on the other side of the Blue Ridge Mountains. They must have looked to Waterford Quakers for spiritual and emotional support in those troubled times.

Existing legislation required all young men to join the militia, but had many loopholes, including exempting Quakers if they could find a substitute. In 1754, Frederick County officials in Winchester jailed eight Quaker youths for one year because they refused military service on any terms. Isaac Hollingsworth's elder brother George was arrested and fined five pounds for disorderly meeting and assembling, when he participated in (and probably organized) a worship service held under the windows of the Winchester jail.

In 1756, six Quaker men who refused to bear arms were brought before George Washington, who arrested and jailed them, threatening to have them flogged. Isaac and Rachel Hollingsworth and Waterford's John Hough visited the young men in jail. Afterwards, Hollingsworth and other influential Quakers petitioned Lieutenant Governor Robert Dinwiddie to release the Quaker prisoners, and pleaded with Washington to await the Governor's decision. Dinwiddie told Washington to give them "a short allowance of bread and water till you bring them to reason." This tactic did not change any hearts or minds, and the six were released into the custody of local Quakers, but only allowed to return home after a six month confinement.

Young Quaker men of military age were "damned if they did and damned if they didn't." Those who actively participated or colluded with the military were judged harshly by the Quaker Meeting. They were either disowned or, if the offenses were relatively minor and the offenders repented by acknowledging their transgressions and promising to be faithful to Quaker Discipline, they were not disowned. Quakers were also forbidden to accept jobs with the government because it was waging the war. The East Nottingham Monthly Meeting Minutes for 1756-1759 contain the following sample of offences committed and action taken:

John Bond, joins militia, disowned
Jacob Bond, enlists military men, acknowledges
Benjamin Chew, becomes justice of the peace, disowned
Jeremiah Brown, wagons haul military stores, acknowledges
Joseph Gilpin, takes oath as Sheriff, disowned
Elisha Cowgill, works on fort at Pittsburg, disowned
Edward Mitchell, takes oath as Magistrate, disowned
Aron Sinclair, enlisted in army, disowned

Their experiences in the French and Indian War convinced leading Quakers they had to return to simplicity, strengthen discipline, use accumulated wealth for charitable purposes, and stand firmer on the great moral issues of the day. Most important were eliminating conflicts of interest arising from Quaker participation in society by publicly rejecting rather than tolerating slavery; refusing to run for or accept any public office; making greater efforts to compensate Indians who had lost their land; providing assistance to those who became destitute; and adopting a "no toleration" policy on deviance from the social and moral codes established by Discipline.

Washington resigned his militia colonelcy in 1758, and set about gaining the fortune he would need to become a leading figure in Virginia. He married widow Martha Custis in 1759, and used Martha's wealth to expand his tidewater properties from 5,000 to 12,000 acres, doubling the number of slaves he owned. The State of Virginia claimed all of what is now Ohio, and had promised 200,000 acres in Ohio to the militia who had fought in the war. Washington's share as colonel was 20,000 acres. Over the next decade, he purchased warrants from his former troops, raising his share to 45,000 acres. He eventually acquired 60,000 acres in the Shenandoah Valley, western Pennsylvania, and Ohio.

# Chapter 6
# Genesis

**"As nature hath given native Indians and their forefathers the possession of this continent of America, they have a natural right thereto"—Thomas Chalkley, Philadelphia Quaker Minister and Elder**

Pennsylvania Quakers were among the very few white settlers who believed America's native inhabitants had a natural right to the land. Thomas Chalkley, an eminent Quaker minister from Philadelphia, was so concerned that Friends who settled in the Shenandoah Valley had not paid the Indians for their land that he sent a lengthy epistle in 1738 to Winchester's Hopewell Friends saying, "...nature hath given them and their forefathers the possession of this continent of America," and native Indians "had a natural right" to possess the land, and therefore no other people had the right to take away or settle their lands "without consent or purchasing the same by agreement of all parties concerned."

Chalkley also pointed out that "Virginians have made an agreement with the natives to go as far as the mountains (Blue Ridge) and no farther; and you are over and beyond the mountains, therefore out of that agreement." He urged his readers to "keep a friendly correspondence with the native Indians, giving them no occasion of offence; they being a cruel and merciless enemy where they think they are wronged," and to buy the land quickly. He warned that if they did not act soon, "some of the blood of yourselves, wives or children, be shed or spilt on the ground."

Amidst all the death and destruction of the French and Indian War, Hopewell Friends historical records indicate *no Hopewell Quakers* "were visited or attacked by Indians," and only one empty house was burned down. The reason for this seeming miraculous survival of the Quakers was that they were regarded by the

Indians as friends, rather than enemies. Most Hopewell Quakers had come from Pennsylvania, where they had a long history of good relations with American Indians going back to the arrival of William Penn in 1682. All existing records of that time indicate no Indian raids at Abram's Delight. However, many years later, when the weatherboarding was removed from the original log cabin built by Abraham Hollingsworth, a five-inch long arrowhead was found embedded in a log.

In William Penn's Quaker Colony of Pennsylvania, all settlers were required to purchase their land from the Indians, who were promised that relations would be peaceful and trade would be open and fair. The use of force was not an option, because it was against Quaker principles and the state had no militia. Religious toleration meant the Indians could worship as they chose. Free trade meant the Indians could purchase weapons and ammunition, and they realized they had nothing to fear from the Quakers. Pennsylvania's system of two separate but equal communities was one of the great experiments of its time, and the colony was at peace for seventy years—despite increasing tensions as ever more white settlers arrived looking for land.

Land speculators tried unsuccessfully to bribe William Penn as early as 1681. In a letter to a friend, he wrote: "I did refuse a great temptation last second day, which was six thousand pounds. To make the purchasers a company, to have wholly to itself the Indian trade from south to north, between the Susquehannah and Delaware Rivers, paying me two and a half percent acknowledgment or rent." This was an enormous sum of money in that era, when a young gentleman of means could live comfortably in London and play an active role in society on an annual income of a hundred pounds.

Everything changed after William Penn died in 1718. His sons Richard, John, and Thomas, gave the Iroquois Confederation, who dominated the other tribes in the region, the sole right to sell Indian land in Pennsylvania, under an arrangement in which the Penn brothers would purchase a large tract of land from the Iroquois at a very low price per acre, and then sell it piecemeal to white settlers at a much higher per acre price. Soon, the sons of William Penn were among the richest men in England. In 1737, they perpetrated what was at the time the biggest land fraud in American history, when they dispossessed the Delaware Indians of almost three-fourths of a million acres of land between the Lehigh and Delaware Rivers. Many Shawnee, who had settled in the Susquehanna Valley of central Pennsylvania after they were driven out of Ohio a century before by the Iroquois, were compelled to move back to their former home at the Forks of the Ohio. By 1740, that area was home to some 2,500 Delaware and Shawnee Indians, whose land in the east had been sold out from under them.

By the mid-18$^{th}$ century, Quakers accounted for one-fourth of all Pennsylvanians, but held over three-fourths of the seats in the colonial assembly. Non-Quakers, led by Benjamin Franklin, insisted that a militia was necessary to protect all Pennsylvania's citizens from Indian attack, and urged the assembly to require all male colonists to be made eligible for military service. The assembly did not concur, yet Franklin was able to raise a militia of 10,000 through private subscription. Without the backing of the government, the militia was ineffective. In 1756, the English governor and his council declared war on the Shawnee and Delaware, and Quaker delegates in the assembly abdicated rather than resort to arms.

The strength of Quaker society lay in its organizational structure. Monthly meetings relied upon a committee of overseers to organize events such as weddings or funerals, ensure members participated in the Meeting's communal activities, and provided "care" for those who needed spiritual or temporal help. Once a year, delegates from Waterford would reunite with all their brethren at the Philadelphia Annual Meeting. They exchanged experiences, discussed major issues of the day, and shared the wisdom that would help them maintain the unity of their faith. The structure was pyramidal. Four times a year, Virginia Quakers met at the Baltimore Quarterly Meeting to discuss and deal with both local and national issues. Monthly meetings helped establish and supervise new "preparative" meetings.

When the Fairfax Meeting achieved monthly status in 1746, it assumed responsibility for the Monocacy Preparative Meeting on the Monocacy River 15 miles northeast of Waterford in Frederick County, Maryland and for the Goose Creek Preparative Meeting eight miles southeast of Waterford. Goose Creek had no meeting house, and all three met alternatively at Waterford and Monocacy, until the wooden Monocacy Meeting House burned down in 1759. The Goose Creek Meeting became a separate monthly meeting in 1785.

Spurred by the rapid growth of the Evangelical movement in Virginia, the 1755 Philadelphia Yearly Meeting reformers played a leading role in revising the Book of Discipline. Quaker historian Glenn Crothers called this a "moral reformation" which remained "a work in progress in northern and western Virginia" until the American Revolution spurred even greater efforts to reform. Evangelicals insisted the Virginia Legislature ought to adopt a plan for the gradual emancipation of slaves. Only in 1795, did the Baltimore Yearly Meeting establish an Indian Affairs Committee to raise funds to support Indians in the Northwest Territories and encourage "school education, husbandry and the mechanic arts among them."

In 1757, Isaac Hollingsworth purchased 300 acres on "the South side of the Beverdam branch of Kittocton" from Lord Fairfax for "ninety pounds current money of Virginia." The deed was witnessed by John Hough, and was only the third land transaction in the recently established County of Loudoun, which had been named after Lieutenant General John Campbell, Fourth Earl of Loudoun, recently appointed the new governor of Virginia by King George II. He also replaced Braddock as commander-in-chief of British and Colonial forces in America. Both men were dedicated and demanding soldiers, yet neither had proven himself on the battlefields of Europe, nor were they prepared to face an enemy that had mastered the techniques of American frontier warfare. Both were aristocrats who believed British troops properly led by British officers using conventional military tactics could overcome any obstacle. Loudoun refused to give commissions in the British Army to George Washington or his staff.

The Earl infuriated colonials by prohibiting trade on U.S ships sailing from American ports to Europe. His tenure in America was, like Braddock's, marked by continuous and acrimonious disputes with provincial officials, legislatures, and militia over royal prerogative and colonial rights. But the Earl was not discouraged. Like young soldiers unaccustomed to discipline, American colonials would simply have to be shown their duty.

The Earl differed from Braddock in that he was a keen observer, and he soon realized the provincial company from New Hampshire, called Rogers' Rangers, had much to offer the British in terms of fighting in hilly, forested country. He doubled their size to two battalions, and put them on the British Army payroll. He discarded massed musketry firing volleys on order, and required British regulars to fire at individual targets, to march in a loose single file in the forests, in a spread-out skirmish line in open country, and to take cover when they heard the command "Tree All!" The ten best sharpshooters in each company were given rifles instead of muskets, and told to pick off the officers during combat, which was an unheard of breach of military etiquette at that time. Soldiers were also allowed to substitute tomahawks for swords in hand-to-hand combat, and carry powder horns instead of having to rely on supply wagons hauling cartridge boxes. Still, Lord Loudoun adamantly refused to include colonial militia in his army—although he did establish a light infantry militia battalion modeled on Rogers Rangers.

# Chapter 7
# In the Service of Truth

**"I expected no other than that my life would be taken for the testimony I should have to bear"—Ann Herbert More, travelling Quaker minister**

The Earl of Loudoun never set foot in Virginia or the county named after him. He did, however, meet Maryland Quaker and frequent visitor to Waterford's Fairfax Meeting, Ann Moore, who went all the way to Albany, New York, to see him shortly after his arrival in America in 1756. The Earl must have been gracious, for a change, because as Moore described it in her diary: "And a sweet time it was. He was put in mind who was the preserver of all mankind to which he readily agreed to, returning us thanks which I know through divine mercy belongs to God only."

Her objective was to convince Lord Loudoun that because God was present in all human beings, he (Loudoun) should rely on appealing to the unity of the Holy Spirit that both British and French shared, rather than warfare, in dealing with the French. Although the Earl seemed to agree with her, he was not inclined to pursue her suggestions, Ann Moore became very disturbed about the consequences of this long war. She traveled through deep snow to New York again in 1758. She was well received by Major General James Abercromby, who had replaced Lord Loudoun as commander-in-chief of British forces in America. Abercromby gave Moore permission to preach to the British troops. Moore visited three forts on the frontier, and found Rogers Rangers to be very welcoming. Major Robert Rogers mustered his battalion of Rangers to hear Moore speak; invited her to dinner, and provided lodgings and "a 'waiting man' to see we had anything we wanted."

Although at one fort she was only allowed to speak to officers, otherwise British Regular Army officers were also friendly and cooperative. Local clergy, however, were quite hostile, and tried to prevent the Army from holding any meetings to hear her. They deeply resented her speaking as an authority about Christianity, not only because she was a woman, but also because she was not ordained, and did not have the requisite university degrees they considered as fundamental to preaching the Gospel to the less educated.

In 1761, Moore set sail to minister in England, but her ship was boarded by Frenchmen, who "came on board our ship with drawn swords in their hands, as tho' they meant to kill all before them." Afterwards, she wrote to her children that she "expected no other than that my life would be taken for the testimony I should have to bear." The French took the vessel as a prize of war, and imprisoned the captain and crew.

Moore was very ill from a great storm and weeks of sea-sickness, and was put ashore by the French in Spain with four others. She was too weak to walk, and rode on the back of a mule to the city of Bilbao. She wrestled with the "idolatry" she observed during Lent, when images of the saints were paraded through the streets of the city, "trembling as one in a strong ague [fever)," and praying "Oh Lord, let them see as my poor soul sees that Christ *within* is the hope."

She wrote an epistle to British residents, warning them to cease doing evil and save their souls, and debated the meaning of the New Testament with a Catholic priest who stayed in the same lodging house. The fact that any debate took place is testimony to More's determination to "serve the Truth." Ann More knew no Spanish, and the priest could not speak English nor read his own Latin Bible.

In 1765, 1767, 1768, and 1774, Ann Moore visited Fairfax Meeting in Waterford, where she spoke and "exhorted in the Authority of Truth to the Edification of Many." She used Waterford as a base for visiting other Meetings, and making many individual visits to Quaker families.

In the 1760s, when few roads existed, Quaker travelling ministers—many of them women—covered great distances on horseback, mostly over Indian/buffalo trails to give "peace testimony" in time of war, and to provide moral and spiritual support to fellow Quakers. Some of these journeys could take a couple of years and reach virtually every Friends meeting in North America.

What motivated these Quaker women? They set high standards for themselves. They believed they were the equal of men, at a time when women had few rights and were believed to be inferior to men. They believed their lives would be judged by what they did in bringing the light of God to those living in darkness. They believed God was within each person, and that conflicts could be resolved and violence avoided if the combatants considered the humanity that bound them together, rather than their differences. Their faith gave them the courage to conquer seemingly insurmountable obstacles and hardships. They justified long periods of hardship, danger, and separation from their families, as answering God's call to deny self "in the service of Truth." In the Quaker religion, revelation came from within, and these women believed they were guided by the Holy Spirit, which one Quaker woman said "was to me like a needle of a compass, touched with a loadstone [lodestone]; for so it pointed where I ought to go, and when I came to the far end of the journey."

Still, it was a man's world, and they had to develop the skills that would enable them to debate the issues of the day with powerful men. Quakers were known for their emphasis on education, and women received the same education as men. They learned to say what they thought during worship services, and to discuss and manage their own affairs in separate women's business meetings. Women assumed leadership roles in a variety of ministerial, charitable, and organizational activities, and Waterford's Fairfax Meeting often had more women elders and ministers than men.

The Fairfax Meeting's Visitor Log Book, 1761–1812, reveals how interconnected internationally the Quaker world was at that time. There were almost as many visitors to Waterford from "Old" England as there were from New England. They were also visited by a Quaker from Waterford, Ireland.

When twenty-six-year-old British traveler Nicholas Cress-well visited Waterford, he attended a Quaker meeting. In his diary he wrote: "*Saturday, Feb. 10th, 1776*. This is one of the most comfortable places of worship I was ever in, they had two large fire places and a Dutch stove. After long silence and many groans, a man got up and gave us a short lecture with great deliberation. Dinner at Jos. Janney's, one of the Friends." Not long before visiting Waterford's Fairfax Meeting, he had gone to church in Leesburg, "to hear Bombast, Noise and Nonsense uttered by a Methodist and an Anabaptist."

Quakers valued education so highly they often sent both girls and boys to private schools far away. In 1830, it took Rebecca Jane Walker and her father four days to travel from Waterford to the Quaker school at Kimberton, near Philadelphia. Rebecca was terribly lonely at first. "Oh dear mother," she wrote, "thee does not know how badly I want to see you all sometimes...as I lay on my pillow last night the tears would insensibly come into my eyes."

Rebecca was lucky; however, she got a bed all to herself. Once the girls were up and dressed in the morning, the dormitory was locked until bedtime. Discipline was strict and the food, while wholesome, was insufficient. Rebecca made a dress with a big pocket. She wrote her mother, "Thee don't know how handy it is at meal times. I fill it with bread to eat between times."

Rebecca also got caught up in the split that was dividing Quakers into those who adhered to the individual search for the inner light of Christian revelation, and those who adopted a more formalized worship service of a redeeming Christ, which characterized the evangelical movement. Rebecca went to hear speakers from both sides of the controversy, and was unhappy with the accusatory attitude of speakers towards Friends on the opposite side. She decided to stay well clear of the debate.

Rebecca became good friends with Maria Mott, whose mother was Lucretia Mott, a famous Quaker minister and fierce opponent of slavery. The Motts introduced her to the life of Philadelphia society. Still, she missed her family, and it was not until two years later that she seemed ready to enjoy herself. When some girls teased her about her clothing, she wrote her mother asking for "yellow bonnet strings, a black bonbazette apron, and good full patterns for my dresses, and not light color. No more little dotted calico please...I think there is something in your dress towards making you popular here, although I think it is a very foolish practice."

Rebecca returned to Waterford, married Quaker miller James Janney and had nine children, but she died in Philadelphia, which had become home for most of her children.

In 1842, Lucretia Mott and her husband visited Fairfax Meeting to speak about the evils of slavery, before journeying to the White House to speak to President Tyler. Although Mrs. Mott felt "fulfilled by her southern reception," the Philadelphia Quaker leadership was so disturbed by her growing militancy, they never again authorized her to travel and speak on the subject again.

After Rachel Hollingsworth became pregnant, husband Isaac must have known he was likely going to die before she gave birth. He bequeathed to "the Child my Wife is now with," the remaining 200 acres of his Winchester tract when he or she should reach the age of twenty-one. Son Jonah was also instructed to pay 30 pounds a year for the child's upkeep until maturity. He gave his "Beloved Wife Rachel," the remainder of his estate, including fifty town lots in Winchester, 100 acres of the land he had purchased near Waterford from Lord Fairfax, and appointed "my Friend John Hough" to assist wife Rachel in selling the town lots.

John Hough and Rachel Hollingsworth were appointed co-executors of the will—evidence of the close connection between the two families. Isaac Hollingsworth divided among his wife and children the 582 acre tract of land and fifty town lots "on the East side of Winchester Town" he had inherited from his father Abraham. His son Jonah received 190 acres, his Winchester mansion house ("Abram's Delight"), and fulling mill. Daughter Ann was given 200 acres. To daughter Lydia he gave "my Plantation whereon I now dwell in the County of Loudoun and containing two hundred acres." Isaac Hollingsworth died in 1759, aged thirty-seven.

Hopewell Friends had this to say after Isaac's death:

He received a gift in the ministry when about 21 years of age, and was we believe, a fruitful laborer in his master's work; being much concerned with the promotion of truth and the eternal well-being of mankind; of sober and grave deportment, diligent in religious meetings. He visited the churches in divers parts of the neighboring colonies; and we find by accounts from thence his services and labours of love were well accepted among them.

High praise indeed from his Quaker brethren.

Rachel became very active in the Fairfax Meeting, was highly respected, and was appointed overseer in 1762.The joining together of the prominent Quaker families of Hollingsworth and Hough took place when John Hough Jr. and Lydia Hollingsworth were married at Fairfax Meeting House in 1772. Five years later, Rachel Hollingsworth sold her 100 acre farm to her son-in-law for 110 pounds, and returned to Hopewell Meeting in Winchester with her daughters Phebe and Mary. John Jr. and Lydia's first major project was building a mill for grinding corn and grist for animal feed.

In 1775, the leading issue of the day was whether or not to go to war to obtain independence from Great Britain. Quakers were not in favor of the violent overthrow of the British colonial government. In 1775, the Yearly Meeting for Pennsylvania and New Jersey issued an epistle "to Friends and brethren in these and other provinces" urging maintenance of the status quo and "declaring against every usurpation of power and authority."

After July 4, 1776, the newly independent colonies required all males over the age of sixteen to "take The Test," by swearing an oath of allegiance to the new government. The penalty for swearing *any* oath was expulsion from the Society of Friends. John Hough's son, John Jr., was asked by the Fairfax Meeting whether he had sworn such an oath. He admitted he had, and was put on probation. Eventually, the Meeting restored him to full membership. Fifteen other men were expelled from Fairfax Meeting for fighting in the Revolutionary War. These unfortunates were shunned by their families as well.

Quakers were becoming very unpopular for refusing to fight or acknowledge the authority of the new Continental government, or to accept its "greenback" currency. Many young Quaker males were imprisoned, and some even flogged. But the Continental Army was always short of men, and conscription was the only way to fill the ranks. When an angry Continental Army captain named Snickers presented his reluctant Loudoun Quaker conscripts to General George Washington at his Valley Forge, Pennsylvania, headquarters with the comment, "They swear they will not fight," Washington is said to have replied, "Quakers will neither swear nor fight," and sent them home. During 1777-1783, Virginia county sheriffs seized goods and collected fines totaling 11,221 British pounds (about $28,000) from Virginia Friends who had failed to obey the new laws.

In addition to intense pressure from federal and state governments to meet the needs of a nation at war, local Quakers were also under threat of disownment by the Fairfax Mens Monthly Meeting if they did not conform to Quaker Discipline. Many of the discipline violations had to do with behavior, such as dancing in public, drinking strong liquor to excess, using unsavory expressions, and fighting in a public place. Sexual violations were fewer. To avoid disownment, male transgressors were required to prepare a paper condemning their conduct, which they would read at Meeting, hoping for forgiveness if they returned to Discipline.

Unlike their Tidewater neighbors, Quakers living in the Piedmont were better able to enforce a prohibition against slave holding and only three males were singled out at Fairfax Meeting during 1745-1800. Owning a slave only became grounds for being disowned from the Quaker faith in 1774.

The most unusual complaint made at the Fairfax Monthly Mens Meeting was leveled at John Hutton, who was "in the habit of carrying a cane with a sword in it, which he acknowledges is for self defense and that he once used it in that way." Perhaps the saddest complaint was one made against Moses Cadwalader "for attempting bestiality." He was not finally condemned and disowned for his habit until six years later.

At the Fairfax Women's Monthly Meeting the major issue was "marrying out of unity." It provided grounds for dismissal, as did much less common violations of Quaker discipline like "fornication," and having an illegitimate child. Between 1747 and 1800, the Fairfax Monthly Meeting filed complaints against about 115 young women for "outgoing in marriage."

During 1745-1800, only two complaints were recorded against women for buying or selling a slave in company with their husband. Under Virginia law, women were able to own slaves, but were not allowed to sell them. In 1785, a complaint was made against Lydia Tribby for "dancing." Three years later she was still "dancing," according to the minutes of the Fairfax Women's Monthly Meeting 8th mo 1788. One wonders if she ever stopped.

Friendly persuasion to induce repentance could take years, and was often unsuccessful, so it is difficult to determine what actual outcomes were. What seems clear is that many young people did leave the Quaker faith, and it was becoming increasingly difficult to enforce strict Quaker Discipline when life was becoming more urban and cosmopolitan. Temptations were greater, and the Evangelical Movement was offering young Quakers new religious choices more in tune with a changing society.

# Chapter 8
# Slaves and Servants

**"In a world fraught with conflict...friends tolerance and compassion...retains its relevance and significance."—Glenn Crothers, Quaker Historian**

Quaker historian Glenn Crothers is convinced that "the interest of many Virginia Quakers in slavery insured that prior to the mid-1750s anti-slavery made little headway in the colony."

Although the Quaker faith took the equality of all human beings under God very seriously, owning slaves did not become a disownable offence until 1774 Fairfax Meeting in Waterford had tackled the problem in the 1750s. But Quakers wishing to free their slaves faced almost insurmountable problems. In Virginia, it was illegal to free a slave except for "meritorious service," which had to be approved by the governor and his council in Richmond. It was not until 1782 that the Virginia State Assembly voted to allow owners to emancipate their slaves.

In 1790, when Eli Whitney invented the cotton gin—the most famous labor saving device of the early industrial revolution––it had the unintended consequence of creating a huge demand for more slave labor. The gin mechanically separated the seeds, husk, and other debris from the cotton fiber, and reduced processing time so much it became economical for cotton growers to greatly expand their cotton production—requiring ever more slaves. Virginia had far more slaves than any other state, and it became a magnet for slave traders. Cotton was "king," and became America's number one export.

In 1798, the Fairfax Quarterly Meeting asked the Baltimore Yearly Meeting to clarify if hiring slaves was allowed. Baltimore replied that "the practice of hiring slaves is Contrary to our Christian Testimony and Discipline," and those who do so should be disowned. This practice continued to be a problem in some Meetings, and the Baltimore Yearly Meeting in 1805 and 1806 sent a cautionary note to all its members against "hiring black people who are slaves." Fairfax Meeting records, however, reveal only a few cases of the hiring of slaves; and when discovered, the perpetrators were requested to give up the practice. Local historian John Divine was convinced the practice was more widespread, and that "while Quakers didn't own slaves, they *hired* them; and didn't pay them very high wages."

Many 18th century Quakers had large farms and families, all of whom were expected to work on the farm. Friends relied upon instruction and persuasion rather than discipline in bringing up their children, hoping to instill in them a lifelong commitment to their faith-based community. Upon the death of the parents, the Quaker custom was to divide the land and property as equitably as possible among the surviving children—providing another incentive to stay put. This strategy was never easy to accomplish, because the deceased's assets were often difficult to liquidate and divide, and had to be sold at auction, with the proceeds divided among the beneficiaries. It was rare that it could be subdivided yet again for yet another generation. The search for new land was therefore a major factor in Quaker migrations, especially after new non-slave states were created further west.

Waterford Quakers did use indentured labor, often orphans or free Negroes who had difficulty in finding gainful employment. They could be "bound out" to a master by their relatives, or to intermediaries like churchwardens or overseers of the poor. Rachel Lane, a free Negro woman living in Waterford in 1790, bound out her three male children to the Overseer of the Poor. Indentures were usually limited to age eighteen for women and twenty-one for men, but indentured servants had no real legal protection or supervision. If they were mistreated and ran away, local law enforcement officials were required to find and return them to their masters.

The first documentary evidence of a free Negro individual in Waterford was the appearance on Loudoun County tax rolls of Nero Lawson in 1787. He apparently was literate, paid taxes for himself and another free Negro man, and on two horses and three cows. He was a farmer, and took on a young Negro orphan as his apprentice in 1795. In 1818, he was able to buy a lot on Water Street and build a house on it. Later, he purchased another lot and constructed a house.

After 1804, Virginia law required all newly-freed slaves to leave the Commonwealth within a year or risk being sold back into bondage. For those already free, the only legal protection they really had was a local government certificate attesting to their freedom. Freed slaves were subject to harassment and worse; being kidnapped and sold south was a constant fear. Children were especially at risk, and disowned Fairfax Quakers Nancy Griffith, who had one slave, and Thomas Lacey, who had seven slaves, stipulated in their 1811 and 1815 wills, that their slaves be freed when they reached twenty-one years of age and were able to care for themselves. Freed slaves also had to make sure their children were properly certified as free. Physical abuse was always a potential problem, but was not mentioned in Fairfax Meeting Minutes, except when Sarah Canby was disowned in 1802 "for the instigation of the abuse of a black boy." Her husband was eventually tried for killing the boy.

The outlook for freed slaves seemed so grim that some of Waterford's leading Quakers believed they should be sent back to Africa. In 1811, prominent citizens formed the American Colonization Society, whose purpose was to return freed slaves to the newly formed colony of Liberia. The society attracted not only abolitionists, but also slave owners who saw freed slaves as a threat to the institution of slavery, and colonization a means to get rid of them. Several prominent Waterford Quakers and one slaveholding non-Quaker joined the society.

Non-Quaker Noble Braden encouraged several of his own slaves to emigrate, and accompanied them to Norfolk, Virginia, where they embarked for Liberia. But the African colony proved to be a harsh alternative to slavery. The freed colonists were ill prepared for the tropical climate, rampant disease, hostile inhabitants, and difficulty of wresting a living from a strange land. While some adapted, one former Braden slave returned. He complained bitterly of his experience; but changing one's mind was not a real option, and the unfortunate colonist was only allowed to return when he lied, and begged to be allowed to bring back his wife, whom he said had been unable to make the voyage to Liberia with him.

In the 1830s, Waterford grain mill owner and prominent Quaker Edward Bond, was disowned when he repeatedly refused to stop hiring a local slave to work in the mill. In 1855, Mary Jane Hough "had in her service a female slave," and a committee was appointed to persuade her to admit the error of her ways. Six months later, the committee reported that despite numerous visits "she feels no condemnation," and the Meeting disowned her." Meanwhile, Mary Jane's husband Isaac Hough was forgiven after he apologized and promised never to hire a slave again.

Non-Quaker newcomers brought with them their religious beliefs and slaves. Scottish and Scotch-Irish migrating south from Pennsylvania founded the Kittocktin Presbyterian Church in 1765. In 1768, a log church was built on a plot of land two miles south of Waterford. No trace of this building remains, but grave markers bearing the date 1776 still stand on that spot. In 1814, the Presbyterians bought two lots on High Street and built a brick church, which was "free for all denominations." Baptists and Methodists also held services there. The Baptists erected their own brick church in 1852, and the Methodists built a wooden church in 1877. When the Presbyterian Church burned down in 1878, the congregation met in the Baptist Church, until a new church was built in 1882. This ecumenical spirit also extended to Waterford's Union Cemetery, where the name "Union" meant open to all denominations.

Waterford became a haven for free Negroes, whose numbers tripled from twenty-four in 1810 to seventy-eight in 1830. Most of Waterford's free Negro population worked as male laborers on farms or mill, or as female domestic servants. In the quarter century before the Civil War, Waterford's biggest employer of free Negroes was Quaker farmer and miller Thomas Phillips, who employed twenty-two; including entire families, such as Forest Griffith, his wife and daughter for $120 a year in 1846.

Quakers living in slave states were particularly susceptible to "Ohio fever," because Ohio was the first state created by the Northwest Ordinance of 1787, which prohibited slavery. To many Quakers, Ohio seemed to be a "promised land." In 1782, Thomas Jefferson wrote: "The Ohio is the most beautiful river on earth. Its current gentle, waters clear and bosom smooth."

In the first two decades of the 19th century, one to two families a year left the Fairfax Meeting for Ohio. Quakers could not join another Meeting unless they had a certificate signed and approved by their present Meeting. Many Waterford Quakers heading west travelled Braddock's Road, and then the National Road, crossing the Ohio River at Wheeling, West Virginia, and settling in what became Belmont County, Ohio. When Indiana (1816)) and Illinois (1818) became non-slave states, they also became destinations for Fairfax Quakers.

Although their families were large, infant mortality among the Quakers was surprisingly low, especially when compared to America's cities, which had become so unsanitary that the death rate often exceeded the birth rate, and total population levels failed to decline only because of the seemingly endless inflow of new immigrants. Thomas Jefferson's warning that great cities would become "great sores" on the body politic, was about to be fulfilled. John Hough's grandson Samuel and all five of his siblings survived their father and mother, and all eleven children of Samuel's uncle William Hough lived to maturity. All of Isaac Hollingsworth's children also outlived him.

Nevertheless, the loss of a new life was always hard to bear. Mary Dutton Steer, born to a prominent Waterford Quaker family in 1840, was cleaning out items collected under her kitchen stair a quarter-century later, and wrote a long poem "Old Memories" including the following verses:

> Back in the corner under the eaves
> An old fashioned cradle my eye perceives
> Of solid walnut, strong and good,
> And part with it—do you think I would?

> It was sixty years old when it came to me,
> And that's been twenty five years you see.
> And six little darlings have hush'd their cry
> At the sound of mother's lullaby
> As she rocked them gently to and fro
> And knit by the fire light's ruddy glow
> While one little darling's spirit fled
> From this same treasured bed.

Meanwhile, the larger world of the Society of Friends was suffering its own inner turmoil. It had been profoundly affected by the Evangelical Movement spreading rapidly across America in the late 18th and 19th centuries, and by the increasingly more cosmopolitan society of the cities, which influenced many city-dwelling Quakers to reject Quaker individualism and replace the absolute authority of Discipline with the absolute authority of the Bible.

"Hicksite" Friends—named after Elias Hicks, eloquent defender of traditional Quaker beliefs—retained their simple service focusing on achieving individual revelation through the "divine light of Christ" within themselves. They were opposed to any creed "that impeded the leadings of the inward Christ or the explorations of the rational mind." Prolonged debates between "Hicksite" and "Orthodox" only resulted in the hardening of attitudes, and travelling ministers fanned the fires of controversy. Soon there was no middle ground between the absolute authority of the Bible versus the absolute authority of Discipline, or between accepting a historic or a mystical in-born in-dwelling Christ.

In 1827, the Philadelphia Annual Meeting split into Orthodox and Hicksite factions. This schism had a ripple effect down the rigid Quaker hierarchy, causing quarterly Meetings to split and in turn, disown monthly Meetings that did not adhere to their particular faction. The Fairfax Quarterly Meeting, including Fairfax and Goose Creek (the meeting house at Monocacy had burned down in 1759) were all predominantly Hicksite, which greatly reduced internal conflict over the schism.

The rural-urban character of the split is epitomized by what happened in Waterford and nearby Winchester. Waterford's Fairfax Meeting did not lose a single member to orthodoxy while, Hopewell Meeting in Winchester was devastated. Only 12 percent of its nearly 700 members remained after the orthodox members left. Isaac Hollingsworth's grandson, David, who had inherited "Abraham's Delight," did not have a problem. He had already left the Quaker faith, had become a "Kent Street Presbyterian and had relaxed somewhat the strict way of living of [his] ancestors."

By and large, rural Hicksite Friends were disturbed by the worldliness of citified Orthodox Friends, reflected in the extremes of wealth, social position, ambition, and pride of city elders, who greatly influenced quarterly Meetings. These differences became very personal. Travelling Orthodox ministers no longer visited Hicksite Meetings, and vice versa. Like most religious schisms, each side believed its adherents were "the genuine successors" of the early founders and that their opponents had departed from "original doctrines." This perception nourished the belief that those on the other side were apostates, and left no middle ground for accommodation.

Each individual felt his or her religious freedom was at stake, and discussions became extremely acrimonious. Years later, Samuel Janney, Virginia's leading Quaker educator and abolitionist, lamented that words were "an imperfect medium for the conveyance of thought," because so many theologians "had attached meanings not intended by the original writers."

# Chapter 9
# Innovation and Mechanization

**"[Waterford flour] was fine, clean, and pure, and not mixed with meal of Indian corn, pease or any other grain or pulse"**
**—Oath sworn before a Justice of the Peace**

Quaker wheat farmers and millers from Pennsylvania's Brandywine Valley settled in western Loudoun County because its piedmont valleys contained more fertile soil than the neighboring tidewater plain of eastern Loudoun and Fairfax Counties. They brought with them clover to plant, deep plowing; a mixture of burnt lime, plaster of paris and dried manure; and crop rotation techniques—all of which greatly improved the fertility of the soil. Their white spring wheat produced a fine very durable wheat grain. With proper industrial processing, it would retain its freshness on the longest voyages.

The Quaker system was first published in a *Treatise on Practical Farming* by Loudoun farmer John Alexander Binns in 1803. Thomas Jefferson read Binns' book and was so impressed he described it as "the Loudoun method" in his correspondence. Ironically, it was one of the Earl of Loudoun's ancestors who was credited with first introducing burnt lime to help improve agricultural fertility in the 17th century. The Earl was elected to the prestigious Royal Society in 1738, for his contributions to scientific agriculture.

Welsh immigrant Oliver Evans in the 1780s built the world's first fully mechanized flour mill at Greenbank (now part of Wilmington, Delaware). The mill was powered by water wheels driven by the fall of the river, and the wheat was converted mechanically into flour without a human hand intervening. This process relied on a series of automated cups, belts, and wheels to move the wheat instead of human hands. It greatly reduced labor costs and vastly improved flour quality. Congress passed the first national patent law in 1790, and Oliver Evans received the third patent issued by the U. S. Government. Among the first of Evans's clients were the millers on the Brandywine River. So innovative was Evans's automated flour mill, that it set the standard for other mills for almost a century, until the roller process was introduced in 1870. By the late 1700s, bread made from "Brandywine Super-fine" was appearing on dinner tables of wealthy planters in southern states and the West Indies.

Flour exports had become such an important part of its economy, that Virginia passed legislation in 1765 and 1782 requiring the farmer to swear an oath before a justice of the peace that "the flour was not mixed with meal of Indian corn, peas, or any other grain or pulse, and that his casks are justly tarred."The farmer was then given a certificate which he showed to an inspector at the port of embarkation. The Waterford area's terrible dirt roads and the 45 mile trip to the ports of Washington, D. C. required a six-day roundtrip by wagon. When the Leesburg-Georgetown Turnpike (today's Routes 7 and 193) was completed in the early 1800s, the trip was reduced to three days. In difficult weather, wagons with heavy loads could get stuck for a long time. In early colonial Virginia, road-building was the responsibility of the county courts.

In 1748, the Virginia legislature gave the responsibility for building and maintenance of roads to local governments, which deeply resented paying to build, repair, and maintain thoroughfares for folk just passing through their communities. In 1762, the Loudoun County Court appointed four surveyors to "site a new road from Jenny's [Janney's] Mill into the main Road leading from Leesburgh to ferries on the Potomac River." Nevertheless, poor transportation remained the major issue hindering development for a half-century more, until angry merchants convinced the Virginia legislature to issue charters to private road companies to build and maintain roads for profit by charging tolls. Turnpike companies eventually linked Loudoun County with the ports of Alexandria and Georgetown in the east, and west to Ashby Gap. Because of the costs involved in road construction and maintenance, almost not one of the turnpike companies was profitable. One company that did pay dividends to its shareholders was the Little River Turnpike Company owned by Quaker Phineas Janney, who operated 34 miles of road between the towns of Aldie and Alexandria from 1806 to 1896.

The center of Waterford's economic activity was the mill on Catoctin Creek at the north end of town. A small log mill was first built in the 1740s by Waterford founder Amos Janney. His only son, Mahlon, inherited the mill in 1752, and in 1762 had a mile-long mill headrace dug to improve the flow of water. Also in 1762, he built a two-story stone house with a three-room floor plan known as the "Quaker" or "Pennsylvania" plan. The original house with its horsehair plaster and oak floors is still there today. Mahlon Janney built a second, larger mill on the same site, after the new "merchant milling" technology became widespread in the 1790s. The current mill building dates from about 1817, and was rebuilt by Thomas Phillips in 1832. Phillips sold it in 1859 to Samuel Means, a non-Quaker.

Waterford millers would have been in contact with their counterparts in Pennsylvania's Brandywine Valley, receiving early intelligence about Evans' revolutionary technological breakthrough. Mahlon Janney and Samuel Hough built, owned, and operated merchant mills using Evans technology, and exported their "American Superfine Flour" from the port of Alexandria. Strict inspection requirements ensured their flour would maintain its quality in reaching such faraway places as Lima, Peru, which required a four-to-five-month sea voyage around the continent's southern tip through the Straits of Magellan, and up the west coast of South America. This increased shipping costs some 600 percent more than a trip to Europe.

The three decades after the American Revolution were a time of great innovation and change in the application of new scientific discoveries and development of new inventions. Leading the way was U. S. Secretary of State and later President, Thomas Jefferson, who had been influenced by the French Enlightenment, a movement dedicated to unlocking the mysteries of the universe for the benefit of all mankind. Jefferson himself was an inventor, and hated the monopolies that characterized the economies of the Old World. He had become convinced that new ideas were as incapable of being the possession of a single individual as was the air people breathed. To his way of thinking, an invention was a cumulative process rather than the product of a single genius.

Thomas Jefferson was elected president in 1800. In his first annual message to the American people, Jefferson's theme was growth, peace, and prosperity. But America was at war with Tripoli over the capture of American vessels by Tripolitan pirates, and Jefferson cleverly blended both themes. He praised the schooner *Enterprise,* which had defeated a Tripolitan cruiser without any American loss of life; concluding that "agriculture, manufactures, commerce, and navigation, the four pillars of our prosperity, are the most thriving when left most free to individual enterprise."Jefferson did not go one step further and consider what might happen when legions of individuals, each pursuing their own interests, collided with the rights of others.

In 1790, Jefferson became Secretary of State, and took charge of the newly established Patent Office. Shortly thereafter, Oliver Evans received the third patent issued by the U. S. Government for his fully mechanized grain mill. Millers from all over the country—including Jefferson himself—proceeded to copy parts or all of the patented process. Evans was furious, and attempted to collect fees from his adversaries. Evans sent the President a bill, which Jefferson reluctantly paid. Evans was indeed a genius, who also invented a high pressure steam boiler capable of driving river boats and railroad trains. Yet, he spent much of his life scrambling for financing, and in litigating against all those, whom he correctly believed were stealing his ideas.

Pursuing "individual enterprise" and its corollary, "free enterprise," led to a belief in "individual entitlement, which fueled contempt for government regulation of any kind. Patents were viewed by many as a government obstacle to be overcome in the search for riches and success. A century later, such attitudes were more entrenched than ever. After Alexander Graham Bell invented the telephone in 1876, his father-in-law, who was a brilliant lawyer, fought over 600 legal actions against Bell's patents in courts of law. He won every single one.

The period 1792-1818 was the time of Waterford's greatest prosperity. Its population grew 60 percent, but the population dynamics of the town were changing fast. At the beginning of the 19$^{th}$ century, Waterford experienced an in-flow of non-Quakers and a building boom along Second Street or "new town," as it was known then, almost doubling Waterford's size. In the speculative frenzy that accompanied the boom, the two lots totaling 0.3 acres upon which Samuel Hough built his mother's house, were sold five times between 1810-1817, with the price increasing from $100 to $240, when Samuel Hough bought it in 1817.

The Second Bank of the United States, which had been chartered in 1816, could issue paper currency, which then was redeemable in specie (gold or silver coin), and make loans to state governments, businesses, and individuals. It expanded its lending and printed new bank notes so fast that by 1818, it was responsible for 20 percent of all lending by banks, and 40 percent of the bank notes in circulation. Many of its loans were politically motivated, and were granted without assessing the creditworthiness of the recipients. The Second Bank's directors decided in 1818 that it was overextended; and it began calling in its loans, creating a cascading effect down the chain of debtors, spelling ruin for many thousands of investors and hundreds of banks.

The "Panic of 1819" is considered to be the first boom-and-bust business cycle in American history. It affected everyone, from wealthy banker and landowner, to the most humble trader and holder of a mortgage on a log cabin. The banking crisis and speculative fever in land and investments in new production—especially cotton—which had been going on for decades, was brought to a sudden halt by a fall in cotton prices of 60 percent, between 1818-19 when British investors shifted to Indian cotton. Meanwhile, European agricultural production was recovering, and the price per barrel which Alexandria Quaker merchant Phineas

Janney paid Waterford millers for their "American Superfine Flour" fell 65 percent during 1818-1820.

Prussia emerged as a major European power after Napoleon was defeated in 1815. Its enlightened monarch, King Friedrich Wilhelm III, decided to make Prussian industry the equal of Great Britain's, the world's leading industrial country. In 1827, he sent students from the Prussian Industrial Institute to "infiltrate the flour mills of America, and learn the secrets of the American millers' success." Carl Friedrich Ganzel was selected to seek employment at Virginia's merchant mills in Alexandria, Falmouth, Fredericksburg, Richmond, Charlottesville, Staunton, Winchester, Shepherdstown, and Harpers Ferry. Ganzel was unsuccessful as an industrial spy in Virginia, but when he visited a Baltimore mill, he finally admitted his goal was to copy all production drawings and data. To his surprise, he was warmly welcomed: "they kindly took me by the hand and showed me everything having to do with the production of fine long lasting flour."

By the mid-1830s, Waterford farmers had abandoned the long wagon ride to the ports of Georgetown and Alexandria. They were taking their wheat eleven miles north by wagon, crossing the Potomac at Point of Rocks, Maryland, and using the C&O Canal and B&O railroad to get to market. Residents of Waterford had been complaining for almost a hundred years about the physical danger and economic losses suffered when trying to cross Catoctin Creek in high water. When Waterford was incorporated in 1836, it had the political clout to ask the county for a bridge. The county court agreed to appropriate $1,400 for "a substantial covered bridge, "while requiring citizens to raise the balance, but individual contributions fell short. A new petition in 1838 insisted that "no person could be found to construct a suitable bridge under $2,200." The county eventually appropriated $2,000 and the bridge was built in 1838-39. In 1889, the great Johnstown Flood elevated the water to a height never seen before, and the covered bridge was lifted up and carried away, last seen floating downstream into the broad Potomac. A replacement bridge was built, but it lasted only nineteen years, when a large threshing machine caused one end of the bridge to slide off its base and submerge the threshing machine. Today's concrete bridge was built in 1959, and is the fourth bridge built at this crossing.

# Chapter 10
# One Round Trip Out of Three

**"Mr. Gunner give them an answering shot!"**
**—Captain of the *Betsy Jane***

In 1793, France and Britain declared war on each other. President Washington issued a proclamation of neutrality declaring it was "the disposition of the United States to pursue conduct friendly and impartial to the belligerent powers." American ship builders took advantage of the reduction in trade between the two adversaries, and during 1793-1807 the number of U.S. merchant ships tripled to 10,000 employing 68,000 sailors. U.S. exports quadrupled. Merchant ships under 200 tons, such as the Baltimore Clipper *Betsy Jane* owned by Charles Taylor, could pay for all their building and outfitting costs in one successful trip. Idle British "able seamen" were also enticed by the fifteen dollar monthly wage paid by American merchant ship captains, as compared to the Royal Navy's seven dollar wage. By 1807, most of Europe was under the control of Napoleon Bonaparte, and Britain announced a sea blockade on all ports controlled by the French. Napoleon responded by declaring all British ports under French blockade. Both countries also forbade any neutral countries to trade with their enemy.

After America went to war with Britain in 1812, the British Royal Navy extended its blockade to include major American ports. President Thomas Jefferson placed an embargo on all overseas trade with Britain. The embargo was a disaster, and was ended fourteen months later. Like most economy-wide restraints on trade, it had the unintended effect of creating a vast "shadow" import-export trade involving smuggling, trading with the enemy, operating with counterfeit licenses, and privateers replacing legitimate trading vessels. The combined effect of blockade and embargo was to drive most legitimate American trading vessels from the seas until the war ended in 1815.

Local Quaker ship owner Charles Taylor was not intimidated. His *Betsy Jane* clipper ship managed to make it back with a valuable cargo from the East Indies. In 1814, *Betsy Jane* was off the coast of Virginia heading for Philadelphia, when a lookout spotted a sail on the horizon. The captain went aloft with his spy glass, came down, called the crew together, and told them the other ship was a British Man-O-War with sixty to seventy-four guns. He told the crew:

> Everyman stand at his post, be quick to obey orders, and if I don't fool that Englishman, my name isn't Jason...Now, put every stitch of canvas on you can find with a place to fasten it, and every man who can carry a quart of water get to work and keep those sails wet. And one thing more, that Englishman shall never have the *Betsy Jane*...I will scuttle and sink her first.

The British vessel was gradually gaining, but darkness was approaching even faster. BOOM!! Came the sound of a British cannon, but the ball dropped three cables short [about 500 yards]. "Now Mr. Gunner, give them an answering shot! All hands were [wear] ship!" The *Betsy Jane* turned to the east and then south, doubling back on her tracks in the dark and heading for the port of Baltimore.

The Royal Navy needed to get the British Army on dry land, before they could pursue the conquest of Washington, but the British commanders feared landing a large force of soldiers and being ambushed in the "boundless forests" and "numerous creeks" of Tidewater Virginia; "losing men without show [in] an inglorious war," while denouncing American preference for shooting from behind cover as cowardly and effeminate They chose instead to launch amphibious surprise attacks, targeting shipping towns and villages. To carry out this strategy, they needed a ready supply of fresh water and provisions, and found most Tidewater Virginians quite eager to sell them goods for British gold. They also found that slaves were equally eager to serve as their guides through the maze of deep forests and creeks. During 1813, at least 600 Tidewater slaves stole boats and canoes to seek refuge with the Royal Navy.

Tidewater slave owners rationalized the departures of so many slaves by emphasizing the slaves credulity and childlike nature (and therefore their own superiority), and by denouncing the British as cunning deceivers who meant to sell them into harsher slavery in the West Indies.

Many male former slaves chose to join the Colonial Marines. They were paid six dollars a month less the cost of their uniform. They were happy to exchange their rags for a bright red coat, white jacket, and pantaloons, black gaiters and stocks, and black hats with narrow brims and white feathers. The British daily ration of meat, wheat bread, and a tot of rum, was a great improvement over their cornmeal diet as slaves. They were also promised promotion as noncommissioned officers based on performance.

Still, British Rear Admiral Sir George Cockburn had his prejudices, believing "Blacky hereabouts is neither very valorous nor very active."Not long after, Cockburn wrote "They are getting on astonishingly, and are really fine fellows...They have induced me to alter the bad opinion I had of the whole of their race." The Colonial Marines justified Admiral Cockburn's new optimism when they successfully attacked an American militia battery and burned their barracks in Accomack County, and burned tobacco barns and liberated slaves along the Patuxent River.

Admiral Cockburn decided the Colonial Marines would play a role in major engagements by serving as light infantry skirmishers who led the advance of British regulars, guarding their flanks in wooded terrain and surprising American snipers. Their white platoon leader, Lieutenant James Scott, recalled: "The enemy, who prided himself on his skill in bush-fighting, was completely foiled." More ex-slaves were enlisted, and within a month their unit numbered 300 men. They then became part of the Third Battalion of Royal and Colonial Marines, which included 200 white Royal Marines. Cockburn escalated his shore raids, targeting the Potomac and Patuxent Rivers and threatening Washington.

President James Madison instructed Stephen Pleasanton, Clerk of the State Department, to remove the nation's most important records to a safe haven. Terrified Washingtonians were searching for any way to get out of the city, and Pleasanton was fortunate to find a wagon and team of horses, as well as bolts of linen, which he and his assistants sewed into bags which could hold and protect the precious documents. He first took the documents to Alexandria, but decided he was too close to Washington. After consulting with local farmers, he decided to head west.

On August 14, 1814, a weary Pleasanton arrived in Leesburg, Virginia, looking for a safe haven for his precious cargo. Charles Binns Jr., Clerk of the Loudoun County Courthouse, knew what to do. His father, Charles Binns Sr., had constructed in 1757 a mansion house near Leesburg, When Loudoun County was established in 1759, Binns Sr. became its first clerk of court, and he conducted most of his business from his home. He built a brick vault in the basement, in which he stored the county's earliest records, installed an iron door leading to the basement, and placed iron bars over basement windows. When a courthouse was built in Leesburg in 1811, all Loudoun County records were moved there and the basement vault was left empty.

Charles Binns Jr. and Pleasanton carefully stored in his father's empty vault the original Articles of Confederation, Declaration of Independence, and U.S. Constitution, George Washington's copy of the Declaration of Independence with his marginal notes, Washington's letter to Congress reporting the victory at Yorktown, and his letter resigning his commission as commander-in-chief; and other important documents.

Admiral Cockburn sent his army up the Patuxent River to Bladensburg, Maryland, where 7,000 raw American Militia faced 4,000 battle-hardened British veterans of the Duke of Wellington's Spanish campaign, on the opposite side of the Anacostia River. When the British constructed a bridge of boats and crossed the river, the militia turned and ran, and chaos reigned in Washington.

When the British reached Washington and broke into the White House, the delighted officers sat down and ate the meal left behind by President and Mrs. Madison. That night, Cockburn ordered the building torched by fifty sailors and the Colonial Marines, who broke the windows with long poles and hurled in incendiary devices "so that an instantaneous conflagration took place and the whole building was wrapped in fire and smoke."

The next British objective was Baltimore, but the attack failed. When the British sailed away, Francis Scott Key commemorated the American victory in what became *The Star Spangled Banner*. His third verse mocked the British use of runaway slaves in the British army:

> No refuge could save the hireling and slave
> From the terror of flight or the gloom of the grave
> And the star-spangled banner—O! Long may it wave
> O'er the land of the free and the home of the brave.

Slaveholders condemned pacifist and anti-slavery Quakers as traitors, who inadvertently or not, were aiding and abetting the enemy. In Loudoun County, Fairfax and Goose Creek Meetings held to their principles, and disowned ten young men for participating in the militia. Quaker men who did not join the militia received stiff fines; and if they could not pay, their property was seized.

Although most Americans proclaimed victory after General Andrew Jackson defeated the British Army at the Battle of New Orleans, the contest between the two nations was at best a draw. The real losers of the War of 1812 were America's Indians. Shawnee brothers Tecumseh ("Shooting Star") and Tenskwatawa ("The Prophet") had called for a united resistance of all tribes against the wave of white settlement that threatened to engulf them. Tecumseh's ultimate goal was to establish a separate Indian nation. He saw the war with Britain as an opportunity to achieve his goal by siding with the British. He was a great orator, but never was able to attract sufficient followers among other tribes to achieve his ambition. The British were more interested in defending Canada than helping the Indians; and in 1813, Tecumseh was defeated and killed at the Battle of the Thames. The Shawnee and their allies were forced to move west. Ironically, Indians who had sided with Jackson, like the Creek and the Cherokee, suffered a similar fate.

The 1814 Treaty of Ghent ended the war, but the British conceded nothing else. Their restrictions on American trade and impressment of American seamen only ended with the defeat of Napoleon in 1815. Virginia slave holders who had lost their human property attempted to get their former slaves back, but the British refused, unless the slave was willing to return. Only *nine* of 3,400 former Virginia slaves decided to go back.

Most Americans celebrated the end of the war as a second war of independence from Britain, and as vindication of their identity as a nation. U.S. Navy Commodore Stephen Decatur spoke for the nation when he made his famous toast: "Our country! In her intercourse with foreign nations may she always be in the right, but our country, right or wrong." America had gained a new self-respect, and President James Madison's residence received a hasty coat of white paint over its stone exterior to hide the black smoke marks," and forever after has been known as the "White House."

Meanwhile, in Waterford, the end of war was followed by catastrophe, when the biggest volcanic eruption in recorded history—25 times more powerful than Mt. St. Helen's last eruption — occurred at Mt. Tambora in Indonesia in April 1815. The ash column rose an amazing 28 miles in the sky, creating an ash blanket that eventually spread around the world, and profoundly affected world climate. Loudoun County in May 1816 suddenly turned extremely dry and cold, with killing frosts and no rain. These conditions persisted through September. The creeks stopped running, and only a few very deep pools had any water. Ironically, the wheat crop was good, but it was so cold, farm workers wore coats all summer, some even for the exhausting work of cutting, binding, and shocking the wheat by hand.

In the Waterford area, the only springs left were one in Leesburg and another on Samuel Purcell's property north of Purcellville. Farmers would come from all over north Loudoun to the two springs, and line up their wagons, waiting their turn, for a limited amount of water. Pastures became dusty, barren wastelands. Desperate farmers turned their cattle into the woods, and when all the leaves of the lower branches of trees had been eaten, trees were cut down to give the animals access to leaves from the upper branches. Finally, at the end of September, the rains came back. Loudoun farmers remembered 1816 as the "year of winter" In recent times, Waterford farmer Bruce McIntosh remembers only one time, during the drought of 1956, when his grandfather had to cut branches from trees to provide feed for his cattle.

# Chapter 11
# Between Life and Death

**"Milly Winters/ five foot one inch high, has a mole on the right side of her nose, one on the left cheek near the corner of the eye, two small ones on her chin, one larger one on the back of her neck, a scar under her left jaw"—Certification of Freedom, signed by Loudoun County, Virginia, Clerk of Court, Charles Binns, Jr…October, 1823**

After Congress prohibited the importation of slaves in 1808, the slave trade in Virginia became big business. One of the law's unintended consequences was that other southern states turned to Virginia as an alternative source of slaves, because it had three times more slaves than any other state. In Alexandria, slave dealers Franklin and Armfield moved 1,000-1,200 slaves south each year. Most walked the Carolina Road, barefoot and in chains.

William Walthall, from Gravelly Run Meeting near Richmond, described what many Virginia Quakers felt:

> I was accustomed to seeing droves of slaves on their way to southern market. The circumstances in my mind were frightful. Noble men, manacled and handcuffed, driven to market like beasts. About the year 1828 my parents finding themselves left alone as members of Friends' church in a dense slave holding community, and realizing the danger that would attend their effort to raise their children under such circumstances, resolved to move to Ohio.

In Virginia, "a prime field hand" sold for $400. At the end of the Carolina Road, the price rose to $600. Free Negroes in Loudoun County lived in constant fear of being kidnapped and "sold south." The risks of being sold and of the breakup of slave families had increased dramatically after a 1792 Virginia law defined slaves as personal property. They were no longer "real property," which had to be sold with the land, and as "personal property" could be sold separately.

African slaves first had to survive a dangerous sea passage, in which they were stowed like cargo in the holds of ships and fed only enough to prevent starvation. The slave traders had to navigate the dangerous currents and storms around Africa's Cape of Good Hope, before crossing the Atlantic to the New World. Many ships never arrived at their destination. Marine archaeologists have determined that at least 600 [slave] ships with names like *Our Lady of Mercies, The Meermin, and L'Aurore* were wrecked somewhere along their voyage.

According to author Alan Taylor, between 1790 and 1810, after the cotton gin made cotton cultivation much more profitable, at least 100,000 Virginian slaves were sold south and west. Thomas Jefferson was among the plantation owners who sold slaves. Jefferson favored and protected slaves who were obedient and worked hard. But when a slave became disruptive, Jefferson would make an example and a warning to other slaves, by selling the slave to a "quarter so distant, as never more to be heard from among us." Between 1784 and 1796, Jefferson sold—or gave to relatives—161 slaves.

The greatest demand and highest prices were obtained for 17 to 26 year-old slaves, and many thousands of Negro families suffered the horror of being separated forever from their maturing children. Even when slaves were offered the opportunity to leave their families and escape their bondage, such as occurred in the War of 1812, "most slaves stayed behind" because of their families. America's Constitution did not offer slaves any protection. It defined them as "three-fifths of a Person. The word "person" was synonymous with "human being," and therefore slaves were "three-fifths human" and "two-fifths" non-human.

Even when free, former slaves faced grave danger. The only legal protection a free slave had was a document attesting to his/her identity, which was signed and certified by the clerk of the county court. The importance of this document cannot be underestimated, because it was designed to provide incontrovertible evidence of the identity of the bearer. The name and age—birth dates of non-whites were not recorded—of the individual, parents' names, the mother's maiden name, and the parents' marital status, had to be clearly indicated. The certificate had to indicate that the white person attesting to their free status had sworn an oath to that effect in the presence of the clerk of court. But the real protection provided by the certificate, was that it contained a detailed description of those aspects of the individual's physical appearance which made him/her *UNIQUE*:

On October 14, 1823, Clerk of the Loudoun County Court Charles Binns Jr. certified:

> Milly Winters, age 25, of a very bright complexion [code for white], five feet one inch high, has a mole on the right side of her nose, one on the left cheek near the corner of the eye, two small ones on her chin, one larger one on the back of her neck, a scar immediately under her left jaw, and no other apparent scars or marks, was this day registered [No. 463] in my office according to law.

This piece of paper, this passport to freedom, folded and refolded, a patchwork of faded stains and cracked seams, upon which the humanity of an individual was reduced to the smallest imperfections on the surface of her body, was the difference between life and death for Milly Winters. Her Certification of Freedom was signed by Charles Binns Jr., Clerk of Loudoun County. Binns had beautiful handwriting and wrote his letters large. The writing is clearly legible and the paper is of good quality because it was an important legal document, enabling what was written there to be seen and read almost two centuries later. To survive a lifetime or more, the paper was made out of heavyweight cotton.

Similar certificates, as well as advertisements for the sale of slaves or the return of slave fugitives, provide a great deal of evidence that scars, deformities, and other evidence of prior injury were common among Virginia's Negro population before the Civil War. Whether or not they were caused by physical abuse, accident, or mistake cannot be determined. Only if a slave owner caused the death of a slave, would the matter have been investigated. Even if the owner was brought to trial, the odds were great he or she would be found innocent of any crime.

The new owner of Samuel Hough's house was Israel Thompson Griffith. In 1830, he had opened a new variety store, selling dry goods, groceries, clothing, shoes, hardware, crockery, and much more, "at low prices, for cash." He apparently was no businessman, because one year later, he closed his Waterford store, selling his stock at cost. He certainly had sufficient funds to lend Samuel Hough $1,568 in 1833. The loan had to be repaid by 1835, and as security for the loan, Hough gave Griffith a deed of trust for "the Fairfax meeting house lot and two others adjoining the town of Waterford. This document is of particular interest because, Samuel's wife Jane was a co-owner of the properties, and the law required two justices of the peace to determine whether or not she had been coerced by her husband into signing the deed of trust.

At Waterford's July 4th celebration in 1834, the Declaration of Independence was first read by George Washington Hough (Samuel's nephew), followed by Israel Griffith's toast to "The present political revolution. May it result in the extermination of dishonesty from the executive and legislative branches of our government." His concern for good government was also local, and when Waterford became incorporated in 1836, he was one of nine councilmen selected for Waterford's first town council, and was appointed recorder. In 1837, Israel Griffith bought the three-quarter acre lot across the street from the Samuel Hough House, and three other lots in town. It seemed he was there to stay.

In 1831, Nat Turner, a Negro slave and deeply religious visionary, who believed God sent him messages, led his followers in cutting, stabbing, beating, or shooting to death 57 white men, women, and children. The first to die were his master, mistress, and their three children, killed with an axe as they lay in their beds.

As they went from house to house, killing quietly and quickly, Turner's band swelled to more than fifty slaves. Turner himself wounded several victims with a sword, later confessing to killing only one person. Local militia eventually broke up the group, killing or capturing most, but terrified white people all over the South who believed a conspiracy existed, killed at least 200 innocent Negroes wrongly identified as conspirators. Nat Turner stayed hidden in the woods for weeks, but was finally discovered, tried by a jury, and hung for his crimes.

While in prison, Turner was interviewed by lawyer Thomas Gray, who published his account in *The Confessions of Nat Turner, the Leader of the Late Insurrection in Southampton, VA.,* in 1831.Turner told Gray that "Joseph Travis was to me a kind master. I had no cause to complain of his treatment of me…the murder of this family, five in number, was the work of a moment…I viewed the mangled bodies in silent satisfaction."What really shocked Southern whites was that in Turner's mind there seemed to be no contradiction between the brutality of his crime and his apparent affection for the white family who owned him. Many slave holding whites came to the conclusion that every Negro slave was a potential murderer.

The Virginia State Assembly received many petitions on how to deal with the situation. A petition to gradually abolish slavery, submitted by the Virginia Yearly Friends Meeting, was the only one considered by the Assembly. It was voted down, 65 to 58. Only *seven* votes separated Virginians who were willing to end slavery, from those who would not. How quickly that would change.

For most of Virginia's white population, the only alternative left was to ensure that another Nat Turner could not rise again. Legislation followed, restricting almost every activity Negroes could undertake. On matters of race in Virginia, a middle ground for discussion was fast disappearing. Virginia's infamous "Black Laws" were designed to prevent people of color from gathering together for any purpose, and were especially restrictive against "teaching them reading and writing, either in the day or night. "

Black Laws" also outlawed religious services for Negroes, stating that "any slave or free Negro [who]…shall preach or hold a meeting for religious purposes…shall be punished at the discretion of the justice of the peace with not exceeding thirty nine lashes."

Henson Young was born a slave in 1811. He was owned by Jacob Mock, whose farm was located just north of Waterford. Henson was listed on census records as a "mulatto." In 1831, Mock must have been seriously ill because he made his will and died within a year. An entire paragraph in the will was devoted to. .

> My boy Hanson [sic] I will o be free at the age of 26 years and that my executors prov de for him so that he shall not fall into a state of slavery again by the operation of the laws of the state in which we live. And I further will that my executors shall give the boy Hanson at the time of his emancipation ten dollars in cash and a good suit of woolen cloth clothing.

Jacob Mock's will was probated September10, 1832. He bequeathed to his wife Elizabeth "a full life estate in and to all the land which I bought of Saml and John Taylor...two feather beds of her choice and such other furniture necessary to her comfort...and two milk cows." Mock had nine children. Five children who were twenty-one or older had already been given legacies when they reached their majority. His four children under the age of twenty-one, and Henson, were given "specific legacies:" Henson received the ten dollars in cash and eighteen dollars to buy the suit of clothes, as stated in Mock's will.

The probate occurred not long after Nat Turner's rebellion in 1831, and, given those circumstances, what is so unusual is Henson being included in the will as a recipient of a "special legacy." This meant he was considered by Jacob Mock to be a "legal person" rather than as his "property." This act, as well as Mock's deep concern expressed in the will that his executors do everything to keep Virginia laws from preventing "my Boy" Henson gaining his freedom, clearly indicate Henson was Jacob Mock's natural-born son. Why then was Henson not given his freedom in accordance with the will at age twenty-six?

After Nat Turner's Rebellion, it was extraordinarily dangerous and difficult for a free Negro to survive in Virginia without the protection of a white owner. Also, an 1806 law provided that any Negro receiving his or her freedom after the date of the law, would have to leave the state within a year or forfeit that freedom. Even if Henson had become free at age 26, any children he had would still have been slaves, because under Virginia law it was the mother that determined the status of a child born into slavery. Henson's only alternative would have been to leave Virginia and his family. Henson Young was finally freed on 9th December1850, when he was thirty-nine years old.

Prominent Quaker educators such as Samuel Janney from Goose Creek Meeting, unsuccessfully petitioned the Virginia State Legislature in 1847 to allow Negroes to be taught to read. A lifelong abolitionist, Janney was indicted "for inciting to riot" in 1849, when he published an article critical of slavery in a Leesburg newspaper. Janney eloquently defended his presentation, and the indictment was dismissed. The rationale for prosecuting Janney was based on an official policy adopted by the State in the wake of the Nat Turner uprising that forbade public criticism of slavery on the grounds it could encourage future slave revolts. At the time, Janney was headmaster of the Springdale School at Goose Creek, where he taught a number of Waterford children. Janney was a leader of anti-slavery and free schools movements in Virginia; a man of great ability, well educated, and articulate with both voice and pen. Janney sincerely believed he could change minds and hearts, and that in the 1840s, Virginia was turning towards emancipation. He denounced Virginians who were preaching secession.

In his memoirs, Samuel Janney advised fellow Quakers to take a stand against slavery under the "meek, lamb-like, spirit of Christ." With a tactful and judicious approach, Janney hoped to convince Virginia's slaveholders to gradually liberate their slaves. He acknowledged that many slave owners who supported back-to-Africa colonization were doing so only to remove "dangerous" free

Negroes from Virginia. Yet he understood that rather than condemning his audience, he had to appeal to the benefits manumission would entail. He therefore argued that a free economy would be much more prosperous than one encumbered by slave labor. Janney explained that his zealous pursuit of reform began when "at a very early age I experienced the operation of divine grace condemning me for evil, and inciting me to goodness."

The Panic of 1837 was exceeded in severity and duration only by the Great Depression of 1929. Speculation in land and cotton, long-term infrastructure development financed by short-maturing loans, dependence on foreign credit, and mistrust of our own banking and currency systems during a period of great economic expansion, were at the heart of the economy's downfall.

President Andrew Jackson closed down the Second Bank of the United States by withdrawing all federal funds and refusing to renew its charter. The nation was left without a lender of last resort and with no means of regulating the creation of paper money by state and private banks. Jackson's Specie Circular of 1836 prevented federal land offices from accepting banks' paper money from potential settlers—only specie would do. But banks did not have specie to back up their paper currency, which rapidly lost value, and the liquidity in the banking system dried up. Land sales dropped to one-fourth of the previous year's sales and thousands of land speculators and the banks that financed them, faced financial ruin.

In 1837, America's banks had to depend more than ever on international specie payments to meet their domestic lending needs. When the Bank of England curtailed credit in early 1837 to pay for emergency grain imports after a failed harvest in Britain, American banks dependent on British financing had to call in their loans to satisfy the demands of their foreign creditors. On May 10, 1837 every bank in New York City stopped payment in gold and silver. Newly-elected President Martin Van Buren, who considered himself Andrew Jackson's disciple, refused to take any government action to save the banking system.

Many economists and historians blame Van Buren for prolonging the panic for seven years. Others say boom-and-bust are an inevitable consequence of the business cycle. That debate goes on today. What is not debatable is the human suffering involved. Before the crisis was over, thousands of businesses and speculators had gone bankrupt, millions of ordinary people had lost everything, and 40 percent of America's banks closed their doors forever. The Panic of 1837 was arguably a "depression," because it lasted six to seven years.

Data indicating the economic cost to Waterford of the Panic of 1837 is not available. Population statistics can provide a useful indicator of the impact of economic cycles. Local historians John and Bronwen Souders gathered data indicating that between 1810 and 1830, Waterford's population of both free and slave Negroes increased some 300 percent; but steadily declined during 1840-1860.

On September 9, 1839, Waterford's mayor presided over an inquest, held in the Samuel Hough House, with twelve jurors present to view Israel Thompson Griffith's body. All twelve men swore oaths and signed and sealed an "inquisition indenture," testifying that Griffith "being alone, in a state of mental derangement threw himself into his well on his own premises whereby he was drowned about three or four o'clock in the morning."

We do not know what demons drove one of Waterford's leading citizens to take his own life. A likely explanation for his state of mind would be the recent death of his young wife. He had married Sarah Thompson, a first cousin 15 years his junior, in 1831. Marrying a first cousin was contrary to Quaker discipline, and Sarah had been disowned from the Fairfax Meeting. Why Griffith was not disowned remains a mystery. The Samuel Hough House was sold by Griffith's heirs to Jonathan Cost, who subsequently died. In 1853, the house was sold to Charles and Nancy Hollingsworth. Samuel Hough's mother, Lydia, was second cousin three generations removed from Charles Hollingsworth, so the house was back in the family again.

# Chapter 12
# A Raging Epidemic of Secession

**"We deem it our religious duty to take no part in [this war]."**
**—Fairfax Friends Meeting, Waterford, Virginia**

The Bible was as ambiguous regarding slavery as was the U.S. Constitution. Baptist, Presbyterian, and Methodist Churches split into northern and southern denominations: Each side defending its position as being according to scripture. Congress also passed the Fugitive Slave Law, which prescribed that slaves *were* property.

The Missouri Compromise of 1850 was an attempt to defuse the confrontation between Southern slave-holding and Northern slave-free states over whether slavery should be extended to the territories acquired in the Mexican War of 1846-48. California was admitted to the Union as a free state. Texas, a slave state, gave up its claim to part of the New Mexico territory when the Federal government assumed all of its sizeable debt. The people of the territories of New Mexico and Utah were allowed to determine by "popular sovereignty" whether to be slave or free states, and slavery was abolished in Washington, D.C.

More and more Quakers became involved in politics as the debate over extending or excluding slavery from new states polarized the political scene. They were especially attracted to the newly-established Republican Party. In 1856, Goose Creek Meeting held two Saturday debates on Millard Fillmore's candidacy in the forthcoming presidential election. A large crowd attended the second debate, including both slave owners and anti-slavers. When two Quakers stood up to denounce Fillmore for voting for the Fugitive Slave Law and failing to oppose the spread of slavery into the western territories, slave owners jumped to Fillmore's defense, and the meeting broke up in an uproar. The editor of Leesburg's *Democratic Mirror* claimed the debate was staged "for the treasonable object of proclaiming boldly and impudently the vilest Black Republican Doctrines."Northern newspapers picked up the story, and stirred up angry reactions against Quakers all across Loudoun County. Waterford Quakers managed to keep quiet over all the fuss, but their emphasis on maintaining balance between extremes would not survive much longer.

In 1857, Dredd Scott, a slave in Missouri, with the aid of abolitionist lawyers, filed suit in federal court claiming that as he had previously resided in a free state (Illinois) and a free territory (Wisconsin), he was entitled to his freedom. The case was narrowly defined as jurisdictional, but had broad implications for the status of all Americans of African descent. Seven of nine of the U. S. Supreme Court justices ruled that Scott was chattel, or property, and thus subject to due process of law governing property.

Abolitionists were outraged. Frederick Douglass was one of the few who saw the bright side of this decision. He believed it would polarize the nation and bring the issue of slavery to the forefront of national affairs, thus leading to its ultimate destruction. Abolitionist John Brown agreed with Douglas, but decided *he* would be God's instrument in destroying slavery.

On the night of October 16, 1859, John Brown led thirteen white and five Negro men into Harpers Ferry, where they occupied the arsenal, armory, and railroad depot without opposition. Brown distributed his small force among the major buildings and the bridge over the Shenandoah River, but local militia struck back quickly, overwhelming Brown's men. Several tried to escape, and Brown was left with one-half his force, his "enlisted" slaves, and ten white hostages.

Colonel Robert E. Lee and a detachment of U.S Marines arrived at midnight. At dawn Lee sent his aide-de-camp, Lieutenant J. E.B. Stuart, under a flag of truce, to ask Brown to surrender. Brown refused, and Lee ordered the Marines to attack. The Marines battered down the door, and Lieutenant Israel Greene's sabre cut the back of Brown's neck. He fell senseless to the floor. In three minutes, the fighting was over. Brown's attack on Harpers Ferry defied any strategic or tactical logic. He saw himself as "the sword of the Lord," wreaking divine vengeance upon the wicked of the earth who had violated God's laws. In a letter to a friend just before he died, Brown wrote that to destroy God's enemies "my death may be of vastly more value than my life is."

Brown's enemies wanted him out of the way as quickly as possible. After a speedy trial, Brown was convicted of treason, conspiring with Negroes to produce insurrection, and murder in the first degree. Each of these crimes carried the death penalty. John Brown was perfectly composed as he walked from his jail cell to the gallows. He was not allowed to leave any last written notes or messages, but managed to hand a piece of paper to a guard, on which was written: "I John Brown am now quite certain that the crimes of this guilty land, will never be purged away but with blood. I had as I now think, vainly flattered myself, that without very much bloodshed, it might be done."

John Brown became a national hero, villain, and lightening rod, attracting the worshipful admiration of abolitionists and deep hatred of slave owners. His attack convinced most Southerners that all Northern abolitionists were intent on inciting a slave revolt which would terrorize slave holders and involve the killing of innocent men, women, and children.

Back in Loudoun, Leesburg's *Democratic Mirror* denounced Brown's attack as "one of the most fearful plans for revolution that this or any other country has ever witnessed." Fear that a horde of Northern abolitionists would try to free Brown led to the formation of six volunteer and militia companies in northwest Loudoun near Harper's Ferry. The "Between the Hills" area southeast of Harpers Ferry became an armed camp. In a thirty-day period, Baltimore firearms dealers sold more than 10,000 pistols to Virginians.

Waterford Friends were both appalled and frightened by Brown's insurrection and the furor it aroused among their non-Quaker neighbors. They kept to themselves, and when they hosted a quarterly meeting, the subject of Brown's Raid never came up— much to the disappointment of many of their visitors. Quakers had reason to be afraid. Throughout Virginia, Friends were suspected of secretly supporting Brown's violent attack.

Between 1800 and 1860, it is estimated that about 6,000 Friends left the Southern states to go west. So many Virginia Quakers left, that the Virginia Yearly Meeting in Richmond was "laid down," and that function was transferred to the Baltimore Yearly Meeting. The increasingly intolerant attitude of Virginia slaveholders reinforced by anti-Negro legislation, plus the catastrophic rupture between Orthodox and Hicksite Quakers, caused many Quakers to seek a new start in one of the free states to the west.

In 1860, 63 percent of the Fairfax Meeting membership and 60 percent of Hopewell Meeting members, were females. As a result, Quaker women assumed greater and more numerous responsibilities. Six of the seven ministers recognized by the Fairfax Meeting between 1800 and 1850 were women. Five women and two men became elders after 1850. As slavery became more divisive and polarizing in Virginia, the burden of maintaining the Quaker community's ethical and spiritual concerns depended upon the relations nurtured by women.

In 1860, Waterford was the second largest urban center (after Leesburg) in Loudoun County, and the commercial center for farms within a five to eight mile radius. The federal census of 1860 listed seven merchants, plus blacksmiths, saddlers, shoemakers, tailors, cabinet makers, hotel and tavern keepers, a tinner, an ambrotypist, and a confectioner, among others. Four taverns emphasized how much Waterford had become cosmopolitan and less Quaker. The 1860 census listed 155 free Negroes and 129 Quakers among 990 residents of the village plus surrounding farms. At a time when most Virginia whites considered free Negroes, who represented only six percent of Loudoun County's total population, to be a threat to slavery, Waterford and the farms around it had become part of that threat.

In the 1860 presidential election in Loudoun County, only eleven votes (including just two from Waterford) were cast for Abraham Lincoln, while John Bell of the Constitutionalist Union Party, who promised to preserve both the Union and the institution of slavery, received 69 percent of the vote. Waterford was voting for the status quo, but a year later the status quo had disappeared, and Waterford villagers voted 221 to 30 *against* secession. Waterford's northern neighbors, the Lovettsville "Germans," also voted not to secede, 325 to 46. Communities to the north and west of Lovettsville, like the ironworkers at Potomac Furnace, also voted heavily to stay in the Union.

In Leesburg, the county seat, the vote was 400 to 22 *for* secession. Many Quakers from nearby Goose Creek Meeting, including Samuel Janney, stayed away from the polls in the belief that remaining neutral was the best path to take. The town of Purcellville voted 82 to 31 to secede. The Quakers of Fairfax Meeting in September 1861 resolved: "We deem it our religious duty to take no part in [this war], and abstain from every act that would give aid in its prosecution."

William James was one of thirty Waterford residents who voted for secession. He was born in 1828 and was connected through his father Elijah to the Samuel Hough family. Elijah's brother Levi, had married Samuel Hough's sister Rachel in 1797. James provided much of the initial investment for developing the center of Waterford, where Main Street, Water Street, and Second Street converge. He was operating a Waterford general store in 1855 with a partner, George W. Paxson. In 1856, James purchased Waterford postmaster Oscar F. Reed's storehouse, which he converted into a general store and stable. In 1857, he built the William James House, a wood frame house next to the general store.

By the mid-19th century, John Janney, a former Quaker from Goose Creek, had become one of Virginia's most influential and powerful politicians. Early in his career, he helped draft a bill for the Virginia legislature to abolish slavery, and successfully defended a freed slave who was charged with stealing his wife after her owner refused to sell her. Yet he became a slave owner and was disowned by the Goose Creek Meeting. On February 14, 1861, as the entire nation watched, John Janney presided over the Virginia Secession Convention to decide whether Virginia ought to secede from the Union.

On April 12, 1861, Federal Fort Sumter in the harbor at Charleston, South Carolina, was attacked. The day after the fort surrendered and the stars and stripes were hauled down, President Lincoln called for the mobilization of 75,000 volunteers to crush the rebellion. This forced Virginia's Secession Convention to decide whether it would send Virginia's quota of volunteers to fight the rest of the South; and the debate turned in favor of secession. John Janney supported the Union, and twice voted against secession. But on finding his second vote was the only negative one cast, he reversed himself to make it unanimous for secession. It was Janney who greeted General Robert E. Lee at Virginia's House of Delegates, remarking that in his will, George Washington had left his swords to his favorite nephews, instructing them only to draw them from their scabbards "in self defense, or in defense of the rights and liberties of their country." Lee responded "trusting in an almighty God, an approving conscience, and the aid of my fellow citizens, I devote myself to the service of my native state, in whose behalf alone, will I ever again draw my sword."

Virginia called for all volunteer companies to mobilize, and put into effect secret plans to seize the Harpers Ferry Arsenal. The Arsenal's commander burned it down and escaped across the Potomac River with his troops. Eppa Hunton, Virginia Commonwealth Attorney and brigadier general of militia, wanted to join the regular army, and resigned from the militia. When Governor John Letcher did not accept his resignation, Hunton responded that he would join the army as a private soldier. The governor duly appointed him as Colonel of the 8th Virginia Infantry Regiment. On May 23, 1861 the Ordinance of Secession was ratified by the State of Virginia.

All young males in the County had been required to attend militia meetings, but Quaker youth simply stayed away and paid a fine. Most of Waterford's young men refused to join the Confederate army, and the July 16, 1861 issue of *The Baltimore Sun* described what happened next:

The reign of terror in Loudoun County is at its height...citizens were told to be ready to be drafted into the militia for an immediate march to Manassas Junction, to fill up the ranks of General Beauregard's forces. All the Union men of Waterford determined to escape. Twelve fled from their homes night before last, and evaded the Confederate pickets for nine miles, arriving at the ford of Point of Rocks, which they crossed and soon got inside the lines of the First New Hampshire Regiment...Forty more Union men were to run away yesterday and try to cross the above mentioned ford last night...Confederate pickets on the other side were seen to stop and drive back several squads of men of the escaping party.

Meanwhile, the young men and boys of nearby Leesburg, were flocking to enlist to fight the Yankees. The new Provisional Army of Virginia set up a recruiting office on King Street, just opposite the county courthouse. These recruiters had to compete with the local militias, and offered applicants two dollars if they were accepted. But service in the regular army was not attractive to the young men of Leesburg, who wanted to fight to preserve *their* state from the Yankee invaders, and had no interest in being sent to fight elsewhere in the country. When Colonel Eppa Hunton arrived in Leesburg, he solved the problem by absorbing all the militias into his new state regiment, the 8th Virginia Volunteer Infantry Regiment. Six of the ten companies which made up the 8th Virginia were Loudoun County men.

The Civil War has been called the first modern war. It could also be called the first industrialized war. By 1860, the U.S. was the second largest manufacturing country in the world after Great Britain, and American inventiveness in developing machines to do jobs formerly done by skilled workers, was second to none. Without specialized machines that could produce thousands of parts with the same dimensions and tolerances, and machine tools that could do the job far faster and better than any human being, neither Union nor Confederate armies could have armed the hundreds of thousands of volunteers they needed to fight the Civil War.

The War also saw the introduction of the world's first reliable rapid-fire gun patented by American Richard Gatling in 1862, the land mine, the field telegraph, steam-driven "ironclad" ships, revolving gun turrets, and the first submarine. The use of railways and steamboats to transport troops rapidly played a crucial role in the war. Never more so than when President Lincoln rushed Federal troops to Baltimore as a show of force to prevent Maryland's possible secession from the Union in 1860; or when the Yankee Sixth Corps travelled from Richmond, Virginia to the Monocacy River in Maryland, and arrived just in time to disrupt and delay Confederate General Jubal Early's unopposed march on Washington in 1864.

The Civil War tore apart the fragile social fabric that had enabled non-slave holders and slave holders in Loudoun County to ignore their differences most of the time. Some families were so deeply divided over their loyalties that the emotional scars never healed. Disputed border areas such as northern and western Loudoun County suffered the most. Law and order and regulated commerce were undermined by smuggling and looting by troops from both sides. The Waterford mill and post office shut down, and commercial enterprises had their goods taken at gun point and all eventually closed. Even more traumatic was widespread seizure of farm wagons, horses, and drivers. Confederate authorities used local poll books to target individuals who had voted against secession, and many farmers in the Waterford area gave up farming altogether.

Local historians Bronwen and John Souders point out that the region became a "no-man's land," which neither Confederate nor Union forces could effectively control for any length of time. Waterford's citizens felt increasingly isolated as Confederate troops burned both nearby bridges across the Potomac at Point of Rocks and Berlin (now Brunswick) Maryland. Waterford's free blacks were especially anxious they would be arrested and "sold south."

President Abraham Lincoln had suspended *habeas corpus* and imposed martial law in border states at the beginning of the war. Although the Confederacy did not do so until ten months later, Confederate commanders in Loudoun County felt free to imprison or confiscate the property of anyone suspected of supporting the Union. Because roads radiated from Waterford to principal Potomac River crossings at Point of Rocks and Berlin, Maryland, it became a key point in the Confederate defense in 1861. Confederate cavalry from Brigadier General D.H. Hill's brigade were stationed in Waterford to counter Union patrols from Point of Rocks and Harpers Ferry.

The Confederates billeted their cavalry troop in Waterford's Fairfax Quaker Meeting House, and used the Quaker cemetery as a pasture for their horses, which knocked over and broke many of the gravestones. Because the Quakers had voted overwhelmingly against secession, they were viewed with outright hostility by the Confederate troopers. During the cold winter of 1862, Waterford became an armed camp. Through friendly persuasion and fair dealing the Quakers managed to establish a basis for mutual respect with the troopers, who agreed to move to the opposite end of the meetinghouse when meetings were taking place, or attend them if they so desired. Some of them did, and Susan Walker, daughter of James and Eliza Walker of Talbott Farm, described what happened:

> Almost all [the soldiers] had curiousity to be present, having heard of Quaker meetings. When the members entered, the scenes presented were strange ones for the interior of a Friends Meeting House, and had it not been for the solemnity of the occasion would have been truly amusing. The old ladies ascended the steps into the gallery and took their seats, though rather daintily, as arms were stacked behind them, muskets and swords stored away beneath the benches. In one corner of the room, the "Stars and Bars"

was unfurled. In the opposite one was a large fireplace with a blazing fire, over which was roasting a large turkey, also some hominy cooking. Overcoats were hanging all about, knapsacks and saddles were strewn around, while a suppressed titter or an amused whisper of some of the more mischievous soldiers regarding the peculiar shape of their plain bonnets could be distinctly heard. But when all were seated it was perfectly quiet, and when an aged and feeble lady [Miriam Gover] rose, every countenance wore a thoughtful aspect and each attentively listened to her words of truth and love. When she invoked a blessing on the little band there assembled, she also prayed that the wings of peace might be spread over our prosperous and happy land, also for the strangers that were that day gathered in their midst, until loud sobs broke from strong men and great tears forced themselves down their sunburnt cheeks.

Miriam Gover was unusually eloquent, and when she rose to speak with the dignity of her 70 years, she made a deep impression. The Confederate officers had met her carriage and escorted her inside, their glittering uniforms contrasting with her plain Friends 'dark dress. The Confederates called the meeting house "Camp Quakeress," and both sides became accustomed to each other and developed a mutual respect. The soldiers were actually a boost to the local economy, as they paid a premium for eggs, butter, and other items that had disappeared from their diet. However, they paid in Confederate scrip (paper currency), which had less purchasing power than Federal notes, and the Quakers got rid of it at first opportunity.

One Confederate soldier was quite happy to be billeted in Waterford during the hard winter of 1862. Sergeant Robert Parker of the Second Virginia Cavalry Regiment wrote to his wife Beck (Rebecca) in Bedford, VA: "We have never been to a better place, and the people kind as you could wish. They send great baskets of provisions ready prepared for eating in camp, and on picket our men have dinners furnished them almost every day." Waterford's hospitality extended to its homes. When Sergeant Parker missed his dinner while seeing Waterford's Quaker physician, Thomas Bond, the good doctor invited him to dine, and to Bond's brother's house for dinner on the following evening. During the war, Dr. Bond tended to many wounded soldiers, both Yankee and Rebel.

Sergeant Parker liked the town and people so much, he wrote Beck they should consider settling there after the war was over. Waterford's farmers, however, were not pleased about sharing their bounty with soldiers, Rebel or Yankee, who arrived like a swarm of hungry locusts. When the 13th and 17th Mississippi Infantry Regiments arrived at Talbott Farm, at the southern entrance to Waterford, unhappy hostess Eliza Walker informed her brother in New Jersey that "hundreds of their men have visited our orchard & premises," adding more charitably, "Some very gentlemanly men from Mississippi have eaten with us.

Sergeant Parker had joined the Southern cause at the outbreak of war when his wife was pregnant with their first child. Although he strongly believed it was his patriotic duty to protect home and family from the Yankee invaders, he felt very conflicted about leaving his family, closing many of his letters with "From your devoted but unworthy husband." Parker's letters are very revealing about the life of a Confederate soldier. They show how the Confederate Army was incapable of clothing and feeding its soldiers, although, cotton from the Southern states accounted for three-fourths of all America's exports and two-thirds of the world's supply.

Next to the welfare of his family, clothing and food were uppermost in Parker's correspondence with his wife. Beck made all his clothes and sent them by mail. But she was unable to find the material to make him an overcoat, and every letter he wrote during that terrible winter asked about the status of the overcoat. He would always hedge his request, "Don't trouble yourself anymore, I can get one made here, and if I don't I will be sure not to suffer." But he never had the money to have one made. He wore just a shawl in the most bitter, wet weather, and finally asked Beck to send him "the other half of my shawl. His letters also reveal how much his regiment was plagued by illness. Many more soldiers were disabled or died from natural causes, especially typhoid fever, diphtheria, measles, and dysentery, than military action. Parker made light of his own infirmities, while seeming to be unwell much of the time.

Meanwhile, the 8th Virginia Infantry had distinguished itself at the First Battle of Manassas and at Balls' Bluff, both of which were resounding Confederate victories. Colonel Hunton's home was only five miles away from Manassas. Colonel Hunton wrote in his diary that his wife Lucy was suffering from a painful liver disease, "and still more from anxiety for her husband and her country, and she lay down and put a feather pillow over her head to try to keep out the sound, but she heard the firing.all day long and knew I was in the fight. Her anxiety can be better imagined than described.""

After President Lincoln appointed General George B. McClellan to command the Union Army of the Potomac, he moved his troops south into Virginia in March 1862. Colonel Hunton's home was in the path of the Union Army. The Colonel was not well, and his wife was still ill. Hunton wrote:

> I was home sick. I could not make preparation to give up my home or to save any of my property. I moved my wife and son—my wife on a bed in a wagon…to take the last train that went out. My wife suffered intensely on the way. I feared at times she might die on the train.

The 8th Virginia Volunteer Infantry Regiment joined Brigadier General George Pickett's brigade, and in the Battle of Gaines Mill, Pickett was wounded and Colonel Hunton led the entire brigade in a charge that broke the Union line and insured a Confederate victory. Hunton was "mortified "when he was not promoted to brigadier general, after Pickett was elevated to major general.

# Chapter 13
# Hurrah for the Union

**"Hurrah for the girl who hurrahs for the union!"**
**—Union Infantry Marching through Waterford**

In February 1862, Col. John W. Geary's 28th Pennsylvania Infantry crossed the Potomac with the owner of the Waterford mill, Samuel Means, as their guide. Confederate troops stationed in Waterford decided to leave town, and Maggie Gover, whose husband Sam Gover had closed his store and fled to Washington the previous summer, overheard a Rebel cavalryman threatening to burn "the cursed Quaker settlement." She asked a fellow Quaker to go to Col. Geary's headquarters eight miles away in Lovettsville for help. The reluctant Friend refused to take the risky ride. "Lend me thy horse then," she said. He declined again. "I shall steal thy horse," she said, "and go myself." She instructed a servant to bring her the horse, and rode through the night past Confederate pickets, who did not stop her.

Colonel Geary complimented her for her "fearless act," and later reported to his superiors that a large Confederate force of 1,000 infantry and 200-300 cavalry was in Waterford preparing to burn down the town before destroying the B&O railroad line at Point of Rocks. When his regiment approached the town, he reported it "created a panic among the [Confederate] troops at Waterford, who fled precipitously to Leesburg, without applying the torch."

In their book, *Between Reb and Yank*, local historians Taylor Chamberlin and John Souders, claim that Geary had a penchant for overstating the forces against him and exaggerating the threat they posed, thus inflating his own successes. Geary was one of many politicians who had been given command of troops in the

Union Army, and he understood the value of public relations. Geary was soon promoted to brigadier general.

When Geary's men marched into Waterford, the whole village turned out to welcome them. Lisa Dutton recalled these were "the first Union soldiers we ever saw," and wrote in her diary that she and her sisters welcomed the soldiers by having them record their names in an autograph book. She and her family "stood watching the long lines of soldiers in blue as they marched through town," and how her shy sister Mollie "called out from the porch in a voice not loud, but yet heard by the soldiers below, 'Hurrah for the Union.'" Back came a voice from the ranks, "Hurrah for the girl who hurrahs for the Union," and cheer after cheer went up as each succeeding company passed."

Geary's objective was Leesburg, where he received a very different welcome. Women crossed to the other side of the street to avoid the bluecoats, little boys sang "Dixie" as loud as they could outside their barracks, and stores closed their doors to the troops. One Union artilleryman wrote, "But if the white folks didn't want to see us, the colored did," and five slaves joined his battery.

Samuel Means had fled Virginia in 1861 not only to escape arrest for refusing to fight for the Southern cause, but because he was suspected—with good reason—of being a Union spy. Means was providing important information on Rebel units stationed in and around Waterford, and Lieutenant Colonel Gabriel DeKornay of the 28th Pennsylvania Regiment, described him as "one of our principal and most valuable scouts in Virginia." When a Confederate picket was shot to death near Means's Mill; that was too much for Richmond authorities, who offered a $15,000 reward for Means, dead or alive.

Means's adherence to the Union cause was brought to the attention of Edwin M. Stanton, President Lincoln's Secretary of War, who granted him a commission to form a Union cavalry company, which Means did in June 1862, naming them the Independent Loudoun Rangers. According to local historian John Divine, creating a Union military unit in the Old Dominion "had the immediate effect of drawing the undying hatred of those who followed the fortunes of Virginia, and border warfare takes on a new dimension of hatred, for there is never a feud so bitter as a family feud."

Most of Means' recruits were from Waterford or nearby Lovettsville. The latter was known as "the German Settlement" because it had been founded by immigrants from the Rhineland Palatinate. Twenty-eight of the Lovettsville recruits were members of Lovettsville's New Jerusalem Evangelical Lutheran Church. One of them, Luther Slater, was elected First Lieutenant (second-in-command) of the Independent Loudoun Rangers. Slater was certainly the best educated of the new recruits, having spent a year each at two Lutheran colleges, Roanoke and Pennsylvania (now Gettysburg College). About twenty of the recruits "were of Quaker lineage" and there was also a large contingent of Scotch-Irish recruits.

In his personal account of the Loudoun Rangers, Briscoe Goodhart explained how it was that peaceable Quakers came to serve as Union cavalry scouts:

> The Quakers on account of their religious faith, were strictly opposed to war, but when brought to the threshold of their own home the flesh grew stronger than the spirit, and in the late war quite a number laid down their lives that the Nation might live...In one of the early battles of the late war one of that faith found himself on a skirmish line, with the bloodthirsty enemy in front. He selected his man and raised his trusty Enfield. With the remark, 'Friend, it is unfortunate, but thee stands exactly where I am going to shoot,' he pulled the trigger, and when the smoke cleared away, the enemy had one less to draw rations.

Cavalry units require horses, and Means' instructions from Secretary Stanton were to "press" only horses owned by supporters of the Confederacy. When Means captured a horse from the Confederates that previously had been stolen from John Dutton, one of Waterford's leading Quaker citizens, Dutton only got his horse back when the Union general commanding federal troops in the area gave Means a direct order to return the horse. Complaints about Means reached the War Department, and Quartermaster General Montgomery Meigs sent him detailed instructions about commandeering horses. There is no indication Means became more accountable for impressing horses, because stealing horses was simply a fact of life when cavalry units were raised and equipped at the local level. Over a hundred years earlier, during the French and Indian War, Samuel Hough's grandfather, "Old John" Hough, had his horses pressed by the Fairfax Militia.

After the War was over, the Federal Government had to deal with claims totaling $40,000 for 227 horses taken by the Loudoun Rangers from petitioners who said they were "loyal citizens" (many were not). Since Means had kept no records of these transactions, the claims were judged to have no merit. Of particular interest is the $1,120 claim filed by Henson Young, one of Waterford's free Negroes, for five horses taken in 1862 by Means as mounts for his Rangers. The claim was prepared by former Union officer Edwin A. Atlee of Waterford, in the presence of Samuel Means, who acknowledged taking the animals. The claim was filed with the U.S. Southern Claims Commission, which disallowed it on the grounds Young had filed a similar claim with the Quartermaster General, and Means was considered an unreliable witness.

What was going on? The Commission believed that Means, who was in the process of submitting multiple claims to the government, was using an uneducated Negro to submit a bogus claim. The Commission found it hard to believe that a free Negro in Virginia in 1862 would have had the resources to own five horses. The Federal Government was also aware Means was working with Atlee in preparing the claims and fixing the prices, and believed the two were in cahoots in a scheme to defraud the Government.

If times were difficult for white residents of Waterford, they were far more so for those of African descent. Waterford had provided a venue for people of color since the mid-18th century. Quakers' religious convictions welcomed people of all races, and the prospect of cheap labor was an added inducement. The free

Negro community in Waterford had increased dramatically in the early 19th century, but then sharply declined after the Nat Turner Rebellion and the Panic of 1837.The slave population showed a similar, even sharper rise and fall. The 1860 federal census listed only twenty-eight free Negroes employed in the village: fifteen of nineteen men worked as unskilled laborers, and all but one of the nine women were washerwomen. The others were a wagoner, a cook, a mill hand, a blacksmith and a barrel maker.

Henson Jr. was the son of Henson Young, and lived with his mother on William Russell Sr.'s farm. When Union cavalry came to Russell's farm in 1864 looking for horses, Henson Jr. slipped away with them. He was twenty years old, and managed to make his way to Baltimore, where he enlisted for one year on September 22, 1864 as a private in H Company, 1st U. S. Colored Troops Infantry Regiment. National Archives Combined Military Service Records describe him as "Black eyes, woolly hair, yellow complexion, 5' 4". He agreed to be a substitute for John Sanderson, 114 York Avenue, 8th ward, 3rd district, Baltimore, MD, "for a sufficient consideration paid and delivered to me.".

Henson Young Jr. was one of about 200,000 men of African descent who fought for the Union during the Civil War. He participated in the siege of Petersburg and Richmond in 1864, in the Carolinas Campaign of 1865 which included the assault and capture of Fort Fisher and Wilmington, North Carolina, and the occupation of Raleigh. Henson was mustered out on September 29, 1865 at Roanoke Island, North Carolina, returned to Waterford and took over his father's teamster business. Local historian John Devine said "Henson junior inherited his father's way with horses. I remember him driving a fine team when I was a child."

With a few exceptions, slaves did not officially marry. After Emancipation, many couples married any way they could, with the ceremonies being performed by the ministers of local churches, or by travelling ministers responding to the greatly increased demand for their services. It was a chaotic time, and no attempt was made to record the process through the existing court system. On December 2, 1871, Henson Jr., laborer, married Mary Colston.

Henson Jr. and Mary Colston Young had two children, a daughter Susan, who was born on March 20, 1883, and a son who lived only one day on May 20, 1889. County records also show that Henson Young became the father of Daisy Young on 1 March, 1880. The baby's mother was recorded as Anna Young; we are left to wonder whether Henson Jr. and Henson Young may not have been one and the same person.

Several free Negroes from Waterford joined the Loudoun Rangers as non-combatant "auxiliaries," who were not officially enlisted and therefore not entitled to a government pension. When former Loudoun Ranger auxiliary Richard Collins was included in the 1890 federal list of veterans as a drummer in a regular army unit, his widow Marietta tried to obtain a pension, but her request was denied by the Federal government, on the grounds that he never enlisted. In 1993, an archaeological excavation of the remains of the Collins house on Waterford's Main Street by Dan Kent, a history teacher at Loudoun County High School, unearthed a Union military belt buckle and button.

When the general commanding Confederate troops in Leesburg, the county seat, announced in early 1862 that all able-bodied males were required to build fortifications to protect Leesburg from a Federal attack, this order led to another exodus from Waterford, especially among Negroes, who correctly believed the announcement was simply a ruse to send them "south." Many who did not leave suffered this fate.

In April, 1862, after Virginia passed a conscription act that did not exempt conscientious objectors, Friends were allowed to find substitutes, but this was contrary to Quaker discipline. The law was later amended to exempt males practicing pacifist religions, but they still had to pay a fine of $500. The fine was payable in Confederate scrip, and one local Quaker quipped it cost him "$200 in greenbacks." Confederate money was only worth forty cents on the dollar. Small wonder Waterford merchants were reluctant to accept Confederate dollars.

# Chapter 14
# Wild Riding and Ear-Splitting Yells

**"You are too brave a man to take from you your sword."**
**—Major White, 35th Virginia Cavalry, to Sgt. Webster, Loudoun Rangers**

By mid-1861, the U.S. Congress had prohibited virtually all commerce between North and South, except where justified by the "public good." By the end of the year, all five Waterford stores had been closed, and its desperate citizens were looking elsewhere for essential supplies. Early in 1862, Colonel John W. Geary brought Union troops to Loudoun under a Union policy that "commerce should follow the flag." Waterford's citizens were able to cross into Maryland and buy what they needed without having to undergo loyalty checks. But when General Lee marched north, U.S. Secretary of the Treasury Salmon Chase announced that commerce between North and South would henceforth require a federal permit to be given only to persons of unquestioned loyalty to the Union, and control of the cross-border trade was left in the hands of the Army.

The demands of the Antietam campaign, however, left military provost marshals with little time or interest, to implement the Federal Permit system. Unionist as well as Confederate smugglers were given permission to cross into Maryland and trade if they claimed to be escaping conscription into the Rebel army. Cross-border trade in contraband goods was thriving, and many "Copperheads" (secessionists who claimed to be loyal to the Union) played a major role in getting critical supplies from the North for the Confederacy.

An investigation ordered by Secretary Chase revealed there were many irregularities and omissions in the customs process, and abuse of the system was widespread. Meanwhile, Captain Samuel

Means had been able to get Lieutenant Luther Slater appointed as provost marshal and "permitting officer" at Point of Rocks. When a new Union military commander was put in charge of Union troops in the region, however, he brought in his own people. Lieutenant Slater was out of a job and Samuel Means and the Rangers were transferred upriver from Point of Rocks to Berlin (now Brunswick), Maryland.

The prospect of easy money, in a situation where rules and authority were never very clear, attracted a large cast of colorful characters of dubious morality. When Means arrived at Berlin, he found that two Secret Service detectives had been sent from Baltimore to assist the provost marshal there. One of the detectives was Mrs. Frankie Abel. She had started the war as a Union spy, been captured, and exchanged for the notorious Confederate spy, Belle Boyd. She always carried two loaded pistols and a dirk (a short dagger) hidden in her clothing, and was said to be able to ride, drink, and carouse like a man, and often dressed like one. She also had the feminine charm to attract the men she worked with, and the male detective travelling with her was her lover.

Frankie Abel came to Berlin straight from a successful spying mission that earned her 300 gold dollars. Her main task at Berlin was to make sure women did not cross the border at Berlin, Maryland, with contraband goods. She was not popular with the women she searched, and one female who went through the process described her as "a *creature* calling herself a woman." One day, a Maryland woman, Lucy Ann Baggot, accompanied by her widowed sister and her sister's small children, crossed from Virginia into Maryland and was taken into a room in the provost marshal's office. She was confronted by Frankie Abel, who asked her to undress. When she refused, Frankie drew both pistols, pointed them at her, and demanded she remove her outer garments. Frankie found a belt under Mrs. Baggot's dress with gold coins, Federal greenbacks, and Confederate money sewn into it, as well as a note addressed to Capt. Elijah White. When all the money was counted by Union Lieutenant Benjamin, who was in charge, Mrs. Baggot claimed it was $160 less than she had sewn into the belt.

The lieutenant ordered the travelers to go back to Virginia; but when the children started to cry, he relented and allowed them to board the next train to Baltimore.

Later that day, Union Captain Ford had Frankie search two sisters, and when $310 in gold bullion was found hidden in a trunk, Ford took the gold. When it was returned to the sisters, they claimed that sixty gold dollars had been removed. Both parties filed formal complaints, and shortly thereafter Secret Service detectives arrested Captain Ford, Lieutenant Benjamin, and Frankie and her detective paramour. All four were sent to Washington's Old Capitol Prison. The lieutenant died in prison. During the trial, Frankie claimed that Captain Ford had tried to force himself on her sexually and then had tried to frame her paramour. Both defendants claimed the other was intoxicated most of the time. Less than a year later, Captain Ford was dismissed from the Union Army for drunkenness. The defendants were acquitted for lack of evidence, and the Union Army continued to employ Frankie Abel as a spy.

Like other Unionists in Loudoun, the citizens of Waterford had little food or medicine, and were suffering greatly from the Federal blockade of trade with the South. They appealed to Washington, and after General McClellan's Army of the Potomac forced the Confederates to retreat toward Richmond, Waterford Unionists were allowed under military supervision to purchase ten dollars worth of necessities per family per week, at major Potomac River crossing points in Maryland after swearing an oath they were for "family use" only. Trade surged, both regulated and illicit, among Copperheads, as well as Unionists.

William James was one of the tiny minority of Waterford citizens to vote to secede from the Union in 1860, and local Confederates considered him for the job as Waterford postmaster. However, when Union Colonel John W. Geary occupied northwestern Loudoun County in early 1862, James was one of just three Waterford secessionists persuaded to swear allegiance to the United States of America. A year later, the Loudoun Rangers searched his home and found a dozen pairs of boots usually worn by soldiers, and three kegs of Virginia tobacco. They found no mail, but

Samuel Means arrested him for "keeping a house for the distribution of contraband (i. e. Southern) mails," and sent him under U.S. Cavalry escort to the Union Army Provost Marshal in Baltimore.

James swore "the charges against him are false, that he neither carried the mail himself, nor knows anyone that in any way is connected with the same, and promised that if released will never aid or abet the South." The U. S. Provost Marshall, Major W.S. Fish, believed James and dismissed the charges. The verdict was not surprising, considering Samuel Means had found no evidence to support his case. Yet four years later, former "Comanche" Major Frank Myers had this to say in his diary: "I rather think I don't like Bill James much. I know he is a coward because he is afraid to vote against the Waterford Ruffians. I don't believe he has any principles that he would fight for."

When General McClellan failed to capture Richmond in the summer of 1862, he took his army back across the Potomac. General Robert E. Lee pursued him, and the Confederate advance into Loudoun County was spearheaded by Major Elijah White's 35th Battalion Virginia Cavalry, which joined Brigadier General Thomas Rosser's Laurel Brigade. Rosser had witnessed their wild riding and ear-splitting yells during a charge against Federal troops, and dubbed them the "Comanches."

At Talbot Farm, just outside Waterford, Eliza Walker was up at "½ past 4 AM" on August 27, 1862, writing a letter to her absent husband James. She had written a single sentence lamenting his absence, when "my ear was startled by a bark & growl from Ring (their dog) on the front porch—the report of *musketry*.

> I stepped to the front door & there heard so much din clamor & noise & rapid firing—with the *orders to charge* then rapid riding & firing of pistols as they rode, or *dashed* along the road by the lower gate. I went to the trap door in the garret & could see dimly in the grey dawn the shadowy forms of horses as they galloped by the gate. The children were all instantly awake & Elisha [her son] went to the corn house but has learned nothing further...1/4 before

8AM—Another period of the *most intense excitement.* Just now the string of apparently perhaps 100 *guerrillas* passed our gate towards Leesburg, leading many horses & loaded with blankets &c. I dropped my pen in haste this morn and went with the children near the stacks by the barn & there in C.H.'s [Charles Hollingsworth farm] field we dimly saw horses & men stationed and *heard firing* about the church...My chief personal concern was for Elisha. He attended to his morning duties in a quiet calm way. E. T. [hired help] was like a crazy man. He and several others are hiding about the corn & woods.

What was upsetting Eliza Walker was Elijah White's 35th Virginia Cavalry. The "Comanches" had decided to teach the Loudoun Rangers a lesson they would never forget. They set a trap for a unit of the Loudoun Rangers which had spent the night inside Waterford's Baptist Church. The Comanches avoided Ranger pickets by approaching Waterford through a cornfield just opposite the church. Major White then sent some of his men down the road to create a disturbance and draw the Rangers from the church. When the Rangers rushed out of the building, they were met by a volley of gunfire, and Lieutenant Luther Slater, who commanded the Ranger unit, was gravely wounded in his temple, shoulder, arm, chest, and hand. Slater narrowly escaped certain death when a sixth bullet passed through his hat. He ordered the Rangers to take cover inside the church. He was bleeding profusely, and was carried inside, where he told Sergeant Charles Webster to take command.

White's Comanches concentrated their fire on the large windows and the plaster portico that framed the wooden doors of the church. Sergeant Webster rejected demands they surrender "in rather emphatic language not usually heard in church." Slater and he agreed to a third surrender demand only after the Rangers ran out of ammunition. Webster emerged from the church with a white handkerchief on the point of his sword. Major White refused to accept it, remarking, "you are too brave a man to take from you your sword."

Lieutenant Slater accepted White's surrender terms, but only on condition all his men were paroled and released, and the officers were allowed to keep their side arms. Major White agreed, as his men were also running out of ammunition. Such courtesies between enemies were a tradition going back to the American Revolution, French and Indian War, and beyond. They would not survive the first year of the war.

Two brothers of the Snoots family fought against each other, one in each unit. After the Yankees surrendered, the brother in White's cavalry had to be prevented from shooting his sibling. Lieutenant Slater was carried to a house in Waterford, and a week later was transported to a nearby farmhouse. Three weeks later, ten of his neighbors fastened poles on either side of a rocking chair and carried him about four miles to his father's farm north of Waterford. When he was strong enough to travel, he was taken to a hospital in Gettysburg, Pennsylvania, where he was nursed by Mollie Yount, whom he married in 1864. Although still recovering from his wounds, he accepted the position of U. S. Army Provost Marshal at Point of Rocks in December 1862, with responsibility for enforcing Federal regulations governing cross-border trade. In 1863, he resigned his commission when he reluctantly concluded that the disabling gunshot fracture of his right arm he had received at the Baptist Church, prevented him from returning to active duty with the Loudoun Rangers.

Brother versus brother was a tragic issue in many families. Waterford saddler Amos Brown, had a son Charlie, who had joined the 8th Virginia Infantry Regiment and was badly wounded at the Battle of First Manassas. Amos also had another son Turner, who was an ardent Unionist. Probably to keep from killing each other, Charlie moved to Richmond, where he became a harness maker for the Confederate Army, and Turner went north to Maryland. Samuel Means's brother George was a lieutenant with the Confederate Loudoun Cavalry. When Samuel was informed George had been shot by a trooper of the 1st Rhode Island Cavalry Regiment, he remarked that the shooting had "saved him the trouble of doing it."

After the battle, rumors in Waterford spread like a wild fire: Major White's Comanches were going to burn down the town; its stars and stripes flag had been torn down and desecrated; all Unionist sympathizers were going to be robbed of their valuables. Eliza Walker gathered the family money and valuable papers and hid them in her and daughter Susan's clothing. That night she and Susan went to bed with their clothes on, ready to jump up at the first alarm. Eliza kept getting up during the night to look toward Waterford to see if Elijah White was carrying out his alleged threat to destroy the town.

Loudoun Ranger Sergeant Charles Webster, who had been praised for his bravery by Major White after he surrendered, is described by local historian Taylor Chamberlin, as "a psychopath loyal to none." Webster achieved notoriety after he led a group of Rangers on a looting spree in nearby Leesburg, and fatally shot a Confederate officer allegedly after he surrendered. When Captain Samuel Means blocked his attempt to obtain a commission in the Rangers, Webster obtained a fraudulent commission as "captain," and convinced Governor Pierpoint of West Virginia to sign it and appoint him Captain in the 3$^{rd}$ Cavalry Regiment of Virginia Volunteers. Meanwhile, the Union Army Provost Marshall at Berlin, Maryland, reported that "when last heard from [Webster] was in Washington 'in full dress' selling horses he has stolen from Union men." He was arrested, but released for lack of evidence.

Webster seems to have decided his luck was running out with the Yankees, and he tried to join White's 35$^{th}$ Virginia Cavalry. Major Elijah White would have nothing to do with him, and had him bound and thrown in jail. When Lieutenant Frank Myers and other Comanches visited Webster, he was suffering terribly and his hands had turned black. Myers convinced White to untie him and leave him in his custody, and that evening Webster sat around a campfire with the Comanches and regaled them with stories of his adventures. Myers commented in his memoir of the war, "I doubt in the annals of rascality a more finished character than Webster ever had a place." Webster was incarcerated in Richmond's notorious Castle Thunder Prison, where he convinced fellow prisoners to escape. After two failed attempts, Webster was placed in irons. He unlocked his shackles with a key made out of dinner bones, but did not get far.

Webster was charged with murder, stealing horses, and violation of parole. No detailed record of the trial exists. The Government would have had difficulty proving the murder charge (Webster claimed it was self defense), and horse stealing was rampant among both blue and grey troops (Webster claimed he was just following orders). But breaking parole during the war was a capital offense, and he was sentenced to hang. He made a final attempt to escape by jumping out a window, but broke both ankles on the pavement below. He was carried tied in a chair, to the gallows, dressed in his blue Union captain's uniform. He "died bravely," it was said, throwing down his hat to signal that the scaffold's trap door be sprung.

Eliza Walker and many other townspeople were furious with Samuel Means for quartering his troops in Waterford and drawing the attention of White's Comanches, for fleeing Waterford when the attack began, for not returning to save his outnumbered and trapped troopers, and for failing to prevent the destruction of the Baptist Church. These emotional fires were stoked when former neighbors and friends were recognized among the attackers. From then on Waterford's Unionists regarded White's Comanches not as real soldiers, but as brutal "guerrillas, "who preyed upon the civilian population.

When General Robert E. Lee's Army of Northern Virginia defeated Union Major General John Pope at the Second Battle of Manassas and headed north in late August 1862, Colonel Dixon Miles at Harpers Ferry did not believe a word of what he heard. He was sure a Union victory had occurred, and ordered Major Henry Cole and three companies of cavalry to link up with Samuel Means's Loudoun Rangers to harass any Rebels fleeing west through Loudoun County. Cole's force, totaling about 200, ran up against the advance guard of Lee's victorious army at Leesburg. They were quickly surrounded by the larger Rebel force, and Major Cole gave the order "every man for himself."

In the melee that followed, eight Loudoun Rangers were captured. Four were paroled, but the other four were falsely accused of breaking an earlier parole and were sent to Castle Thunder prison in Richmond. Three died in prison of starvation, and the fourth was "so near death's door that he was totally unfit for service when he was released." Loudoun Ranger Private Briscoe Goodhart wrote in his memoirs that "The Waterford and Leesburg engagements came in such close succession, before the company had attained proficiency in discipline and drill, that they almost broke up the organization." Recruiting for the Rangers fell sharply, and there were less than twenty men fit to fight. Captain Means never did achieve his goal of having the unit reach battalion strength, which would have justified his promotion to major.

Back in Waterford, citizens were attempting to deal with having either blue or gray on their doorstep almost every day. Eliza Walker said it was "one of the most trying periods since the war began." Lee's cavalry placed pickets at the gate of Talbot Farm, where Cole's Maryland cavalry had stationed its own pickets two days before. According to Eliza," some of Lee's soldiers demanded the keys of closed stores in town, & the females of the families went in and waited on them. They took what they wanted of groceries and cotton goods & paid for them in Confederate money—that is not worth anything here...all is doubt and confusion here." But when White's Comanches broke into Samuel Gover's store one month later, they had no such scruples, and "pillaged" the store. After the war, Gover sued Elijah White for $3,000 in damages and stolen goods.

Quakers had been wrestling with the issue of neutrality since the Civil War began. The turning point came when Elijah White's troopers took the lead in conscripting local males between the ages of eighteen and thirty-five into the Confederate army. Most of the Quaker young men remaining in Waterford either went into hiding, enlisted in Union units or fled to Maryland. With no more help coming from the north, Waterford Quakers' feelings of isolation, despair, and helplessness were only deepened upon hearing the distant thunder of cannon at the battles of South Mountain and Antietam. Although the November 1862 Baltimore Quarterly Meeting continued to support a neutral stance in the War, many Waterford Quakers could no longer turn the other cheek.

When the dilatory George McClellan was replaced by Ambrose Burnside as General of the Union Army of the Potomac, the Yankees moved south on their way to Fredericksburg. White's Comanches followed in their wake, and Captain Frank Myers claimed they captured 1,000 Union stragglers and a great quantity of arms, horses and supplies. Most paroled soldiers went home until formally exchanged for prisoners from the other side, but in contested areas like northern Loudoun, where there was no strong civil or Military Authority exchange became a long, drawn-out process. It was at this time that some Comanches awaiting formal exchange with Union parolees, decided to step outside the law and go into the business of horse stealing on their own account.

In a lengthy plea to Brigadier General Geary, prominent Waterford Quaker John Dutton complained:

> We have been annoyed to death with these horse stealing bands under White, Grubb, Trayhern, Myers [all Comanche officers] and God knows who else…Cannot you put a stop to this thing—for we are too good loyal a people to be left to suffer in this manner.

Shortly after Dutton wrote the letter, the Comanches raided his store and took all his goods, while he barely escaped out the back. Dutton closed his Waterford store and fled north, crossing the Potomac at Point of Rocks, Maryland, where he established a new store. Another prominent Waterford Quaker, Samuel Steer, who like Dutton was a well-known abolitionist, fled to Point of Rocks, where he became the U.S. customs agent.

One victim of the Comanche "desperados" who got his horses back was James Walker of Talbot Farm. He complained to White, who had his adjutant write a letter authorizing Walker to retrieve his horses. It was not the only time his horses had remained untouched during a Comanche horse stealing raid. Walker had established a good relationship with White to protect his family and farm. In a frank letter to his brother, he wrote about agonizing over having to keep quiet about his pro-Union sentiments, because "we knew not whom to trust, hardly a brother. Indeed, I felt my [Unionist] friends had lost confidence in me. It was an unhappy state, but that all is past." Waterford's Quaker farmers kept their neutrality longer than their non-Quaker neighbors.

The U. S. Government was in dire financial straits. Confederate artillery batteries near Quantico, Virginia, closed the Potomac River to Union shipping from October 1861 to March 1862. In Washington, "supplies withered and prices soared, as the overwhelmed B&O Railroad was its only link with the rest of the world." There was no national currency, and the government had been financing the war through the sale of U. S. government bonds and Treasury notes. With the government's public debt increasing at an annual rate of 400 percent, a Republican-dominated Congress enacted the Revenue Acts of 1861 and 1862. The laws imposed an income tax to be levied, collected and paid, upon the annual income of every person residing in the United States, and created a progressive tax of three percent on income above $600, and five percent on incomes above $10,000.

The war was becoming more and more expensive, and there still was no end in sight. When a gold crisis with Great Britain, in December 1861, sparked a run on New York banks, the latter suspended payments in gold and silver. The Federal Government had to act quickly and decided to end its reliance on precious metals. The Legal Tender Act of February 25, 1862 created the government paper currency "greenback," and the Internal Revenue Act of July 1, 1862 empowered the government to tax a whole range of new items, such as jewelry, liquor, tobacco, playing cards, billiard tables, and professional licenses.

Federal greenbacks were driving bank notes issued by Virginia's state-chartered banks out of circulation, and Virginia currency was discounted forty percent, as was Confederate currency. Waterford's citizens tried to rely on greenbacks as a medium of exchange, but they were hard to find. Confederate currency was also in short supply, because Waterford men who had enlisted in the Rebel army were not receiving enough pay to even meet their own basic needs, and their families were in a desperate situation. According to local historian John Devine, "many deeds of kindness were shown toward these families by their Union neighbors, especially Quakers."

The new year of 1863 found Waterford empty of occupying troops. The two great blue and grey armies had moved south, and were face-to-face at Fredericksburg, Virginia. The Loudoun Rangers had moved to Point of Rocks, Maryland, and White's Comanches had been incorporated into Confederate Brigadier General W. E. Jones's Laurel Brigade to fight in his West Virginia campaign, causing great dissension within their ranks. Many Comanches did not want to leave their families to the mercies of occupying Yankees. Many deserted. Their morale suffered even more when they lost many men in the biggest cavalry battle of the War at Brandy Station, although they fought with great distinction. Major Elijah White left Loudoun without the renegade elements of his 35th Virginia Cavalry, who had no interest in fighting the war somewhere else. Although they were deserters, White never reported them to his superiors.

In March 1863, The War Department was so concerned with the diversion of cross-border trade into Confederate hands, it cancelled the privilege it had granted to loyal Unionists to buy "family supplies" in Maryland and take them back to Virginia. This total blockade of north-south Potomac trade imposed an even greater hardship on Loudoun loyalists. At the same time, raids carried out by renegade elements of White's 35th Virginia Cavalry and other small bands of Confederate deserters, parolees, and armed civilians, created a reign of terror in northwest Loudoun. Federal authorities across the Potomac were deluged with complaints against these "desperadoes," bushwhackers," and "guerrillas."

No one better deserved these epithets than John Mobberly, former member of White's 35th Virginia Cavalry. Major Henry Cole's Maryland Cavalry Battalion was looking for Mobberly and his band, whom they considered to be "outlaws." One of Cole's troopers later wrote why: "Mobberly, with his few men, were never known to take a prisoner; anyone falling into their hands would be instantly shot, as they wanted nothing but the soldier's horse and arms." Mobberly's band terrorized Loudoun for almost two years.

During a Loudoun Ranger skirmish with John Mosby's Rangers in 1864, Mobberly's band heard the firing and approached. They found Loudoun Ranger Sergeant Charles Stewart lying in the road with bullet wounds in the chest and left leg. Mobberly rode his horse back and forth over Stewart's prone body, firing at him with his pistol and piercing his left hand and shattering his jaw. He then dismounted and pulled off Stewart's boots, leaving him to die. Rachel Steer had Stewart brought into her house and called Dr. Bond. Under the care of Bond, Rachel, and other Quaker women, Stewart eventually recovered and swore he would get even.

The Baptist Church was damaged so badly it was not until 1876 that the congregation was reorganized and the repairs completed. Worse yet, the physical destruction of the church led to a much longer-lasting spiritual decline, because "believers here had become so few that they had become pastor less and scattered to other churches." In 1876, the Reverend R.R. Acree was appointed "to revive the congregation and repair the House of the Lord." After the Reverend C. T. Herndon became pastor in 1882, "the church grew to great strength and good works." His ministry lasted for twenty-six years. In 1926, the church celebrated the 50th anniversary of its reorganization, and the Reverend Dr. C.T. Herndon returned to Waterford to preach the sermon, praising local believers, who, "like Nehemiah, held to the purpose of rebuilding the walls and re-establishing their organization."

Despite and because of their loyalty to the Union, Loudoun Unionists suffered terrible hardships inflicted by both sides. Their personal possessions and means of making a living had been taken from them, and their very survival was in jeopardy. They could count on no one but themselves.

# Chapter 15
# Ten Men Still Standing

**"Don't forget boys that you are from Old Virginia!"**
**—Confederate Major General George Pickett at Gettysburg**

In June 1863, after General Robert E. Lee defeated Union Major General Joseph Hooker's Army of the Potomac at Fredericksberg and Chancellorsville, he headed his Army of Northern Virginia north to Pennsylvania. Colonel Eppa Hunton, commanding officer of Leesburg's 8<sup>th</sup> Virginia Infantry Regiment, was riding at the head of his brigade—the brigade commander being injured and carried in a cart—when General Lee rode up beside him.

> We had a half hour's conversation. I expressed to him my disinclination to the movement into Pennsylvania. I told him that I was afraid that if we had a disaster in Pennsylvania it would be very serious, and difficult for him to get his army back into Virginia. General Lee replied that the movement was a necessity; that our provisions and supplies of every kind were very nearly exhausted in Virginia, and that we had to go to Pennsylvania for supplies. He believed that the invasion of Pennsylvania would be a great success, and if so, it would end the war, or we would have rest for sometime to come. General Lee was so enthusiastic about the movement that I threw away my doubts and became as enthusiastic as he.

General Lee was rightly concerned about supplies. According to Hunton, the Army was "without shoes, without clothes, and without blankets."

When Lee's Army of Northern Virginia marched into Pennsylvania, J.E.B. ("Jeb") Stuart's cavalry had not showed up, and Loudoun's 35th Virginia Cavalry Battalion was the *only* cavalry unit in all of Lee's Army. So it was that Loudoun County's "Comanches" found themselves at the head of the Army of Virginia, scouting in advance of the lead infantry brigade. They were about to meet for the last time, one of their arch enemies, former lieutenant of Waterford's Independent Loudoun Rangers, Luther Slater. These antagonists would be among the first to clash in the biggest and most decisive battle of the war.

President Lincoln had become convinced General Joseph Hooker was not the man who could defeat Lee. "Looking sad and careworn," the president told his cabinet that Hooker had turned out to be another McClelland, and named General George Meade as commander of the Army of the Potomac.

When General Lee finally found out that General Meade and his Army of the Potomac had crossed its namesake river, Lee's forces were widely dispersed. General Ewell's corps was attempting to destroy and disrupt railroad facilities at Carlisle and York, Pennsylvania; while Generals Longstreet's and A.P. Hill's corps were near Chambersburg. Lee sent an urgent message ordering Ewell to join the rest of the army. One of Hill's divisions had heard that the town of Gettysburg had a good supply of shoes, and General Hill gave his permission to the division to "go get those shoes" on July 1st.

Meanwhile, Pennsylvania Governor Curtin called out the militia. Former Loudoun Ranger Lieutenant Luther Slater, who had been discharged from the U.S. Army as disabled, and whose wounds were still healing, was attending Pennsylvania College in Gettysburg. Yet with one arm still in a sling, he was among the first to respond to Governor Curtin's call, and joined the 26th Pennsylvania Volunteer Militia Regiment, which had been ordered to slow the Confederate advance towards Gettysburg along the Chambersburg Pike. The 26th Volunteers were vastly outnumbered and made up mostly of college students and other civilians. Because of his past experience, Slater was immediately appointed second lieutenant.

Both Independent Loudoun Ranger Private Briscoe Goodhart and 35th Virginia Cavalry Comanche Captain Frank Myers
recorded what happened next. Their accounts differ greatly. History, after all, is recorded through the eyes of the beholder, and de-
pends upon how the beholder wants to be remembered. According
to Goodhart, when the Confederates captured the 26th Pennsylvania
pickets on the Chambersburg Turnpike, Colonel Jennings, who
commanded the regiment, and "was as cool as he was brave," divided his command into several detachments to make as formidable a showing as possible. This maneuver was successful, and the
enemy did not risk a direct attack, but contented himself with following at a more respectful distance and firing an occasional volley.

Colonel Jennings decided to make a stand. The regiment
lost 120 men, and was forced to continue its fighting retreat during
the night, arriving in Harrisburg after marching fifty-four out of
sixty hours. Slater was unhurt. Goodhart concluded "too much credit cannot be given Col. Jennings for this masterly retreat and the
saving of his command from annihilation, for if the rebels had
known it was only one militia regiment opposing them such a fate
would have overtaken the gallant 26th." Years later, a bronze monument was erected at Chambersburg Street in Gettysburg to
commemorate the 26th Pennsylvania Volunteer's valor in first opposing the Confederate advance on the city.

However, according to Captain Frank Myers's account, the
Comanche's, "yelling like banshees and waving their pistols,
charged and scattered the green troops blocking their way," and
chased the Pennsylvania Volunteers all the way back to Gettysburg, where the Rebels celebrated their victory with strong drink,
"as the citizens gave them all they wanted, and more." The celebrating stopped when General Early arrived and ordered them to
"go catch some Yankees." The *Gettysburg National Military Museum and Visitor Center Official Guide Book* does not honor either
of these combatants. It states the battle for Gettysburg only began
when Lee's army was within three miles of the city, and a Union
scout fired "the first shot."

Lemuel Smith moved to Waterford three decades after the Civil War, but he never forgot waking up as a child one summer night in 1863 to hear horses hooves and the jingle of spurs under his window, as Confederate Major General "Jeb" Stuart's cavalry passed by on their way to Gettysburg. Stuart had gained a well-deserved reputation as "the trusted eyes and ears of Robert E. Lee's army." This time he arrived too late to help Lee determine the disposition of the Union forces at Gettysburg, and received a rare rebuke from his commander. In his report about the battle, Lee wrote, "the absence of cavalry rendered it impossible to obtain accurate information...the march toward Gettysburg was conducted more slowly than it would have been had the movement of the Federal Army been known."Jeb Stuart's troubles had only just begun.

Ten roads converged upon Gettysburg like the spokes of a giant wheel. Union General George Meade spread out his Army of the Potomac in a wide arc to the west, north, and east of Gettysburg, wondering which road would reveal the grey shapes of Confederate cavalry. General Meade was unaware General Lee was "blind," having lost his cavalry "eyes."

When General A.P. Hill's "shoe searchers" were finally spotted on the Chambersburg Road by a Union scout, Brigadier General John Buford and 2,700 Union cavalrymen were waiting. Buford had posted his men with their breech-loading carbines on high ground. Fighting dismounted behind fences and trees, they held off three times their number of Confederates until General Reynold's 1st Corps and General Howard's 11th Corps arrived in time to keep the Confederates at bay. After four hours of fierce fighting, the Union line collapsed when Lee ordered Ewell and Hill to attack with their entire corps. The Yankees lost 9,000 men killed or wounded, and retreated up Cemetery Hill as Lee's Army of Northern Virginia marched into Gettysburg. The Union forces regrouped, forming a northeast-north-northwest semi-circle around the high ground above the town.

The next morning, Jeb Stuart's cavalry still had not turned up, and General Lee had no idea how large the Union army was or how he should deploy his forces. When Lee's scouts reported that Meade's troops had not occupied the higher ground to the south at Big and Little Round Top, Lee pointed to Cemetery Hill and told his chief of staff, Lieutenant General James Longstreet, "the enemy is there, and I am going to attack him there." Longstreet replied, "If he is there, it will be because he is anxious we should attack him; a good reason in my judgment, for not doing so." But Lee had made up his mind, and Longstreet turned away sadly with a conviction of impending disaster.

Meanwhile, Union Major General Daniel Sickles had recklessly moved his $3^{rd}$ Corps a half-mile forward, extending and exposing the left end of the Union line. When a furious General Meade rode up and confronted Sickles, he offered to pull back his troops. "I wish to God you could," Meade replied, "but the enemy won't let you." Longstreet's battle hardened veterans attacked, driving Sickles $3^{rd}$ Corps back, and the race for Little Round Top began. Union Colonel Strong Vincent's brigade gained the top of the hill just ahead of Longstreet's men scrambling up its rocky slope. More help in blue arrived, and five Union regiments fought desperately to hold off wave after wave of Confederates.

The $20^{th}$ Maine Infantry Regiment was defending the far left end of the Union line at    Little Round Top. The regiment's colonel, Joshua Chamberlain, had extended his 200 men as far as he could to prevent being outflanked, while under attack from the $15^{th}$ and $47^{th}$ Alabama Regiments. In his autobiography, Chamberlin described what happened next:

> We were enveloped by fire…our last rounds of shot had been fired…I saw the faces of my men turn anxiously toward mine…Not a moment was about to be lost! One word was enough. BAYONET…It caught like fire and swept along the ranks…the grating clash of steel in fixing bayonets…the whole line quivered for the start…It was a great right wheel. Our left swung first. The advancing foe stopped, tried to make a stand amidst the trees and boulders, but the frenzied bayonets pressing through every space

forced a constant settling to the rear...and it turned to full retreat.

Chamberlin's thin blue line of bayonets had swung like a giant scythe, tearing apart the right flank of the advancing Confederates, who tried to re-group in the center of their line, where Chamberlain was confronted by the Confederate commanding officer, who "coming on fiercely, sword in one hand, and big navy revolver on the other, fires one barrel almost in my face; but seeing the quick saber-point at his throat, reverses arms, gives sword and pistol into my hands and yields himself prisoner"

Colonel Chamberlain was later awarded the Congressional Medal of Honor. Meanwhile, Confederate General A. P. Hill had turned his attention to Cemetery Ridge, three-quarters of a mile north of Little Round Top. It was another race against time. The last of General Sickle's artillery batteries (9th Massachusetts) was between the Emmitsburg Road and Cemetery Ridge, and was ordered to stay in place and slow the Confederate advance. For 30 minutes, the 9th Massachusetts laid down such a curtain of fire with "terrible missiles of death...flying thick and fast everywhere."That effort, and a desperate charge by the Union's 1st Minnesota Infantry Regiment, outnumbered five-to-one against Brigadier General Cadmus Wilcox's Alabama brigade, enabled the Yankees to hold back advancing Confederates in time to form a line of battle on Cemetery Ridge. At sunset, Confederates under Major General Richard Ewell attacked Cemetery Hill and Culp's Hill at the northern end of the Union line. Although both sides fought in the dark for hours, aiming at each other's muzzle flashes, Union troops still controlled the high ground, while the Confederates had gained a foothold on Culp's Hill.

On the third day of the battle, General Ewell renewed his assault on Culp's Hill, but was beaten back a second time by the Yankees. General Meade became convinced the Rebels would try again to capture the high ground on Little and Big Round Top, and moved 5,750 men from Cemetery Ridge to meet the perceived threat. General Lee thought differently. He decided to break the back of the Union line by attacking its center at Cemetery Ridge. Three divisions totaling 12,500 men would converge to breach a few hundred yards of stone wall. Major General George Pickett's Division was the only one in the entire Army of Northern Virginia that had not fought in the first two days at Gettysburg. It would attack the very center of the Union line, and Pickett was sure his men could turn the tide of battle that day.

Pickett was something of a dandy. He wore his hair long and perfumed, and had been last in his class at West Point. According to historian James McPherson, "he looked like a cross between a riverboat gambler and a Cavalier dandy." But Pickett was an enthusiastic soldier, and was delighted to have the honor of leading the Confederate attack.

At the forefront of Pickett's Division were the Virginians, including Colonel Eppa Hunton and the 8th Virginia Infantry Regiment; two-thirds of them Loudoun men trained at the fairgrounds outside Leesburg. The 8th Virginia had established their reputation at the Battle of Balls Bluff, five miles north of Leesburg. When they ran out of ammunition, Hunton, gave the order to fix bayonets and divided the last cartridges so each man had one round. They made a charge "as gallant as any made in the war," according to Hunton, and won the day. At the Battle of First Manassas, the regiment earned the proud name of the "Bloody Eighth" "when they made a most gallant and impetuous charge, routing the enemy." They would make another most gallant and impetuous charge that day at Gettysburg, when they attacked Union General Meade's "left center," the weakest point in the Union line.

What became known as "Pickett's Charge" was preceded by the largest artillery bombardment in Western Hemisphere history, involving 160 Confederate cannon aimed at Cemetery Ridge, answered by 100 Union guns. Rifles, cannon, and exploding shells provided a much more accurate and deadly armory than in previous wars, and would take a terrible toll among advancing infantrymen. It was a very hot day, and Pickett's Division had waited all morning in fields out of sight of the Union lines. Pickett had allowed his men to lie down in the grass. As the shells fell among them, "bursting in sharp puffs everywhere," men hugged the ground. It seemed an eternity before the Union cannonade slackened, and Pickett rallied his men, crying out, "Don't forget boys that you are from Old Virginia!"

It was a moving sight. Six thousand men in grey-brown ranks, lined up with their Virginia battle flags. The Virginians had to advance about a mile, marching to the beat of their drummers. Pickett's Division consisted of three brigades: Garnet's, Kemper's, and Armistead's. General Lee ordered all his officers to lead the charge on foot to limit their exposure to enemy fire. The order was ignored by brigade commanders Richard Garnet and James Kemper, who led the charge on horseback; and by Colonel Hunton, who was unable to walk in front of the 8$^{th}$ Virginia Infantry Regiment because of a serious leg injury. Brigadier General Lewis Armistead was the only brigade commander who led his men on foot. He put his hat on top of his sword so all could see it, and waving them forward, each line in perfect order, marched towards the clouds of smoke that hid Cemetery Ridge. Historian McPherson best described what happened next: "It was a magnificent mile-wide spectacle, a picture-book view of the war that participants of both sides remembered with awe until their dying moment—which for many came within the next hour. Pickett's charge represented the Confederate war effort in microcosm: matchless valor; apparent initial success; and ultimate disaster."

As he advanced in front of his men, Colonel Hunton saw the North Carolina Division that was supposed to support Pickett's charge, "disintegrate" under heavy Union fire, and leave Pickett's three depleted brigades "entirely without support." About halfway to Cemetery Ridge, Colonel Hunton's horse was mortally wounded and he was shot in the leg. Hunton's personal courier, Private G.W.F. Hummer, took the bridle and led the dying horse and the colonel to the rear, where he had his wound dressed. Hunton tried to get back on another horse, but could not, and Hummer carried him to the field hospital.

Despite more casualties, the Virginian lines held until they reached the Emmitsburg Road. Before crossing the road, they had to climb over a split rail fence. When they formed ranks again, they were met by the massed fire of hundreds of Yankee rifles behind the stone wall along the top of Cemetery Ridge. As man after man fell, sergeants would yell "close up!" and the lines still stayed firm. At the base of the ridge, the Confederates were met by a fire storm of flanking fire and canister shot, and the lines wavered and began to break. Brigadier General Kemper got close enough on his horse to see the faces of the Yankees, when he was shot in the groin and fell. He was captured, then saved by his own men, and later captured again.

Brigadier General Garnet had previously commanded the famous "Stonewall Brigade," but had been arrested and accused of cowardice by General Stonewall Jackson after he withdrew his brigade while under fire, which he did because his men had run out of ammunition. Jackson subsequently died after he was shot by his own sentries, and General Lee desperately needed seasoned brigade commanders. Garnet had much to prove as he led the charge to dislodge the Yankees behind the stone wall. He was within a few yards of it when he and his horse disappeared into the confusion and smoke. His body was never recovered. Colonel Hunton, who succeeded Garnet as brigade commander, said, "He was the noblest and bravest man I ever knew."

Meanwhile, Brigadier General Armistead had called for "double time" and his men ran up the slope to Cemetery Ridge. With Armistead leading the way, about 150 of them reached the stone wall. Armistead fell, grasping a Union cannon, after he crossed the wall and was hit by three bullets. After fierce hand-to-hand combat, the few men with Armistead were shot, cut down or captured by the 72nd Pennsylvania Infantry Regiment, which had rushed forward from the Union's second line of defense to fill the gaps left by the troops Meade had moved out earlier. Great waves of cheering surged up and down the Union side. Armistead was taken to a Union hospital, where he was told his wounds were not life-threatening. He died two days later. Some say of a broken heart. General Pickett never got over the disaster and blamed Lee for sending his men to certain death.

When the charge was over, Hunton hobbled out to the battlefield on a pair of crutches "to see who was left of my faithful and gallant regiment. Only ten of those who went in responded to the roll call—190 out of 200 were gone (his regiment had actually numbered 205, but five men had been killed in the morning's artillery duel)." He said:

> ...it nearly broke my heart to look over the ten surviving members of the gallant 8th Regiment, that had stood by me in so many battles...I have frequently been invited to go over the battlefield of Gettysburg, but I could never summon the courage to do so. If I were to go...I would say, Here fell Captain Green; Here fell Captain Bissell; Here fell Captain Grayson; Here fell Captain Ayres;—and a host of others. It would nearly kill me to see where so many brave men fell—all of them among the best friends I ever had
> ...We passed Will Adams, a gallant soldier of my regiment who was wounded. He looked into my face and said, Colonel, I'm hit. I shall never forget his appealing look
> ...I called to a soldier and told him to take Adams from the field. I thank God he lived, and is now a prosperous merchant in Middleburg, Loudoun County...thus ended the charge of the 3rd of July—a charge that will go down in history as the most gallant made by any army.

Lee thought that Meade would counterattack, but Meade's plan was to stay put, and he did. While the infantry tended to its wounded, 7,000 cavalrymen clashed three miles east of Gettysburg after General Lee ordered Jeb Stuart to attack the Union rear and disrupt communications. Stuart was intercepted by Union cavalry under Major General David Gregg. Both sides fought to drive the other back, but when the Confederates began their final charge, they were stopped by a fierce counterattack led by newly promoted (from first lieutenant) Brigadier General George Armstrong Custer. At sunset, both armies returned to the positions they had held earlier. After midnight, the streets of Gettysburg filled up with men in grey.

The Army of Northern Virginia was in retreat, but Meade refused to pursue until the next day. When Meade finally caught up with Lee's Army, he was too timid to attack and allowed the Rebel Army to escape across the Potomac River.

President Abraham Lincoln wrote: "I do not believe you appreciate the magnitude of the misfortune of Lee's escape. He was within your grasp, and to have closed upon him would ...have ended the war...and I am distressed immeasurably because of it." Upon reflection, Lincoln wrote "never sent, or signed" the letter and stored it in his desk.

Colonel Hunton blamed General Longstreet for the Confederate defeat. He believed Longstreet had disobeyed General Lee's direct order to send five divisions to attack the center of the Union line, and had sent only two divisions to do the job. Hunton also posed the question: "Did Pickett go with his division in the charge?" Hunton mentioned that one of his 8th Virginia soldiers, who had been detailed to carry water for Pickett and his staff, told Hunton that Pickett and his staff were still in back of a limestone ledge of rocks behind where the division had waited all morning before the charge. Hunton also pointed out that neither Pickett nor any of his staff or their horses were wounded or killed, despite the great slaughter around them, and it was "most improbable they participated."

After the battle, Colonel Hunton was promoted to brigadier general. Three of the 8th Infantry dead are buried in Waterford's Union Cemetery. Also buried there are sixteen Independent Loudoun Rangers—thirteen are white troopers, and three are black "auxiliaries."After Hunton died, his son, Eppa III, had his father's tombstone inscribed, "Wounded in the charge of Pickett's Division at Gettysburg."

Union Major General Abner Doubleday, whose badly outnumbered 1st Corps had held off ten attacking Confederate brigades on the first day of the battle, described the fighting "as being the most desperate which ever took place in the world. Nothing can picture the horrors of the battlefield around the ruined city of Gettysburg. Each house, church, hovel and barn is filled with the wounded of both armies. The ground is covered with the dead."

Michael Ruane wrote in the June 30, 2013 *Washington Post:* "Sheets of musket fire had peeled the bark from the trees. Rocks were scarred by thousands of bullets. Artillery shells and rifle balls had buried into trunks and branches, some to stay hidden for more than a century. Residents carried bottles of peppermint oil to mask the stench from dead horses and men."

In early September, Elijah White's 34[th]Virginia Cavalry ranged across north Loudoun County looking for new conscripts, as well as Confederate deserters who were in hiding after Gettysburg. Captain Frank Myers, White's second in command, was grieving one mile outside Waterford, where his mother was being buried. Myers could not be present because the town was full of Union troopers. The day before, Myers had said goodbye: "I looked on her dear dead face. She was the best earthly friend I ever had."

November 19, 1863 was a fine day at Gettysburg. It was a momentous day. Thousands of people—estimates range from 9,000 to 20,000—had converged on the city to see President Lincoln dedicate the new Soldiers' National Cemetery. The principal speaker was Edward Everett, the most famous orator in America, and a former Secretary of State and President of Harvard College. He spoke eloquently for two hours about the importance of the day, to a spellbound audience.

The night before, President Lincoln had written out the ten-sentence "Gettysburg Address" on a piece of paper. He held the paper in his hand as he rose to speak. Doris Kearns Goodwin in her book, *Team of Rivals*, describes what one listener felt:

...the flutter and motion of the crowd ceased the moment the President was on his feet. Such was the quiet that his footfalls, I remember very distinctly, woke echoes, and with the creaking of the boards, it was as if someone were walking through the hallways of an empty house.

Lincoln spoke briefly, but forcefully. The shortness of the speech startled everyone, and there was total silence at the end of it. When Lincoln stepped away from the podium, the audience began to applaud. Lincoln thought his speech had been a failure.

One person who did not was Edward Everett. He later wrote to the President: "I should be glad if I could flatter myself that I came as near to the central idea of the occasion in two hours, as you did in two minutes." Edward Everett had top billing as the principal speaker because in those days most people considered plain speaking and a short speech to be a sign of a lack of education and/or intelligence.

All three of New York's newspaper giants (the *Times, Herald* and *Tribune*) missed the importance of Lincoln's address, and focused on Everett's speech. The pro-Democratic *Chicago Times* dismissed Lincoln's speech as "silly, flat and dishwatery." The pro-Republican *Philadelphia Press* was alone in describing the president's speech as "immortal."

General George Meade finally moved his Union troops across the Potomac, traveling south through Loudoun County. On succeeding days, thousands of soldiers from the 1st and 11th Corps passed through Waterford. William Williams's daughter Rebecca counted 600 wagons in the supply train. A soldier of the 7th Indiana Infantry Regiment liked what he saw:

> The street was lined with citizens, men in broad-brimmed hats and drab coats, women dressed in the modest garb of their sex, and young misses slightly more fashionably habited than their mothers... a half-dozen of these demure young Quakeresses—all sisters one would judge from their appearance—passing cool cups of water as they passed along. It was astonishing the number of thirsty men in the line; to be honest, even I must plead guilty.

Confederate soldiers continued to fight on without proper food, clothing or shoes. Even the officers were having problems. Brigadier General Hunton wrote, "Confederate money had depreciated to such an extent that my pay would not support my wife, son Eppa and myself. On one occasion [my family] was reduced to a single beef bone." The bone was to provide soup, but son Eppa III spilled the pot of boiling water and bone. That night, he ate only some bread and molasses.

During the siege of Petersburg, Hunton was the target for three bullets: one hit his sword belt; another bent his scabbard double; a third ripped across the shoulder and breast of his uniform. He reported to General Lee, who "looked at my clothes all torn up by bullets, and said: 'I wish you would sew those places up. I don't like to see them.' " Hunton responded, "General Lee, allow me to go back home and I will have my wife sew them up." Lee replied, "the idea of talking about going to see wives, it is perfectly ridiculous, sir" and was rather amused at it."

On April 6th, 1865, General Hunton was captured by troops under the command of Union Brigadier General George Armstrong Custer. When Custer heard that Hunton was ill, he sent his physician with a bottle of imported French brandy and a mattress for him to sleep on. Hunton never forgot Custer's kindness. In 1873, when Hunton was a member of the Congressional Committee on Military Affairs, and charges were brought against Custer, Hunton defended him.

General Hunton and six other Confederate generals were imprisoned in Fort Warren, in Boston harbor. The commander was a Union general from North Carolina, and Hunton and the other Rebel generals refused to speak to him. They were befriended by a Boston family who sent them food every week. Ironically, Hunton's health in prison improved for the first time in years, which he attributed to his greatly improved diet.

When the Rebel generals were released, they paid a visit to their new, but as yet unseen, Bostonian friends. Hunton described the reception:

> ..."wine and cake were handed around, and a very handsome young lady asked me if I would drink a toast with

her. I said, 'certainly'. I was pretty thirsty and was willing to drink a toast with almost anybody—especially with this handsome young lady. She said, "here's to Cousin Sally Ann." I said, "my dear miss, I don't know your Cousin Sally Ann, but if she is a cousin of yours, here's to her." She laughed heartily and then said, "Don't you know Cousin Sally Ann?" I said, "No, indeed." She laughed again and then said, "don't you know C.S.A.?"

# Chapter 16
# Personal Gain or Patriotic Duty?

**"Captain C. S. Means is hereby dismissed the service of the United States, for disobedience of orders"**
**—By Order of the Secretary of War**

In October 1863, Lieutenant Colonel Elijah White received orders for the 35th Virginia Cavalry Battalion to report for duty in the Laurel Brigade of Lee's army. What its commander, Brigadier General Thomas Rosser, did not know was that the 35th was greatly diminished. White had failed to report that 70 of his troopers had been captured by Union cavalry during the summer and fall of 1863, and the battalion was further reduced after John Mobberly and a dozen or more of his comrades deserted rather than join the regular army. Waterford's Unionists were delighted to see the backs of the "Comanches," and hoped the end of the war was in sight. They were to be sadly disappointed.

During the first half of the war, cross-border trade in north Loudoun's agricultural produce had been limited, and largely controlled by Southern authorities. After the Battle of Gettysburg, with two great armies fighting in southern Virginia, the market south was closed, and Loudoun farmers looked north to sell their produce. The Federal greenbacks they earned could also be used to import northern manufactures. Federal military authorities welcomed the northward flow of food and forage for their own troops and horses. According to local historian Taylor Chamberlin, the resulting two-way trade, which had been just a trickle, became a torrent in the fall of 1863.

Under U. S. Treasury Secretary Chase's policy that "commerce should follow the flag," Federal customs agents became well aware it was the volume of trade that justified their salaries. The agents were therefore not too careful about buyers' loyalties, and many purchasers were secessionists. The Union Army Provost Marshal was responsible for ensuring only loyal Unionists benefited from cross-border trade. Samuel Means, who owned a store at Point of Rocks in partnership with his brother Noble, was forever writing his superiors complaining that "a great many goods were passing through without a permit and without paying the 5 [percent] duty." Meanwhile, many Leesburg secessionists had been shipping their crops up the Potomac by canal boat for sale in Georgetown and Washington without paying any duty.

In December 1863 Brigadier General Jeremiah Sullivan placed all trade in corn, wheat and hay grown in Loudoun, under military control. He had the full backing of General B.F. Kelly (Sullivan's father-in-law), commander of Federal forces in West Virginia. Kelly had also placed his nephew in an important customs post. Many complaints were received by the War Department about violations and abuses under this nepotistic structure. But the complaints had little impact, and the Federal Government did not lift the ban on trade until 12 days after Lee's surrender at Appomattox Court house on April 9, 1865.

Local politicians were besieged by Loudoun farmers complaining that Union soldiers had been seizing their hay and grain and compensating them at prices far below market prices. Briscoe Goodhart's history of the Rangers fails to mention their role in this debacle, but post-war claims against the U.S. Government confirm the Rangers' prominent role in taking forage from Loudoun farmers with 14 wagons provided by Samuel Means, and "borrowing" a hay baling press from Waterford farmer Amasa Hough. According to local historians Taylor Chamberlin and John Souders, the Loudoun Rangers "were so heavily engaged in foraging they had time for little else." Meanwhile, the Comanches went into winter quarters after their gallant performance against Yankee cavalry, and 60 of them deserted and went back to their families in Loudoun and Fairfax counties. At Christmas time, Major White sent Captain Myers to bring back the deserters, promising they would not be court-martialed.

In early 1864, "the Grey Ghost," Major John S. Mosby and his Partisan Rangers, suddenly appeared at the Potomac River, carrying out a surprise raid on Major Henry Cole's Union cavalry at Loudoun Heights across from Harpers Ferry. Although six of Cole's men were taken prisoner, none was wounded or killed, while Mosby lost one-fifth of his men. It was a terrible defeat for Mosby. One month later, Mosby set a trap for the Second Massachusetts Cavalry (called the "Californians" because so many were from that state). They were attacked front and rear, with escape blocked on one side by a fence, and on the other by enfilading fire from Mosby's troopers hidden in the foliage. The "Californians" fought bravely and desperately, but 35 of them had been killed or wounded and 72 taken prisoner. Mosby's unit suffered just half-a-dozen casualties. Mosby's audacity caused the Secretary of War to impose a total blockade on trade with loyal Virginians.

Only goods authorized by the Secretary of War could be transported across the Potomac at Harpers Ferry, causing even greater hardship for Waterford's Union loyalists. "Rebel mail" from Waterford was still going north to the Potomac, where a Maryland "copperhead," James Besant, ran the ferry to Point of Rocks. Once across, the mail was placed in the U.S. postal system, and the mail going south was ferried back across. At Point of Rocks, the Federal postmaster had delegated the task of inspecting the mail to Waterford Quaker John Dutton, whom he trusted and who knew the political affiliation of practically everyone in northern Loudoun. If Dutton was satisfied the addressee was a Unionist, he would stamp the letter "J. B. DUTTON," and the letter would cross the Potomac unopened.

The Loudoun Rangers continued their profitable "hay soldiering" activities. They were equally diligent in attending dances and other entertainments. Like their rebel counterparts, the Rangers "had a weakness for such amusement," and the "supply of young ladies seemed almost inexhaustible." Local Federal authorities at Potomac crossing points had to deal with the day-to-day reality of desperate Unionists who could not feed their families. They got around the stringent regulations by moving Maryland pickets back from the shoreline and creating a strip of land where Virginians could trade without actually crossing the line into Maryland.

In March 1864, Major General Franz Sigel was appointed Commander of the Harpers Ferry Military District. Sigel had no time for the petitions and complaints of Samuel Means and ordered the Loudoun Rangers transferred to West Virginia. Means refused, arguing the Rangers were an independent company and not subject to U. S. Army authority. True to form, Means wrote to the highest authority, Secretary of War Stanton, to plead his case.

Means had also heard Stanton was in need of a "fresh milch cow," and sent a squad of Rangers to get the best cow they could find. Means dispatched Sergeant William Bull with a fine bovine and a calf to the Secretary's home in Washington. A verbal mix-up between the sergeant and an aide to the Secretary resulted in the latter being informed Means had sent him a bull. Stanton exploded, damning Captain Mean's incompetence in sending a bull instead of the requested cow. When all was explained, the "Bull" returned to Means minus the cow and calf and with ten dollars in his pocket.

Nevertheless, the War Department concurred with Sigel's recommendation to dismiss Means for failure to transfer his unit to West Virginia in a letter of April 13, 1864:

> By Direction of the President, Captain C.S. Means, 3$^{rd}$ Virginia Cavalry, (formerly commanding "Independent Loudoun Rangers,") is hereby dismissed the service of the United States, for disobedience of orders. By order of the Secretary of War: E. D. TOWNSEND, Assistant Adjutant General

Meanwhile, the Loudoun Rangers all demanded to be mustered out of the military, because the transfer was contrary to their terms of enlistment. Means went to Washington to plead their case, and although Stanton would not see him, Stanton did revoke the transfer order.

Samuel Means was personally courageous and organized a fighting force that stayed loyal to him, but he never proved himself as a military leader. His flight from Waterford during the Rangers' first encounter with White's Comanches, and his failure to return with reinforcements while the Rangers were trapped in Waterford's Baptist church, was long remembered. Means also devoted far too much time to personal business, challenging and attempting to oust those he thought were threatening his interests in north-south trade at Point of Rocks.

According to authors John Souders and Taylor Chamberlin, "if not a born warrior, Means became the Union's valued eyes and ears in Loudoun, and a hated gadfly to the Rebels. In the process, he alienated civilians of all persuasions...He nursed grudges–and, too often the bottle. His early efforts to ingratiate himself with the Union high command enjoyed surprising success...But in the end, Sam Means lacked the skill and luck to ride out a conflict that was devouring far greater men." Also, Means was willing to risk–and lose–his prosperous milling business and Waterford home, to fight for the Union cause. His fundamental problem was in being unable to separate personal advancement from patriotic duty.

While Loudoun Unionists were preoccupied with matters of survival, three courageous Quaker women of Waterford decided to break the blockade. Their objective was to participate in the Maryland State Fair for U.S. Soldier Relief, which took place in Baltimore in April 1864. The Fair's purpose was to raise funds for indigent, wounded or sick soldiers by selling donated "fancy articles" at Fair booths provided by private and local government organizations. Twenty- four-year-old Lizzie Dutton's request to travel to Baltimore representing 60 Union ladies of Waterford, who had contributed 200 articles, was turned down by the War Department. However, Lizzie's father John Dutton, got authorization for Lizzie to cross the Potomac.

She caught the attention of the newspaper *Baltimore American,* which on April 20th reported her arrival "by an underground railroad" with "a large contribution of beautiful and valuable articles from an association of loyal ladies in the very heart of Virginia, who have been three months preparing them for this Fair." She was joined the next day by two other Waterford women, who were also said to have arrived by underground railroad. The Waterford ladies were the hit of the Fair, as the Yankees could hardly believe such personable and respectable young women could have endured the danger and hardship of traveling to Baltimore from Virginia by underground railroad with 200 articles for the Fair.

The Loudoun Rangers were moved outside Loudoun to new camps at major Potomac crossing points, Harpers Ferry and Point of Rocks. With no Union troops to oppose him, Lieutenant Colonel John Mosby descended upon northwest Loudoun like a biblical plague. Mosby told his superiors his men "were mostly employed in collecting forage from the country bordering on the Potomac." What he did not say, was that his quartermaster had been diligent in finding and stealing horses. John Dutton, Lizzie's father, had three horses impressed. Although James Walker at Talbot Farm had an understanding with Waterford's previous tormentor, Elijah White, no such arrangement existed with Mosby. Walker's horses were seized, including a prized Morgan. Walker asked to keep his one remaining wagon and team of horses, but they were impressed to carry corn Mosby's Partisans had expropriated. Mosby left, promising to return on a certain date for the Talbot corn crop.

Samuel Means found out what had happened, gathered some of his former Rangers, crossed the Potomac, and organized a surprise party at Talbot for the corn thieves. When Mosby's men returned, the Rangers were waiting and killed one of the Partisans and captured another. Two days later, Mosby's troopers confiscated Walker's last horse, halting all work on the farm. They returned that night to arrest James Walker for giving information that led to the killing and capture of the Confederates. Walker was released only after secessionist friends interceded on his behalf.

When Mosby's men took two horses from Quaker miller James Janney at nearby HIllsboro, 19 of Janney's neighbors who depended upon his mill, petitioned for the return of his horses. Unlike Waterford, Hillsboro was predominantly secessionist, and the whole town came to his support. Janney had followed Quaker principles in staying above the conflict. He helped his neighbors recover property taken by Union soldiers, and had lent his horses to neighbors who had lost theirs and could not work their farms, and were relying entirely upon him to feed their families in the coming fall and winter. Mosby responded by sending troopers to steal two more horses from Janney. Horse-stealing was a very serious crime in 19th century rural America, because without a horse, a farmer or rancher could not work his farm or ranch to support his family. On the frontier, it was a capital crime. In northwest Loudoun, under Mosby's direction it had become an everyday occurrence.

Famous author and poet Herman Mellville was visiting his cousin, Colonel Henry Gansevoort, who commanded the 13th New York Cavalry Regiment. Melville accepted an invitation to join a scouting party headed for southern Loudoun County in search of Mosby. Melville subsequently wrote a long poem entitled "The Scout Toward Aldie," in which he aptly captured the combination of fear and awe that Mosby inspired among his Union opponents:

> Great trees the troopers felled, and leaned
> In antlered walls about their tents:
> Strict watch they kept: 'twas Hark! And Mark!
> Unarmed none cared to stir abroad
> For berries beyond their forest fence:
> As glides in seas the shark,
> Rides Mosby through green dark.

# Chapter 17
# Damned Abolitionist Den!

"[Our] mission is to cheer the weary soldier, and render material aid to the sick and wounded"
—Sarah Steers, Lizzie and Lida Dutton, Editors, "The Waterford News"

According to local historian John Devine, "with the arrival of John Mosby in mid-1864, hardly a day passed that failed to bring either Blue or Gray, or sometimes both, to Waterford." Mosby's actions reflected an escalation in violence and ferocity as attitudes hardened in both North and South and the war dragged on. Under Captain Daniel Keyes, the Loudoun Rangers fled for their lives in their very first encounter with Mosby. This defeat was especially demoralizing for their new commander, and once again the Rangers had great difficulty finding new recruits. Mosby next seized Samuel Steer, the prominent Waterford Quaker, who was customs agent at Point of Rocks, Maryland.

Captain Keyes responded by arresting three prominent local secessionists and requiring them to post a $45,000 bond as security for Steer's release. A few days later, Mosby's men burned down the house, barn and outbuildings of a known Union sympathizer, Sydnah Williams. John Dutton described what happened in a letter to a prominent Unionist: only Williams's wife was home, and Mosby's men "told her  they had just set fire to the barn and intended burning the whole of the D——d abolitionist den, cursing and threatening her  in the most awful manner, telling her also they had just caught her D—-d old gray bearded son  of a bitch of a husband….and tarred & feathered & burned him….the barn was wrapped in flames  with the wind towards the house. They then told her if she would give them $250 they would save the house, but to her credit, her reply was, 'No, had I thousands under my feet

I would not give you a dollar'." Dutton sent a copy of the letter to the *Baltimore American,* which published it on June 22, 1864.

Four prominent Waterford property owners assessed the damage from the fire at $16,000, and General Weber at Harpers Ferry ordered the rebels of Loudoun to reimburse Williams. Mosby was quite willing to up the ante. While denying his men had been involved, he said any attempt to make secessionists pay damages would be extracted two-fold from the Union men of Loudoun. This threat was enough to persuade the Federal Government to drop the matter. The barn-burning was part of a larger strategy involving 50-100 of Mosby's Partisan Rangers, who were making a sweep from the Potomac down through Waterford, seizing horses, wagons and the corn crop. Their intent was to draw out Federal troops from the Maryland side, who had been too preoccupied with other matters to protect north Loudoun Unionists.

The Loudoun Rangers subsequently fought many actions against Mosby, often joining forces with Captain Henry Cole of the 1st Maryland Potomac Home Cavalry Regiment. Yet they could not prevent the *Grey Ghost* from repeatedly raiding Waterford throughout 1864 and looting the homes and farms of Union sympathizers. Although John Dutton and Samuel Steer had fled to Point of Rocks, Maryland, they would occasionally slip across the Potomac at night to visit their families. But in June 1864, Steer was captured by Mosby's troopers and imprisoned in Richmond's Castle Thunder prison. A few days later, Mosby's troopers crossed the Potomac and ransacked Dutton's store (he was not there).

This was the "last straw" for daughters Sarah Steer, and Lizzie and Lida Dutton. They decided to publish an ardently pro-Union newspaper, *The Waterford News,* which they arranged to be printed by the *Baltimore American,* whose editor was an old friend of John Dutton's. Their goals were to "cheer the weary soldier," and provide financial aid to the sick and wounded by donating the 10 cents each newspaper cost to the U.S. Sanitary Commission, a non-government organization which provided medical care to Union troops.

The editors wrote: "We present to our readers this week the first edition of our little paper, with many hopes and fears. We hope that it may meet the approbation of our friends; that they may uphold us in our hazardous undertaking, and we fear nothing so much as their disapproval. We wish and expect it to meet the *condemnation* of our enemies, for they are averse to the truth, and that this sheet will contain."

They sent copies of the first two issues of *The Waterford News* to President Lincoln with a covering letter informing him they had raised $1,000–a remarkable sum in those days–for the U.S. Sanitary Commission. The package was passed on to a Federal regiment from Maryland, who sent it to the President. We know President Lincoln received and probably read *The Waterford News*, because two copies were found among the Abraham Lincoln papers at the Library of Congress.

Their slogan was "THE UNION FOREVER," and articles and editorials in *The Waterford News* were staunchly Unionist. "The News" column was often devoted to the incursions and sufferings caused by Mosby's Partisans. The young publishers also discovered humor as an excellent way of dealing with adversity. The May and June 1864 issues describe a huge crater filled with mud, which almost blocked Second Street, one of Waterford's two main thoroughfares. It was hazardous to negotiate in a wagon, and was a favorite place for local pigs to congregate and wallow.

A paragraph in *Local Items* thanking one young man for bringing a load of sand to put in the crater, is followed by a plea to other chivalrous Virginia males to bring a dozen more loads. Female readers were nevertheless cautioned that chivalry was almost dead, and "being fearful the gentlemen will get their feet muddy, the ladies will try and remedy" the situation. This was followed by a letter to "Misses Editors of Waterford News" from "a much abused member of the Porcine species," who feared for the future because if the hole was filled in, "there is not another such mud hole in the corporation."

The 10th month 1864 issue had this to say: "Wanted–A plaster [medicinal patch] for the mud-hole, it is breaking out again." The hole was probably never filled in, because the following winter it filled with water and provided a skating rink for the town's people. Village streets at night continued to be dark, muddy, dangerous places. Although people were afraid to walk around at night, it was not until the 1880s, that a public outcry–mainly by women–induced the town council to install a few oil-lit street lamps.

The young Quaker women designed their newspaper to appeal especially to all Union soldiers, not just the wounded and sick. A tongue-in-cheek section in the *News* entitled "Marriages," was blank every issue. The 11th month 1864 issue posed this riddle: "Why are Rebel ranks like our Marriage Column?" Answer: "Because there is little probability of their ever being filled." The *Waterford News* editors often complained it was simply impossible to find eligible men of their generation under any circumstances. Local historian John Devine commented that "when a soldier of the right stripe *did* happen by, it was an opportunity not to be missed, even in less than ideal circumstances."

Divine was referring to Loudoun Ranger Private Roscoe Goodhart's story about falling into a trap set by Mosby's raiders Just south of Waterford. Several Rangers were taken prisoner and marched through town, when "one of the loyal ladies of that burg, and perhaps the most demonstrative, kissed Sergt. James H. Beatty, which made the mouths of Mosby's men water, but it was to no avail, as Miss… was a little particular who she kissed." That night, "Beatty made a break for liberty. He darted through the woods in the darkness like a greyhound. About a hundred shots were fired after him, but he went faster than the bullets. It was two months after he returned from Belle Isle prison, that 'hell on earth.' The thoughts of so soon returning nerved him to outrun greased lightning." He returned to Waterford the next night, and "repaid Miss…with double compound interest, the kiss she so ungrudgingly bestowed 36 hours before. It was a clear case on Miss's part of casting 'bread upon the waters."

It was Lizzie Dutton who chose to be the individual responsible for delivering the first draft issue of *The Waterford News* for printing and distribution. She took the draft to the Virginia shore opposite Point of Rocks, Maryland, but could not find a small boat to ferry her across. Union soldiers across the Potomac did not respond to her efforts to get them to cross the river, so she waded into the river carrying her precious burden. This *did* get their attention, and they came to the Virginia side.

She was not allowed to cross, but the soldiers did agree to take the draft to her father along with instructions for its publication. It was fortunate she was no longer carrying the newspaper, because Mosby's men had been watching what was going on below, from a vantage point high on Catoctin Mountain. They stopped her on her way home, found nothing suspicious and apparently believed whatever story she told to explain her actions. In future, delivery of the newspaper was entrusted to Sarah's handicapped cousin, Billy Steer. The *Waterford News* was an instant success, and was followed by seven more issues. Samuel Steer was eventually exchanged for a Confederate prisoner held by the Union Army, and he returned to his job as U.S. customs agent at Point of Rocks.

By the summer of 1864, the war had reached a stalemate. Union Generals George Meade (Army of the Potomac) and Benjamin Butler (Army of the James) were locked in a desperate, seemingly never-ending struggle with General Robert E. Lee's Army of Northern Virginia, to determine who controlled the Confederate capital at Richmond. Union General William Tecumseh Sherman was attempting to take Atlanta, but Confederate General John B. Hood stood in his way. Lee decided to send Major General Jubal Early up the Shenandoah Valley, and to cross into Maryland and threaten Washington, hoping to induce Grant to withdraw Union troops from Richmond to defend the U.S. capital.

With the presidential election just three months away, General Grant realized something dramatic needed to happen to shift the fortunes of war in favor of the Union, or President Lincoln's chances of being re-elected were doomed. Many in Lincoln's own Republican Party felt he should be replaced. "Radicals" thought Lincoln too soft on the South, while a Republican "peace movement" in Congress intrigued to force a negotiated settlement to end the war, and many spoke of replacing Lincoln with former Union General George B. McClellan or General Benjamin Butler.

Who could stop Early? As late as Independence Day, 1864, neither President Lincoln, nor General Grant nor Army Chief of Staff General Halleck had a clue that Early's army was just a three-day march away from Washington, celebrating "the biggest 4th of July picnic enjoyed during the war," with food and drink taken from the citizens of Martinsburg, West Virginia." Probably the best informed person east of Martinsburg was Baltimore & Ohio Railroad president John Garrett, who used railroad personnel to keep tabs on Confederate troop movements. On June 29th he had sent a telegram to General Halleck in Washington that large Confederate forces in the Shenandoah Valley were moving rapidly north. Halleck did not reply.

Colonel John Mosby was largely to blame for the Union Army's communications problems. He later wrote, "On July 4th hearing of General Early's movement down the valley, I moved with my command east of the Blue Ridge, for the purpose of cooperating with him, and crossed the Potomac at Point of Rocks. I thought the best service I could render would be to sever all communications both by railroad and telegraph between that point and Washington, which I did, keeping it suspended for two days."

Mosby's capture of Point of Rocks was carried out with little resistance from Federal troops, which included the Loudoun Rangers, who were stationed there. The Loudoun Rangers were under the command of Maryland troops, and Ranger Private John Forsythe later criticized the actions of the Maryland commander, who withdrew instead of using the town's natural defenses along the Chesapeake & Ohio Canal bank, where they could have "kept ten thousand men at bay." To add injury to insult, Ranger Captain Daniel Keyes, who had replaced Captain Means, shot himself in the foot as the bluecoats fled to Frederick, Maryland. Meanwhile, Mosby's troopers went on a looting spree, leaving shelves bare, and Quaker John Dutton lost almost $7,000 in merchandise from his general store.

The Rebels took particular delight in a huge cake, which had been baked to celebrate July 4.[th] In the shape of an eagle, it had glass eyes, a mechanical device that screeched every time a piece was cut, and was 25 feet long. It was floated across the Potomac on a raft, was liberated and then re-captured, but destined never to be eaten when the wagon carrying it overturned. On their way south with their loot, Mosby's raiders stopped by Waterford's Talbot Farm to relieve the Walkers of a cartload of corn. They stayed overnight and breakfasted with the Walkers before departing.

Samuel Means' brother Noble met with Mosby in person, to plead for the return of $8,000 in stolen merchandise from the Means brothers' store at Point of Rocks. Despite grumbling from his men, Mosby allowed Noble Means to inspect and remove his goods from the items which the raiders had taken. Noble Means was deeply involved in the "copperhead" trade across the Potomac, but his close connection to Mosby has never been explained. The *Waterford News,* as it so often did, had the last word in its "WANTED" column: "Why is our Maggie like the last stick of candy I got at Point of Rocks? Because she is short and sweet."

# Chapter 18
# Water Below
# the Bridge Turned Crimson

**"Great battles are to be scented far off…and *I will not be there.*"**—Union Major General Lew Wallace, Commander, Eighth Army Corps

On July 5 and 6, 1864, General Jubal Early and his army of 16,000 men waded across the Potomac River at Shepherdstown, West Virginia (the Federals had destroyed the bridge at Harper's Ferry). Early was a West Point graduate who had opposed secession, but joined the Confederate cause after war was declared. At midnight on July 5th, General Halleck received a cable from General Meade at Richmond informing him that two Confederate deserters said General Early was on his way to capture Washington. Halleck sent the cable to Grant, who did not believe it. On July 6, Early occupied Hagerstown, Maryland, extorting $20,000 (the amount was supposed to be $200,000 but a clerical error had left out a zero) from city officials under threat of burning the town down, and on the 7th moved on to the village of Middletown, Maryland, where he accepted $1,500 to leave it unharmed. He was heading for Monocacy Junction, 15 miles northeast of Waterford, where an iron B&O railroad bridge and two wooden bridges serving the roads to Baltimore and Washington, crossed the Monocacy River. Once across the Monocacy, the Washington Pike would lead the Rebels straight to the nation's capital.

Confederate Lieutenant General Jubal Early was a hard man. When Lieutenant General Stonewall Jackson complained that his army had too many stragglers, Early replied that Jackson saw too many stragglers because he rode at the rear of the division. While making a rare appearance at church, Early listened to the minister pose a question to the congregation of what would they do if one of their dear, departed loved ones suddenly appeared. Early turned to a staff officer and growled "I'd conscript every damn one of them". While Washington dithered, Early drove his men relentlessly toward the nation's capitol in the July heat. Confederates stumbled out of their ranks by the hundreds and littered the roadside for miles, many dying

General Lew Wallace had been a rising star under General Grant in the west, but his star plummeted after he received contradictory orders and waited a whole day before coming to Grant's aid in the crucial Battle of Shiloh in April 1862. Wallace was not given another command until two years later, when he became commander of the Eighth Army Corps, which included Delaware, and Maryland from Baltimore west to the Monocacy River. He knew it was a dead end appointment, and i off. and *I will not be there*." Wallace's destiny was about to change. Without informing General Halleck, he went to Monocacy Junction on July 6th, where his own scouts told him Rebel cavalry were east of nearby Middletown. Wallace realized they must be the advance guard of Early's force and that Early was undoubtedly heading straight toward Washington.

On July 7th, Waterford's Independent Loudoun Rangers along with three companies of the 1st Maryland Potomac Home Brigade, were the first Union units to make contact with Early's force at Middletown. At dawn on the 8th, they attacked and drove the Confederate cavalry back into the town, where they came up against a brigade of Early's army. They "fell back in good order," holding their own against much more numerous and experienced troops for several hours, while "the enemy's bullets produced a tornado over our heads."

Help came with the arrival of the 8th Illinois Cavalry Regiment, with a six gun battery that shelled the Rebel cavalry every time they advanced. More help came when the 3rd Maryland Potomac Home Brigade arrived, and they took up a strong defensive position five miles west of Frederick, Maryland. These were troops who had been assigned to guard the home front and had not fought in the great battles and campaigns of the Civil War. Yet they held that position until nightfall, when their senior officer, Colonel Gilpin of the 3$^{rd}$ Maryland, ordered a charge preceded by a cannonade from their six guns, which drove the Rebels back to Catoctin Mountain. General Wallace was very pleased and called it "The best little battle of the war. Our men did not retreat, but held their own. The enemy was repulsed three times."

Generals Halleck and Grant finally realized on July 6$^{th}$ that Early had become a formidable threat. Grant reluctantly ordered a single brigade from the Sixth Corps, commanded by Brigadier General James B. Ricketts, to leave their encampment near Richmond, board fast-moving steamships on the James River, and head for Baltimore. It was a race against time, but no one told Wallace. He did not learn about Ricketts's arrival in Baltimore on the afternoon of July 7$^{th}$ until B&O President Garrett told him he had B&O trains waiting to take them west. Ricketts and his men arrived at Monocacy Junction the next morning. Wallace was overjoyed, but still had only about 5,800 troops to oppose Early's army of 16,000. Except for Rickett's brigade, Wallace's men were mostly rear-echelon soldiers who had never seen action.

General Wallace chose to make a stand on the east bank of the Monocacy River, where the B&O railroad and the roads to Washington and Baltimore all converged to cross the river. His main force, including Waterford's Loudoun Rangers, was opposite the B&O and Washington Pike bridges, where the river was 50 yards wide and 3-4 feet deep. The Confederates stormed the covered wooden Washington Pike Bridge. The fighting was so fierce, according to Loudoun Ranger Private Briscoe Goodhart, that the water below the bridge turned a crimson color from the blood of the dead and wounded. Wallace decided he could not defend both bridges, and burned the Washington Pike Bridge.

Meanwhile, General Early had ordered his main force to ford the river two miles south of the bridges, where, on their third attempt, they successfully turned General Ricketts left flank. Ricketts's men were hardened veterans, and although greatly outnumbered, they held their ground in savage hand-to-hand combat until they were "run over and trampled underfoot by superior numbers."

A Confederate Roman Catholic chaplain later described the Union dead: "Lying in every direction and position, some on their sides, some on their backs with their eyes and mouths open, the burning sun beating down on them and their faces swarming with flies. It was a fight to the death as fierce as any seen by many of the men, among them veterans of Gettysburg and Antietam."

Wallace's defeat was widely criticized, and Halleck, with Grant's approval, demoted him; but shortly thereafter, Grant reinstated him. Wallace believed to his dying day that by slowing Early's advance and forcing his army to stand and fight for one day, he had saved Washington and the Union. Wallace was probably right. Early had won a victory, but his men were worn out and he let them rest until the following morning. Meanwhile, General Grant ordered the two remaining divisions of the Sixth Corps at Richmond to travel by steamer to Washington. The next day, July 10th, despite harassment by Union cavalry and the summer heat, Early's army marched 20 miles to Rockville, Maryland. At noon on the following day, Early finally glimpsed the spire of the US Capitol in the distance. His exhausted troops, many of whom walked barefoot, straggled for miles behind the head of his column. According to author Mark Leepson, Early later claimed he had only about 8,000 men left fit for duty, and only one-half of those were ready to go into action.

At Fort Stevens on the outskirts of Washington, Early faced the most formidable defensive barrier in the Union: a 37-mile-long circle of 68 forts, connected by rifle pits and trenches. Early guessed, but did not know for sure if it was severely undermanned. He sent out skirmishers to test its defenses, while waiting for the rest of his exhausted army to catch up. As he pondered what to do next, the rest of the Union's Sixth Corps disembarked at Washington and marched north up Seventh Avenue. Until the Sixth arrived, the *only* troops facing Early's Army were the 25th New York Cavalry Regiment. They exchanged fire with Rebel sharpshooters until the Sixth Corps arrived and immediately engaged the Confederate skirmishers, driving them back while the big guns at Fort Stevens and other forts began to tear holes in the Confederate line. As darkness fell and the sky was lit up by hundreds of brilliant artillery flashes, Early decided to wait until "first light" before making a decision about invading Washington.

President Abraham Lincoln seemed to be the calmest person in the capital. He had briefly stood with his wife on a parapet at Fort Stevens, in full view of the Confederate pickets, when they first engaged the Union defenses. The next day, July 12, he again stood on the parapet with his tall stove pipe hat, attracting the immediate attention of Confederate sharpshooters. A surgeon standing next to him was hit, but Lincoln only stepped down after Major General Horatio Wright, commanding the Sixth Corps, insisted he do so. Meanwhile, General Early had received dispatches warning him two Federal army corps were on their way to Washington from Petersburg, Virginia, and called off his attack. To Lincoln's disgust, General Halleck made no effort to pursue the retreating Rebels. Major General Wright had, in earlier battles, demonstrated a crippling inability to take decisive action, and the Sixth Corps was so slow getting started they not only failed to harass the retreating enemy's rear, they gave Early a twenty-four-hour head start!

Early's army continued west, living off the land and taking everything they needed and much more from the local population. They crossed the Potomac with 3,000 horses and mules and 2,500 head of cattle. On the night of July 14, 1864 Confederate Brigadier General Bradley Johnson's Brigade numbering 2,000 mounted troops arrived in Waterford, after providing the cavalry screen for General Early to re-cross the Potomac River. .Johnson was the highest ranking officer of either side to spend the night in Waterford. He stayed at Talbot Farm, and once again, Eliza Walker had to provide breakfast for a Confederate commander and his staff. General Johnson arrived at 9am wearing U.S. army pants and a gray jacket with no rank insignia, and "behaved gentlemanly," according to Walker.

Author Scott Patchan writes that the Union general with the best chance of catching up with Early was Brigadier General Jeremiah Sullivan and his division of 7,000 Yankee soldiers. Sullivan had already "distinguished himself" by leading his men to a place on the Potomac River where he was certain there was a crossing–only to find out he was mistaken. He finally got his men across at the town of Berlin, but sent his artillery and wagons to cross at the Harpers Ferry Bridge; apparently forgetting it had been destroyed earlier in the war. At Harpers Ferry, Union Major General David Hunter sent Sullivan's wagons and artillery *back* to cross the Potomac at Berlin. A Union officer wrote in his diary "What orders! What command! What commanders!" At sunset on July 16, Sullivan's weary infantry plodded into Hillsboro, 15 miles west of Waterford. An "old Lady" told one of Sullivan's officers that "the rebs were out at Waterford 10 or 15,000 strong moving on toward us." But Sullivan stayed put, seemingly too "paralyzed" to even send out a reconnaissance patrol without further orders.

General Johnson seemed in no hurry to move his Confederate brigade out of Waterford, only doing so when he heard the Yankees were nearby. When the 15th New York Cavalry Regiment arrived, they met the last of Johnson's troopers. The Federals charged, killing two and wounding one. A young girl ran in front of Yankee trooper John Reilay, hugged his horse, and shook his hand so vigorously he "thought she would shake it off." She ran back to her house and emerged with bread, butter and pie for her newfound hero. When the girl warned Reilay of an approaching Rebel, Reilay cocked and fired his carbine as the Confederate trooper appeared around the corner. He missed, and his intended victim escaped.

The 34th Massachusetts Infantry Regiment marched into Waterford two hours after the Confederates left, and were greeted by wild cheers and cries of thanksgiving from Waterford's citizens. The Federals seemed in no hurry, stayed for two more hours, and never caught Johnson, who also managed to avoid General Crook's army to the west. Meanwhile, General Wright's Sixth Corps troops had crossed the Potomac at Leesburg and established camp at Clarke's Gap three miles south of Waterford, but Wright also seemed in no hurry to catch the Rebels. Poor intelligence, poorer coordination and indecision continued to characterize the Union generals, preventing 23,000 Union troops from finding and defeating less than half that number of Confederates. Not for the first time, the Union was cursed by inept and hesitant commanders.

Lieutenant Colonel John Mosby, meanwhile, was actively harassing the flanks and rear of Yankee units, and sent a squad of his Rangers into Waterford dressed in Union uniforms to pose as Yankees. They joined troopers from the 21st New York Cavalry and at a pre-arraigned signal shot and killed eight Union troopers and captured their lieutenant. Mosby was also joined by notorious desperado John Mobberly, who was reputed to have "bushwhacked" Yankee stragglers, and threatened civilians with death if they did not reveal where they had hidden their valuable possessions. When Mobberly captured a mixed race work gang on the B&O Railroad line, he released only the white workers. There was great concern Mobberly either would kill the Negro workers or "send them south" into slavery, and both General Sheridan and Secretary Stanton were informed of the situation.

The Loudoun Rangers were ordered to find and capture Mobberly and his gang. The Rangers found their quarry, but inadvertently warned them of their approach, and Mobberly and most of his men escaped on foot into the woods. Still, the capture of four of Mobberly's "bushwhackers" was considered a success. The missing workers, however, were never found; it was assumed they had been sent south and enslaved. Although Mobberly had been dropped from the rolls of White's 34th Virginia Cavalry Battalion, and was listed as a deserter, that did not stop Major Elijah White from using Mobberly and his gang later in 1864 to disrupt Federal troops invading Loudoun and Fauquier Counties. Mobberly's specialty was to arrive at a Union campsite after midnight and break up the picket line. He would commence at one end of the chain [of pickets] and make the entire circuit of the camps, driving in every picket, and keeping the regiment under arms the whole night.

Early defeated a Union force under Major General David Hunter near Winchester, and in retaliation for mistreatment of Southern sympathizers by Hunter's army, who had burned several houses in the lower Shenandoah Valley, he sent a cavalry brigade to burn down the city of Chambersburg, Pennsylvania if its citizens did not pay $100,000 in gold or $300,000 in Federal greenbacks. The money had to be raised in three hours. The deadline was not met, and the city was burned to the ground. There was a huge public outcry, and Grant finally intervened.

On August 1, Grant sent a telegram to General Halleck: "I want Sheridan put in command of all troops in the field, with instructions to put himself south of the enemy and follow him [Early] to the death." Neither Secretary of War Stanton nor General Halleck approved of Sheridan's appointment—he was too young, too junior in rank, and too uncouth with his western drawl and colorful language. Grant liked Sheridan because he was a fellow Midwesterner who was willing to attack the enemy and exploit their weaknesses.

When President Lincoln received a copy of Grant's telegram, he telegraphed Grant back with his approval, insisting that Early's destruction "will neither be done nor attempted unless you watch it every day and hour and force it." Two hours later, Grant was on a boat heading up the Potomac to take personal charge of the operation. In the weeks that followed, Sheridan decisively defeated Early at Opequon Creek and Cedar Creek in Virginia, and General Sherman defeated General Hood and took Atlanta.

Meanwhile, General Sheridan sent the 13th New York Cavalry Regiment to deal with Mosby, who was stealing corn and wagons from Loudoun farmers, and had passed through Waterford on his way south. First Lieutenant John Hutchison was delighted when he was ordered to take a detachment of the 13th Cavalry and find Mosby. He also had a personal motive for going to Waterford. In 1862, he had become separated from his unit near the town, and stopped in Waterford to ask directions from a girl walking down the street. Not being certain who this stranger was, Lida Dutton evaded answering his questions, until the frustrated trooper demanded, "What side would you like for me to be on?" Whereupon Lida burst out, "If you're a Rebel, I hate you; but if you're a northerner, I love you!"

Hutchison unbuttoned his overcoat to reveal his Union uniform, and told Lida Dutton that one day, he would return to hold her to that promise. On August 10th Hutchison and the 13th New York rode through Waterford. He saw Lida sitting on her porch, and renewed his acquaintance. He left, convinced he had found the woman he wanted to marry. He had. Lida Dutton and John Hutchison were married in Waterford's Methodist Church on January 5, 1867.

The Confederacy was desperate for soldiers, the Union was just as anxious to prevent Southern sympathizers from being pressured to enlist, and sent their cavalry units into Virginia to arrest potential Confederate draftees. In August 1864, Union cavalry arrested several Quakers who were on their way to Goose Creek Meeting, eight miles southwest of Waterford. Samuel Janney was so incensed he crossed the Potomac (he had a pass signed by President Lincoln), and met with Assistant Secretary of War Charles Dana in Washington, who sent him to see Lieutenant General Sheridan at Harpers Ferry.

After listening to Janney argue against the arrest of peaceable citizens who had done no wrong, Sheridan responded: "We must all bear the burdens imposed by this war. I and my soldiers have to bear our burden in the field of battle; thousands of bereaved families have to bear the loss of near and dear kindred; and you people of Loudoun must not complain if you have to bear your share." Janney went back to Dana, who suggested he write a letter to General Grant. Janney wrote the letter and was eventually able to secure the release of 48 Virginians who had been wrongfully imprisoned. Janney provided a great service to the people of Loudoun, because his intervention forestalled a further escalation of the imprisonment of civilians who were not charged with any offense.

# Chapter 19
# Win at any Cost

**"I will commence in Loudoun and let them know there is a god in Israel."**
**—Lt. General Phillip Sheridan at Harpers Ferry**

The war had become an increasingly bitter and win-at-any-cost conflict. Union Major General George Armstrong Custer's division began carrying out a scorched-earth policy in Clarke County and the upper Shenandoah Valley in August 1864. In retaliation for an attack by Mosby's Rangers east of Berryville, Custer ordered that the houses of nearby secessionists be burned. Mosby Ranger Captain William Chapman responded by ordering his troopers to "Wipe them from the face of the earth! No quarter! Take no prisoners!" Twenty of the Union house burners were killed, and ten surrendered. Two of the latter had their throats cut, and the other eight were forced to kneel down, and were shot in the back of the head. However, one Union trooper survived to tell the tale.

On October 14, 1864, Mosby's Rangers crossed the Blue Ridge and derailed a train carrying a Federal payroll of $172,000. Each man received $2,000, and soon there were more greenbacks circulating in the county than before the war began. Mosby sent Captain William Chapman into Maryland to repeat the feat near Point of Rocks, but the B&O railroad had stopped all trains. Mosby's Rangers settled for burning C&O canal boats, taking the horses that pulled them, and looting all the stores in nearby Adamstown (the seventh time in the war the town had been pillaged). These activities were observed by a detachment of Loudoun Rangers under Captain James Grubb, who had telegraphed for reinforcements, believing his force of 81 troopers was insufficient to attack Mosby.

Grubb was told to harass Mosby until reinforcements arrived. He moved his troopers close enough to the Rebels to commence firing their carbines. The Confederates suddenly turned and charged, surprising the Rangers, who fled in confusion. They lost eight men, one killed, two wounded, and five captured. The two raids on the B&O stopped all railroad and canal traffic and caused an uproar in Washington. The lackluster performance of the Rangers was big news, and Grubb's superiors at Harpers Ferry made sure he received the blame, regardless of their inability to send him timely reinforcements.

A month later, Mosby demolished "Blazer's Scouts," an elite unit of 100 hand-picked men armed with seven-shot Spencer carbines, under the command of Captain Richard Blazer, whom General Sheridan had chosen to "clean out Mosby's gang." Although Blazer "fought as no Federal soldier ever fought before," according to Former Mosby biographer J. Marshall Crawford, Blazer was clubbed off his horse and surrendered. One-half of Blazer's force was either killed, wounded, or taken prisoner. Articles in the Northern press claimed that Blazer's second-in-command was killed after he surrendered, and that other Union troopers were not given the option to surrender.

Mosby began following a policy of making the Union pay "two-fold" for what he perceived as Union atrocities, such as hanging two prominent civilians and one of Mosby's men for atrocities they were said to have committed. Mosby's "two-fold" response was to hang seven of 17 Union cavalry prisoners. These unfortunates were each made to draw one piece of paper from a group which included ten blanks and seven black balls. One lieutenant and six privates drew black balls. Because the lieutenant was a Mason, he was saved from execution and another private had to draw a black ball. During the night, three of the condemned men escaped, but the next morning, the remaining four "were hung in sight of the enemy's camp...they were amazed the next morning, to see their companions in arms dangling in the air."

The Union military establishment had always underestimated Mosby, and General Sheridan abandoned his policy of hunting Mosby down. Instead, he decided to target those who enabled and supported him, as part of General Grant's broader strategy to "eat out Virginia clear and clean." After Sheridan's cavalry completed a 12-day "scorched earth" burning of farms, mills, crops, and destruction/confiscation of farm animals in the Shenandoah Valley, General Grant instructed him to destroy Mosby's sources of supply in Fauquier and Loudoun Counties. Sheridan sent two cavalry brigades of about 8,000 men under his protégé Major General Wesley Merritt to destroy the agricultural base of Loudoun County.

Waterford's Union sympathies did not deter Merritt, who, like Custer, had been promoted over many fellow officers from captain to brigadier general in 1863 for "gallant and meritorious service," to take what livestock and crops were left, destroy any mill, and burn every barn, corn crib, and haystack in Waterford. Waterford's grain mill was only spared because it had been abandoned in 1861 when its owner, Samuel Means, had fled to Maryland. All Waterford livestock were driven away, and were followed by men, women, and children hoping to catch an animal straying from the herd. Many of the cattle never completed their journey. They were later abandoned and ended up with new owners, mostly secessionist. According to Elisha Walker at Talbot Farm:

> Occasionally a barn could not be burned without endangering the house & then the barn was sometimes left. This was the case with our own. The wind being N.W. Our hay in the field was burned. We were just ready to send it to market and the *Press* at the rick was also burned. Mosby's men we suppose to have taken old Bob [horse], & so Sheridan's men took Bill [horse], his *big foot* and all. They also drove away the cows & oxen. Two of the former have come back, escaped from the soldiers. Most of our neighbor's barns were burned, their grain & forage, and their stock driven off…This burning was ordered that Moseby [sic] might be forced to leave this Country for want of forage provisions–

–but we think it will affect him little. He [Mosby] cooly followed close upon the burners.

Many of Waterford's citizens climbed neighboring hills and watched in horror as the tall flames from burning barns, outbuildings, corn cribs, and haystacks lit up the night sky. The Dutton sisters were not upset. Union Major J.B. Wheeler recalled "two young ladies perched on the wide gate posts in front of their home, waving American flags and said as their hay was being destroyed, burn away, burn away, if it will keep Mosby from coming here."

In a letter to her sister, Carrie Taylor of Goose Creek Meeting described what happened when the Federals burned all their neighbors' barns, and then came to their farm:" We soon spied a soldier riding around the barn, taking a survey of it. We all went to him and began to beg him not to burn it, told him an officer had just said they were not going to burn anymore. He said 'I am an officer, and I have orders to burn.' Alice and I got around him and begged as though we were begging for our lives. He asked to see it opened; he wanted to see what was in it. When the doors were opened, he said, 'Ladies, it will have to go.' Those awful words gave us renewed energy, and we pleaded and implored. Alice with tears in her eyes, but I could not shed a tear. We told him the house would go too, and I hardly know what we did not say. He looked very irresolute for some time; looked as though he might have heart; at last he said 'I cannot burn it,' rode slowly away from it, told his men to mount, and they all rode off."

Northwest of the Taylors' farm, there were no exceptions. The chaplain of the 2nd Massachusetts Cavalry Regiment wrote: "It was heart-piercing to hear the shrieks of women and children, and to see even men crying and beating their breasts, supplicating for mercy on bended knee, begging that at least one cow—an only support—might be left. But no mercy was allowed.

Union Brigadier General Thomas Devin, whose 2nd Cavalry Brigade was responsible for covering north Loudoun, had carried out his grim assignment without any difficulties. Most residents of Waterford felt they had been singled out for retribution. Major

General Wesley Merritt and his staff spent the night at historic Drovers Tavern in White Pump, 20 miles southwest of Waterford. Local farmer John Dillon provided the Union officers with two barrels of hard cider, and his farm was spared.

Quakers at Waterford's Fairfax Meeting lost an estimated $23,000 in property destroyed. Since this round of destruction involved what property was left after two and-a-half years of destruction by both Confederate and Union troops, their situation, and that of Waterford's non-Quakers, was desperate. According to Mosby Heritage Association Director Richard Gillespie, southern Loudoun county suffered considerably less, because elements of Union Brigadier General Peter Stagg's 1st Cavalry Brigade got lost, and were distracted from their task by hit-and-run attacks from Mosby's Rangers. Stagg therefore failed to complete his assignment, and many farms in south Loudoun were saved. In January 1865, Mosby moved half of his forces to survive the winter in Virginia's Northern Neck.

When Union Secretary of War Stanton gave them no encouragement, Loudoun Unionists turned to the U.S. Congress as the only possible venue which could satisfy their claims for compensation. Only 140 individual claims totaling $260,000 (of which Quaker claims amounted to $103,000) passed the scrutiny of the government's petitioning process. The claims also had the strong endorsement of their tormentor, Union Brigadier General Devin. A resolution by the House of Representatives approved the livestock claims, which totaled $60,000, but the Senate did not give its approval until more than *a century* later (1973). The balance of $200,000 for property losses was never approved by either house of Congress.

During the cruel winter of 1864, one of the coldest in memory, Elijah White's entire command deserted from the Laurel Brigade and went home rather than face the winter in the Shenandoah Valley, after it had been burned by Union soldiers. White had no choice but to disband his battalion, putting Frank Myers in charge of the deserters who had returned to Loudoun.

At Talbot, the Walkers were better off than most of their neighbors. Livestock that had been hidden on a mountain farm was brought down, and they had sufficient hogs to butcher for the winter. A friend returned from Alexandria with a gift of two blind horses. They had the only sleigh left in the area, and after the first snowfall, they took their friends out for moonlight rides. Two months later, John Mobberly brought his own horses and stole the sleigh for a joy ride of his own.

When the Federals left, Mosby's officers visited Eliza Walker at Talbot Farm, and discussed how the farm had fared in the "Burning Raid." A Confederate Marylander said it was nothing compared to Confederate General McCausland's burning of Chambersburg, which he had witnessed. This was too much for Eliza Walker, who replied, "McCausland's name would not live so long as Nero's, but he would not be forgotten by this generation." The visitors laughed, and the Marylander joked that "although McCausland did not play the fiddle, his horses' feet beat a lively tune to the burning city"

Two days later, a major in Mosby's command took three more horses from Talbot Farm.. He was followed the same day by Mosby's quartermaster, who had dinner at the house, and then claimed one-tenth of all the bacon stored during the winter as a tax to support the Confederacy. Mosby had ordered his command to take a one-tenth portion or "tithe" of the Quakers' grain, forage, and bacon. Dinner conversation this time was less polite, as their uninvited guests let the Walkers know they were not comfortable dining among Union people.

The desperate Confederate Congress passed a law allowing Negroes to serve in the military, and Mosby began looking for young men of any color. Mosby's conscription detail, which spent two days searching Waterford, was even more traumatic for the town's citizens than the property seizures. The Mosby's men visited Elisha Walker's School, and dragged out two boys aged 17. They let one go, because the lieutenant in charge said "Friends were exempt." The lieutenant asked about Elisha, but when he was told Elisha was teaching 24 students at his school, he exempted him. Elisha was not convinced, and went into hiding with other young men, moving from house to house. One of their female protectors dressed companion Joe Steer in women's clothes, much to Elisha's amusement.

Captain Daniel Keyes, who had replaced Samuel Means as company commander of the Loudoun Rangers, seemed incapable of doing anything to hinder Mosby's continual harassment of Waterford. On April Fool's Day, 1865, Mosby himself came to town, had his picture taken, and left it for Keyes, so the unfortunate captain would at least know what Mosby looked like. The new commander of the Harpers Ferry Military District, Major General Winfield Scott Hancock, made one last attempt to destroy Mosby. He sent a force of 1,000 men, which included the Loudoun Rangers, under the command of Colonel Marcus Reno, to do the job. Mosby, in characteristic fashion, set an ambush for the lead cavalry in the Federal column.

The Federal cavalry was routed, and fled to the town of Hamilton, where they rejoined Reno's main body of troops. Mosby disappeared, and for three days Reno looked for a fight, but Mosby was content to harass Reno's rear. In his report, Reno claimed he had "easily repulsed" Mosby at Hamilton, and kept him on the run. Major General Hancock was not impressed. Twenty-one years later, Reno was second-in-command to Colonel George Armstrong Custer at the Battle of Little Bighorn, and was unfairly blamed for not coming to Custer's rescue. Reno was later tried twice by court-martial for drunkenness and conduct unbecoming an officer. He was acquitted the first time, but was found guilty in the second trial.

The Union command at Harpers Ferry was anxious to get rid of John Mobberly, who had eluded capture for three years and was a great embarrassment to them. He was said to have personally "bushwhacked" 31 Union soldiers. Sergeant Charles Stewart, who had sworn to even the score with Mobberly, and had eventually recovered from the grave injuries Mobberly inflicted, was selected to lead a dozen Rangers and "capture or kill Mobberly and his band." Acting on a tip, the Rangers hid themselves in thickets along a country road. They soon heard a commotion coming down the road, and Mobberly appeared, chasing a Negro boy driving an ox-cart for dear life. Mobberly was swinging his sword over the boy's head and laughing at his fright. The Rangers rose up and fired as Mobberly passed by, but all of them missed, and Mobberly escaped this and other attempts to capture or kill him, because he always surprised his enemies. He was a superb athlete and horseman, and acted instinctively in time of danger. By the time the Rangers pulled the triggers of their carbines, Mobberly was already at full speed and a fast-diminishing target.

Brigadier General John D. Stevenson, the new commander of the Harpers Ferry Military District, was willing to listen when a group of civilians led by Lovettsville farmer Luther Potterfield, offered to capture Mobberly. In return, they asked for weapons and protection from retribution by Mobberly's many supporters. Loudoun Ranger Sergeant Stewart was again selected to lead a mixed group of Rangers and civilians.

There are differing accounts of how Mobberly met his end. The most plausible is that Potterfield let it be known there was a fine horse for sale at his farm, and Stewart got word Mobberly was planning to go there on a certain night and steal the horse. Stewart and his men hid in the barn, and when Mobberly approached, he saw Stewart and two other men standing in the entrance. Mobberly exclaimed, "Oh Lord I am gone," and fell off his horse with two bullets in his head. Mobberly's body was taken to Harpers Ferry, where it was left on display outside U.S. Army headquarters. Relic hunters cut off pieces of his clothing until there was little left. Mobberly was buried in the graveyard at Salem Methodist Church near Neersville. On his gravestone are the words, "Thrice hallowed the green spot where our hero is laid, His deeds from our memory never will fade." John Mobberly was twenty years old.

Whether Mobberly was a hero or a villain has been hotly debated ever since the Civil War. Mobberly biographer Richard Crouch who claims to present a balanced view of the controversy, states that "the opposing ranger or guerrilla bands engaged in Loudoun County are particularly conducive to the growth of apocryphal atrocity stories, because of the poisonous antipathy between [them]." Crouch fails to consider that it is precisely this "poisonous antipathy" between neighbors and family members who chose opposite sides that so often led to the most violent and murderous behavior. Nor does Crouch comment on Mobberly's behavior in twice shooting wounded Loudoun Ranger Sergeant Charles Stewart while he repeatedly rode his horse over Stewart's prostrate body. He only states that "Stewart somehow miraculously survived," implying that the whole story, related by "Union-sympathizing" Quakers, was equally "miraculous."He also singles out Dr. Asa Bond's statement that "hell could not be hot enough for Mobberly," as demonizing Mobberly; but fails to point out that Dr. Asa Bond, who saved Stewart's life, had saved many soldiers during the entire Civil War, regardless of the color of their uniform, and had taken Confederate soldiers into his home, like Sergeant Robert Parker of the 2nd Virginia Cavalry. Mobberly's behavior in shooting and trampling Stewart's prone body was witnessed by four independent, credible witnesses, who were bound by their faith to tell the truth.

# Chapter 20
# Sound Principles and Square Dealing

**"I received many acts of kindness from those I regarded as my enemies"**
**—William Williams, President, Loudoun Mutual Insurance Co.**

The Samuel Hough House was sold for $1,500 in 1857 to Jacob Scott, Secretary of the Mutual Fire Insurance Company of Loudoun County, established in Waterford in 1849 and still doing business today. Scott was born in 1804 to Stephen and Sarah Talbott Scott. He was named after his grandfather, Jacob Scott, who moved to Waterford's Fairfax Monthly Meeting in 1799 with his wife, Elizabeth Hayward Scott. In 1850, Jacob Scott married Rebecca Atkinson. They had two daughters and a son. Jacob was good with his hands, and earned extra income by cabinet-making and cleaning clocks.

Jacob Scott was the highest paid person at Loudoun Mutual. His annual salary of $100 was almost twice the president's and four times the treasurer's; and his responsibilities were prodigious. He accounted for, and booked, all funds coming in, before turning them over to the treasurer for safekeeping. Once the Executive Committee recommended and the Board approved new clients, Scott wrote the insurance policies, as well as the minutes of every company meeting. As "Clerk to the Company" he also received and dealt with all correspondence. There is no modern equivalent to Scott. He was chief operating officer, insurance analyst, policy writer, bookkeeper and sole company secretary. The secretary's bond (amount placed in escrow in a bank) was $5,000, and the treasurer's was $10,000.

Loudoun Mutual played a vital role in the community because fire was the greatest threat to the buildings of Waterford. Local ordinances establishing stiff fines for violating fire safety rules were not enough. The company enabled building owners to become members of the corporation and to share the risk and losses with others, proportional to the amount of insurance they had—hence the origin of the term "mutual." According to Loudoun Mutual President Christopher Shipe, Loudoun Mutual was known as an "assessment mutual" because the company had the right to go back to the policy holder at the end of the fiscal year and make an additional assessment for any losses the company had incurred.

The company covered all fire damage to buildings except when caused by "any invasion, civil commotion, or riot or any military or usurped power whatsoever, or any locomotive engine or engines." Also, the company would "not insure distilleries or any property immediately contiguous to them on any terms whatsoever." Coverage for personal items of value was limited to three-fourths of the cash value of the property, up to a maximum of $5,000. Loudoun Mutual did not insure the full value of a house because insuring 100 percent could tempt the owner to burn it down. The system worked, says President Shipe, because it "was neighbor helping neighbor," something almost unheard of today.

In 1860, Loudoun Mutual was the most successful business in town, with almost $2,000,000 in fire insurance policies in effect. The twelve members of the Board of Directors were paid one dollar for each board meeting they attended, and five cents a mile for travel expenses. At the annual meeting of Loudoun Mutual Insurance Company on May 6, 1861, William Williams was elected president, Jacob Scott was elected secretary, and Henry T. Gover was elected treasurer. The board informed shareholders that war-related losses incurred by policy holders had reduced the amount of insurance in force by 39 percent.

On December 3, 1861, the Board of Directors voted unanimously to suspend operations "in consideration of the many and great difficulties by which communication between the various members of the Company and the Executive Officers thereof is at present surrounded." The resolution passed by the Board emphasized that "rights and privileges of each and every member of this Company as such shall remain in full force and effect."

Loudoun Mutual policyholder Sarah Dawson owned a large farm on the banks of the Potomac River several miles southeast of Point of Rocks. She informed the company that an unknown arsonist had burned her granary and cowshed on November 30, 1861. Five hundred bushels of wheat, valued at $100, had been destroyed. Sarah Dawson was a very persuasive, persistent, and charming woman. She convinced Colonel John Geary, whose 28th Pennsylvania Infantry Regiment was occupying western Loudoun County, to give her written assurance that no Union soldiers had been involved, and therefore her property loss was not an act of war, and was covered by her policy.

At the same time, she was obtaining Colonel Geary's help in arranging to exchange her son Arthur, who was a Yankee prisoner of war, for one of Geary's own men, who had been captured near Harpers Ferry by the Confederates. To make sure the prisoner exchange took place, she bombarded the Confederate War Department in Richmond with messages. Loudoun Mutual honored her claim, since it predated the company's suspension of operations, but insisted upon paying her in Confederate dollars.

The policy of Loudoun Mutual's Board during the Civil War was to maintain the company's solvency, as well as its reputation for "sound principles and square dealing." It was successful in achieving these goals, according to J.T. McGavack, who was Secretary from 1888 to 1908. Expenses had been cut to the bone including a reduction in Jacob Scott's annual salary from $200 in 1861 to $25 in 1863. Despite losses from 1860 to 1866 of policies in force of $828,244, of $35,790 in premium notes, and 50 percent ($8,875) of Company assets, the company paid all its liabilities, and was "in good legal state, solvent, and possessing the good will and the cooperation of its clientele." The loss of assets occurred after the company suspended operations, and represented claims paid for fire losses incurred before that date.

Loudoun Mutual's survival was a remarkable achievement, considering the chaos and disruption inflicted by the Civil War.

How did it happen? The cooperative structure of Loudoun Mutual was a source of great strength and stability. Each policyholder was part owner according to the amount of premiums paid, and had a vested interest in the company's success. The company did not have to satisfy stockholders who could pressure the company to sell their shares at the first sign of trouble. Unlike most modern boards of directors, Loudoun Mutual had a managing board which ran the company based upon majority vote of its 13 members. Five board members including the chairman were Quakers, and this management style fit the Quaker ethos of arriving at consensus through discussion. The system also worked because board members were prominent and experienced local businessmen who knew each other and many of the company's clients personally, and were known for their good character (very important in those days) and business acumen.

Six directors voted in 1861 for secession, while seven voted to preserve the Union (as did non-board member Jacob Scott). This division was in sharp contrast to Waterford as a whole, where almost 90 percent of voters had voted for the Union. While the split among the directors could have been a recipe for trouble, it actually was a great advantage, because the company could not be labeled as either "Rebel" or "Yankee."

Board minutes reveal little of the give-and-take or personalities of board members. What seems evident, however, is that they worked in a tightly structured environment in which rules and responsibilities were very clear, cooperation was essential, and politics was largely left at the door. In the worst of times, Board President William Williams was an outstanding individual who was widely respected for his honesty and fairness. In the worst of times, he was the glue that held the company together.

When a crisis occurred in which the rules were not so clear, politics could become an issue. In July 1861, Loudoun Mutual's Treasurer, Henry T. Gover "left the state of Virginia; and it is not known when he may return." Gover had good reason to leave. He was well known in the county as an ardent abolitionist, and for being *one of only eleven* Loudoun County residents who had voted for Abraham Lincoln in the 1860 presidential election.

On May 23, Virginia voted for secession, and several days later, Henry Gover secretly visited Washington looking for employment in the Treasury Department. Despite letters of recommendation to Treasury Secretary Salmon P. Chase and President Abraham Lincoln, Gover could not get an interview with either. He then wrote Chase a letter, declaring that he dared not return to his family for fear of being arrested, because "I am considered a Republican and therefore the more closely watched. " Chase did not respond, and Gover looked elsewhere for asylum. Waterford's Fairfax Meeting recorded in June 1862 that "Henry T. Gover has requested our certificate for himself & wife & minor children Jesse, Isaac, Martha, Ephriam, Miriam, and Mary, to unite them to Baltimore meeting." The certificate was duly approved, signed and sent to Gover.

Gover's sudden departure without explanation was a shock to his colleagues. He had been one of the six founders of the company, helping draft the company's constitution and by-laws, and serving on the first Board of Directors and executive committee. The company's first offices were in a heated room rented from Miriam Gover for $20 a year. The company's directors immediately elected board member Armistead M. Vandevanter, an ardent Confederate, as the new treasurer.

The leadership provided by Board president William Williams was critical in keeping the Board united in saving the company. But in 1863, he was arrested by Confederate Major Elijah White and sent to Richmond's notorious Castle Thunder Prison, in a tit-for-tat after Federal officials seized two prominent Loudoun secessionists, Henry Ball and Alfred Belt.

It happened one evening, when Williams answered a knock on his front door and was met by a pistol in his face. His wife Mary managed to throw a coat over his shoulders as he was dragged away by White's troopers. Quaker schoolmaster Robert Hollingsworth was also arrested. A number of Williams's friends, both Rebel and Yank, went to Major White's house to intercede for

Williams's release. White was adamantly opposed, but did relent after the intercession of a prominent Confederate supporter (probably Loudoun Mutual board member Nobel S. Braden). White grudgingly granted the two prisoners 30 days parole to allow Mary Williams and Williams's brother-in-law James Walker to convince Federal authorities to release Ball and Belt. Accompanied by Samuel Janney, they visited President Abraham Lincoln to plead for the release of the Southern sympathizers. President Lincoln obliged with a note to the officer in charge of prisoner exchanges: "Will General Hitchcock please see these friends, and effect the special exchange they request, if he can consistently can." Hitchcock was agreeable, but Secretary of War Stanton showed "about as much feeling as a polar bear might," refusing an exchange under any conditions, because, he said, "it would encourage Confederates to take more hostages."

William Williams wrote: "Bidding a sorrowful farewell to our friends, not knowing if we should ever meet again, we commenced our march to Richmond...the men composing our guard were inclined to be rough at first, but by being pleasant with them we disarmed this hostility...they frequently carried our knapsacks for miles, and would occasionally 'ride and tie' with us." (Author's note: The first traveler would ride to certain point, tie his horse for a walking second traveler, and start walking himself until overtaken by the second traveler on horseback, and so on).

Their first stopover was at the Orange County Courthouse, whose basement was the county jail. An old man greeted them kindly: "Gentlemen, you have got into a hard place. They [the guards] will steal everything they can lay their hands on. The guards, he said, were [Stonewall] Jackson's old bodyguard, mostly composed of Irishmen, and what they stole they would pass to their off-duty comrades, so if a complaint were made, and the inmates searched, nothing could ever be found...when the inmates would all be asleep, someone would come around with a candle and appropriate anything that took their fancy." William stayed wide awake, and when "a villainous looking man with a candle came around," he passed Williams by.

The following morning the prisoners were herded into a railroad train for Richmond, where they were incarcerated in Castle Thunder Prison. The new arrivals were put into a room with about 100 other men. The only furniture was "a very few lamps and tubs for use in the night," and everyone slept in their clothes on the floor. The windows had no glass, so Williams did not have to "worry about draughts." The main meal was a half loaf of wheat bread and a small piece of boiled beef distributed on a first come, first served basis. A necessary chore was "the more serious business of lousing which had to be done every day to keep the nits from hatching. I have seen as many as five men, stark naked, engaged in this interesting employment."

After three weeks, the prisoners were moved to a better room on an upper floor, but "no one was allowed to depart day or night." That meant the tubs could no longer be emptied when they were full, and only by a special detail once a day. "Consequently the tubs became very offensive and you were never free of the stench day or night." Every prisoner was supposed to serve on the tub detail, "but if you had money, there was no difficulty in hiring a substitute for a Confederate dollar, so we were saved this unpleasant task." Prison life was hard and tedious, especially because there was no hope of release. Yet Williams wrote, "My spirits never gave way, which was a fortunate circumstance, as the hopeless soon pined away and died."

Nevertheless, the odds were high Williams would die in prison, as did so many inmates, or emerge a broken man. What saved him was meeting a physician he had known before the war, who was able to have him and his companion Robert Hollingsworth moved to "the parlor of the Castle among a different class of prisoners," men with money and connections. One day, Williams was in the prison yard when someone called out at the gate, "Are there any Friends in there?" The caller turned out to be John Crenshaw, a distant relative whom he knew "pretty well." Crenshaw was able to get Williams paroled into his custody. Williams also survived an attack of smallpox, after Crenshaw got a local doctor to admit him to Richmond's Smallpox Hospital. Williams believed that if he had ended up in the prison hospital, he likely would have died.

Williams was visited by "several of our Loudoun rebel friends then in Richmond," who interceded with the Confederate Secretary of War Stanton on Williams's behalf. Two days before Christmas 1863, Stanton released Ball and Belt from Federal prison. When Henry Ball heard Williams and Hollingsworth were being held hostage for him, he wrote a letter stating he did not want the two Quakers to be imprisoned on his account, which his son, who was a captain in the Rebel army, presented to the Confederate Secretary of War. These efforts were sufficient to gain the unconditional release of both hostages. They still had to endure many more tests of their fortitude travelling home through a land occupied by soldiers in both grey and blue.

William Williams arrived home nine months after his imprisonment with a renewed faith in the basic goodness of people, but bitter at the Federal Government for refusing to help him: "I was arrested, incarcerated in a vile prison, but never insulted by any and received many acts of kindness from those I regarded as my enemies, while abandoned by those I considered my friends."

At war's end, Loudoun Mutual Fire Insurance Company had survived the most terrible war in American history. But when it began operating again on January 1, 1866, it had to re-invent itself and reconsider the way it did business. Total property insured was just $325,721, and total premium notes in force amounted to only $23,108. But the Board was hopeful: "The amount of assets has been materially reduced in consequence of the war...but those exhibited are believed to be perfectly good, and the Company is in good legal state, and possessing the goodwill of its clientele."

According to J.T. McGavack, who wrote a history of the company in 1940, those very characteristics that carried the company through the war, would enable it to meet the challenges ahead: "no money, but loads of Southern grit; plenty of opposition, but fifteen years of experience, which put it beyond the experimental stage. Now organized with practically the same Board of Directors...They had vision, confidence, and conservatism."

The company's directors decided the regional scope of operations would have to be greatly expanded outside Loudoun County for the company to survive and prosper. John Dutton had been the sole travelling agent, so the company hired more agents, and by 1867 was doing a brisk business in twelve counties. Meanwhile, Jacob Scott was overseeing the herculean task of rewriting insurance policies which had been suspended for five years.

Jacob Scott's annual salary again reflected the company's fortunes, rising from $115 in 1862, to $300 in 1870, plus 50 cents per new policy. Scott retired in 1871, and the Board voted him a parting gift of $150 "in consideration of his past faithful services and as remuneration for any assistance he may render the incoming secretary." Scott was also appointed to the Board. Today, the walls of the Board room at Loudoun Mutual are lined with the portraits of its founders and leaders—all except Jacob Scott. According to President Shipe, the mystery of the missing picture has never been solved.

Because of the fear of fire, many Waterford houses, including the Samuel Hough House, had a split level kitchen area separate from the main house, with a warming room above ground and a cooking room beneath it. After his retirement, Jacob Scott decided to join the kitchen area to the Samuel Hough House by building a two storey gabled and L–shaped addition, integrating both into a single graceful structure. Tobin Tracey, AIA, and formerly White House Architect, identified the two-over-two, 6 feet high windows on the north side of the dining room as 1870s construction. This date is supported by James S. Odin's 1875 map of Waterford, which shows an L-shaped addition as part of the house.

Rebecca Scott died in 1880, and Jacob died in 1889 after a long illness. The *Loudoun Telephone,* a local newspaper, published his obituary in its October 11, 1889 issue:

Jacob Scott of Waterford passed from work to reward last Saturday morning. He had been very infirm for many months, and for years was subject to epileptic fits. His case seems to suggest the irony of fate, for while he had, for years, yearned for deliverance from his suffering, yet his physical nature held on to life with a remarkable tenacity—until his years numbered eighty five.

At his funeral, William Williams "spoke tenderly of the deceased, taking for his text, 'an honest man's the noblest work of man.' And most applicable were these words for the occasion, for the deceased was recognized by all who knew him, as scrupulously honest in all his dealings with his fellow men."

William Williams died on November 23, 1892, in the 41$^{st}$ year of his presidency. Williams was a remarkable man who is remembered in many ways, not the least of which was that he declined to accept any salary during the Civil War. Williams, a firm Unionist, was succeeded by longtime board member Oscar S. Braden, an ardent supporter of the Confederacy, who had been a captain in the 6$^{th}$ Virginia Cavalry.

# Chapter 21
# Hell on Earth

**"Bodies would freeze quickly and were often left for a week or more."**
**—Union Private Briscoe Goodheart, prisoner-of-war, Belle Isle, Virginia**

If Quaker William Williams experienced the best elements of the human spirit during his captivity, Loudoun Rangers who were captured and imprisoned suffered the worst. Briscoe Goodhart was one of 18 Rangers captured at Charles Town, West Virginia, in October 1863. He wrote a vivid account of his suffering and that of his fellow prisoners. The first day, all their belongings, including coats and blankets were taken away, leaving them only the clothes on their backs.

Their destination was an island in the James River ironically named Belle Isle. A stockade had been built on a two-acre sandy plain, with tents accommodating about 3,000 men. When the Rangers arrived there, they joined some 11,000 Yankee prisoners, most of whom slept on the ground. Each prisoner was supposed to receive a daily ration of two small pieces of cornbread, and very occasionally, a cup of bean soup. Many times there was just one piece of cornbread, and other times there was none. It was rare to find a bean in the "soup." Food parcels from relatives were routinely confiscated by prison authorities.

At night, Briscoe Goodhart slept folded ("spooned") together against two other prisoners, with the weakest sleeping in the middle. They were very fortunate because unlike many other prisoners, they had two blankets—one to place on the cold ground and the other to cover all of them. Briscoe's words best express their ordeal and agony: "As the winter rolled on the prisoners became weaker and weaker, until death by starvation and exposure relieved thousands of their suffering. It was a common occurrence to see poor fellows lie down and die in a few minutes." The weakest of the trio, succumbed in just this way. He  got up one night, re-marked how bright and beautiful the moon was, complained of be-ing cramped in the middle, lay down on the outside, gasped for breath three or four times, and died.

The next morning, it took six weakened prisoners to lift and carry their emaciated comrade and put him on a pile of about 200 others who had died during the night. The bodies would freeze quickly, and were often left for a week or more before they were collected for burial.

Belle Isle had a hospital, but none of the Loudoun Rangers sent there ever came back. Every day, 100 prisoners would be se-lected for transfer. When the Rangers were selected, they were overjoyed, imagining they were going to be exchanged for Confe-derate prisoners. They were not told they were destined for the in-famous Confederate prison at Andersonville, GA. The night before they were to be moved, the prison received a message requesting 100 Yankee prisoners to exchange for 100 Confederate prisoners just arrived from the North. Since the Rangers had already been cleared for transfer, their orders were simply changed to a steam-boat going north. It is highly unlikely any of them would have sur-vived Andersonville. They were saved by bureaucratic indifference and Lady Luck.

So many others were not so fortunate. Five Loudoun Ran-gers were taken prisoner on March 1, 1864. They were sent to An-dersonville, and all were dead, probably from starvation, by July 1964.Goodhart emerged from prison in his own words, "a physical wreck," with both feet badly frozen, and partially paralyzed on his right side. He spent four months in an Annapolis, MD hospital, and another year recuperating from his ordeal. He would carry the emotional impact of his suffering for the rest of his life.

Newly promoted Comanche Major Frank Myers was able to muster only 60 men from the 35th Virginia Cavalry Battalion to join General Lee's Army of Northern Virginia, in a last desperate attempt to stop Union troops from seizing the Confederate capital at Richmond. He wrote in his diary:

"1 April, Hard fighting all day...My God! The enemy are too strong for us. We check them at one point & they break thro at another and still force us back. I wonder when it will end and how. Tonight the cannon are roaring along the line most awfully...4 April, "It is now settled that old Richmond has fallen...I feel more downhearted now than I have since the war began...we have been fighting all day. Have retreated about four miles. Went into camp about 11 o'clock pm. Want something to eat I think."

When General Robert E. Lee surrendered to General Ulysses S. Grant at Appomattox Court House on April 9, 1865, the $2^{nd}$ Virginia Cavalry Regiment was fighting the last cavalry action of Lee's Army of Northern Virginia not far from where Lee signed the surrender document. Moments before a flag of truce stopped the fighting, Sergeant Robert Parker was shot. He is believed to be the last man killed in Lee's Army of Northern Virginia. He was first buried in the field of battle, and then re-interred on a grassy knoll overlooking Appomattox Court House beneath a tombstone marked "CSA Unknown." His wife Rebecca was two months pregnant, having conceived during his last furlough. She never found out what became of her husband's body, and died on January 5, 1867, leaving three small children.

When they received word of Lee's surrender, Waterford's sedate Quakers, for whom dancing and other frivolities were prohibited, "danced a jig." At nearby Goose Creek Meeting, "there is great rejoicing with the Union people in regards to the fall of Richmond and the surrender of Gen. Lee...It is said Samuel M. Janney had the old Gobbler killed and invited many of his Union friends to eat and be merry.

Myers and the $35^{th}$ Virginia Cavalry did not lay down their arms at Appomattox. Myers led them in a charge through the Federal lines and headed north to Loudoun. He wrote in his diary, "I am ashamed to go home, but I can say I did my duty as far as I am capable." When the news of Lee's surrender reached Colonel John Mosby in Loudoun, he swore he would fight on, and did so, attacking the Loudoun Ranger camp and capturing 38 Rangers and 75 horses. General Grant was not amused and gave orders to "hunt Mosby down." The orders were never carried out. When the Appomattox ceasefire agreement was about to expire, Mosby assembled his Rangers, tearfully shook hands with each man, said they were free to seek their own paroles, and rode off. He never did surrender. It was this kind of "I don't give a damn" behavior about rules and regulations that helped make him the romantic figure he has become.

First Lieutenant John Hutchison of the 13th New York Cavalry Regiment was in Ford's Theater in Washington on the night of April 14, 1865, to see a performance of "Our American Cousin." In a letter to his Waterford sweetheart, Lida Dutton, he wrote that when President Lincoln and his wife entered the presidential box, the audience erupted into "one continuous roar for several minutes," until quieted by a bow from the President. He also saw John Wilkes Booth jump down to the stage after assassinating the president, but "everybody was so completely surprised that the assassin was allowed to escape. My battalion was ordered out that night to picket the city." Booth and his companions escaped, evading the thousands of soldiers who were searching for them.

The Loudoun Rangers were involved in the vast manhunt for Lincoln's killer and his co-conspirators, who, at one point, were believed to have fled west to Hagerstown, Maryland. The provost marshal at Harpers Ferry was instructed to arrest the suspected killers, and took 20 Rangers with him. With mission accomplished and the suspects in the Hagerstown jail, the Rangers visited the army commissary, where they imbibed freely of strong drink. Ranger John McDevitt, went outside, climbed up to the top of some boxes, and fell asleep. During the night, he rolled over, and fell twelve feet to the pavement below. He was hospitalized for several days, but his injuries apparently were not life-threatening.

The Loudoun Rangers were mustered out of the Union Army on June 3, 1865. They had been poorly led. Captain Samuel Means and his successors had little military aptitude, and Lieutenant Luther Slater was a great loss. After their initial defeat at the

Waterford Baptist Church, the Loudoun Rangers managed to hold their own against Major White's Comanches, although they were no match for Mosby's Partisans. Yet they never deserted or failed to do their duty, despite being outnumbered and outmaneuvered time and time again by Mosby. With the exception of Cole's Maryland Cavalry, neither an elite U. S. Army unit nor regular army cavalry units did any better against Mosby than the Loudoun Rangers did. Their casualties were far higher (36 percent) than most other Union cavalry units operating in northern Loudoun.

One of their own, Private Briscoe Goodhart, wrote their history which, in the words of historians Taylor Chamberlin and John Souders:

"captured the independent fighting spirit of these men of Loudoun Valley (along with their convictions and biases)...vividly portraying the Rangers' sacrifices and losses, particularly the harsh treatment many suffered as captives...making it all the more remarkable that these Virginians (and they never considered themselves anything else), resisted any change in their status that would have taken them to safer assignments farther from their homes."

Participants also tend to put the best light they can on events; and both Goodhart's and Myers's accounts suffer from failure to reveal the less savory aspects of their service. Lieutenant Colonel Elijah White's Comanches will always be tainted by their close association with Mobberly and his band of outlaws. Mobberly is barely mentioned in Frank Myers's history of the Comanches, and the single incident he describes casts Mobberly in the best possible light.

Elijah White apparently tolerated these abuses among his former troopers because his unit had recently been incorporated into the regular army and would be leaving Loudoun, and he felt the presence of the renegades was needed in Loudoun to keep Union sympathizers in check. Since renegade and regular often acted in concert, the line between the two was blurred in White's battallion. In May 1863, when White led the 35th Virginia Cavalry Battalion back through Loudoun on the way to the Battle of Brandy Station, he had no problem incorporating Mobberly and his men back into his unit.

Frequently, during the annual Waterford Homes Tour and Craft Exhibit, members of the 20th Massachusetts Volunteer Infantry, the 8th Virginia Volunteer Infantry, and Stonewall Brigade re-enactors march through Waterford to the Union Cemetery to remember and lay a wreath on the graves of the honored dead. The first sergeants call out the muster saluting the names of the fallen. The captain of the 20th Massachusetts invites the visitor:

> Come closer: read the faded name and the regiment. Suddenly the old weathered stone takes on a different appearance. It stands as steadfast as a soldier in the battle line ready to face his foe. Now the battle is against the elements erasing the soldier's name from the stone, reducing his name to obscurity.

The Union Cemetery in Waterford is the last resting place for twelve white and three black Union soldiers, at least five Confederate soldiers, and one from the Spanish American War. The wreaths were made for many years by former resident Jan Kitselman.

# Chapter 22
# Forgive and Forget

**"I committed treason and am proud of it."**
**—Former Confederate Lt. Colonel John S. Mosby**

Lieutenant Colonel John S. Mosby was unsurpassed as a guerrilla strategist. He had great mobility–he insisted on fine horsemanship and "dash"—and he had no base, living off the land and sleeping at the homes of Confederate supporters. He was constantly on the move, and filled his ranks with young men not tied to home and hearth. He was a master of tactics and surprise, arriving in Waterford like some dreadful apparition, or luring Union cavalry into carefully prepared ambushes.

To confuse and separate his opponents, he liked to trap his enemies in confined spaces, while launching coordinated attacks on their front and rear. He believed sabers and carbines were useless in guerrilla warfare. His men were armed with pistols tucked in holsters, belts or boot tops. He ordered them to charge straight at the enemy and shoot as soon they were within range. There was no time to reload, and when there were no bullets left, the pistol was reversed and used as a club. In the showdown with Union Cavalry Major Richard Blazer, Mosby Trooper Sidney Ferguson knocked Blazer off his horse by hitting him with the butt-end of his pistol.

The development of a rapid-fire gun or pistol raises an interesting issue about the importance of innovation–or lack of it—especially in wartime, when the success or failure of an entire nation can be at stake. Confederate and Union officers shared the widely held belief among their European counterparts that no weapon could defeat the effect produced by "the speed of the horse, the magnetism of the charge, and the terror of cold steel." Mosby, however, was unique in combining "the magnetism of the charge" with greatly increased firepower. But he was only effective fighting at close range, and following a strategy of surprise, surround and overwhelm.

Due to the development of much more powerful and accurate artillery and infantry weapons, Colonel Eppa Hunton's 8th Virginia Infantry Regiment was left with just ten men standing after Pickett's charge at Gettysburg, and Hunton had watched two North Carolina Divisions "disintegrate" under the storm of Union fire. Yet he continued to believe that if General Longstreet had charged earlier in the day with more divisions, the battle–and the war—would have been won. Although Hunton understood that the war had become a matter of attrition, he saw no contradiction with his belief that a gallant charge by enough individuals can overcome any enemy, regardless of the killing power of the enemy's weapons.

In the Confederacy, justification for the deaths of so many had to be found in a higher ideal—the gallantry of the individuals who died. Pickett's "most gallant charge" became the defining image of the Confederate soldier. It was the highest accolade that could be paid, and it became the model for the idealized Confederate soldier.

A new South had emerged from the War. Historian W.J. Cash said "out of that ordeal by fire, the masses had brought not only a great body of memories in common with the master class, but a deep affection for these captains, a profound trust in them, a pride which was inexorably intertwined with the commoner's pride in themselves." These beliefs acquired legendary status as the "Lost Cause," which Cash aptly described as a "deeply felt southern nationalism growing out of the shared sacrifices, the shared efforts, and the shared defeat."

The Virginia General Assembly which convened in December 1865, passed laws designed to turn back the clock. They repealed the recognition of West Virginia, passed anti-vagrancy laws designed to return Negroes to near slave status, refused to finance public education or measures to rebuild the economy, and guaranteed payment of state debt financed by state bonds held by the plantation class. In March 1867, the U.S. Congress overrode

President Andrew Johnson's veto to pass the Reconstruction Act, which divided the South into five military districts, each under a U.S. Army general. Each state would remain under martial law until it met Congress's terms for re-admission into the Union: enfranchising Negroes, barring ex-Confederates from office, and adopting state constitutions that met Congressional guidelines.

In October 1867, elections were held to choose delegates to draft a new state constitution. In Virginia, the old party structure was a casualty of war, and demoralized conservatives hardly participated. Republican delegates (including 24 blacks) won 68 of 104 seats at the constitutional convention. In Loudoun County, conservatives were more unified, and reflected a willingness of men like former Confederate Major Frank Myers to swallow their pride for the greater good. But the proposal for a new constitution failed by 97 votes, because the constitutional convention in Richmond was dominated by radical Republicans, who insisted on a constitution that would meet Federal requirements, including the 14th amendment, guaranteeing the rights of all Americans, regardless of race.

With a national election coming in 1868, Republicans in Washington were not eager to seat more Democrats before it took place, and approval of the new Virginia constitution was put on hold. This delay gave Virginia's establishment time to organize a Conservative Party of Virginia, made up mostly of *ante bellum* Democrats. When Ulysses S. Grant was elected President in 1868, he set a date in July 1869 for a referendum on the Virginia state constitution. This time, conservatives won a resounding victory, and they approved the new constitution after removing the restrictive clauses that would have prevented them from taking political office. Virginia thus mocked the Reconstruction Act, yet was re-admitted to the Union in 1870.

Political historian Dewey Grantham described the South's transition in political terms: "the political hegemony of the conservative Democrats who redeemed the South from Radical Reconstruction was formidable. Having restored all of the ex-Confederate states to home rule, southern Democrats moved to liquidate their Republican opposition in the region…in the presidential election [of 1880] the Democrats carried every southern state."Confederate veterans held most state offices. In Virginia, Confederate hero James Lawson Kemper, was elected governor in 1869, and was followed by six other Confederate "brigadiers" as governors of Virginia.

In 1874, former Brigadier General Eppa Hunton decided to run for Congress on the Democratic ticket. Former Lieutenant Colonel John Mosby supported his opponent, Republican James Barbour. According to Hunton, "through Colonel Mosby hundreds of people throughout the district (especially in the County of Fauquier) were promised office if they would vote for Barbour." In Barbour's own county of Culpepper "there was almost a reign of terror, and persons were afraid to vote for me; their business was threatened and their official position was endangered…Under the circumstances it is very wonderful that I was elected.

The antagonisms and hatreds engendered by the Civil War persisted long after the war was over. In Loudoun County, the defeated were placed in charge of law and order. Former Confederate scourge of Waterford, ex-Lieutenant Colonel Elijah V. White, was elected sheriff in 1867. It was no surprise when he chose his former second-in-command, former Major Franklin Myers, as his deputy. But Myers had a problem. Because U.S. President Andrew Johnson had not required those who had fought against the Federal Government to acknowledge their defeat and swear fealty to the United States of America, Myers was extremely reluctant to take the amnesty oath required to hold office. Worse yet, he would have to swear the oath before Justice of the Peace and Waterford Quaker John Dutton, who had been held in Castle Thunder prison and then driven out of Virginia for his Union sympathies.

Myers hated Dutton, and vice versa, with Dutton calling him "one of the worst rebels in Va," and demanding he either take the amnesty oath or leave the U. S. Myers wrote in his diary, "I've a great mind to kill him & go."Myers was seriously considering going to Mexico and joining the army of Mexican Emperor Maximilian. Myers's humiliation was complete when he acquiesced and swore the oath "before the grand high priest of the Devil."

The fact that a prominent Quaker like John Dutton accepted such an assignment, showed how much the Civil War had liberalized Quaker discipline. Prominent Waterford Quakers William Williams and Dr. Thomas Bond broke with discipline and ran unsuccessfully for local office in 1865: Williams for the State Senate; Bond for the House of Delegates. When Fairfax Quaker Mary Bond married "out" in violation of discipline in 1864, the Meeting did not disown her, as was the practice, but decided that "the unhappy civil war causes much difficulty in travelling and communicating with different sections being the cause of the transgressions of discipline...and she is continued as member." Unlike their brethren at nearby Goose Creek Meeting, most Waterford Quakers had either tacitly or explicitly supported the Union cause, violating Quaker discipline and their original commitment to remain neutral in the War.

Sarah Steer and Lizzie and Lida Dutton found it hard to forgive and forget:

> Can we forget the ones whose hearts
> Are blackened by those deeds of madness
> Once cherished as our neighbors–now
> The cause of all this gloom and sadness.
> (Waterford News, 5th mo. 28, 1864).

Both Lizzie and Lida Dutton married the Union soldiers they met during the war and left Waterford.

John Mosby thought there was nothing to forgive or forget. He said: "I never apologized for anything I did or said during the war. I committed treason and am proud of it. I am not ashamed that members of my family were slaveholders, neither am I ashamed that my ancestors were pirates and cattle thieves." Mosby believed the South should accept defeat and leave the past behind, and supported Ulysses S. Grant for president.

Unlike Mosby, almost all followers of the Confederate cause believed they had done nothing treasonable, and they deeply resented Mosby's association with the Grant administration. Resentment turned to hatred in many cases, and Mosby was no longer welcome at the annual gathering of his battalion. Mosby had moved with his family to Warrenton, Virginia. When someone tried to shoot him, he decided to leave Virginia for the safety of his family, and accepted an appointment from President Rutherford Hayes as U.S. Consul in Hong Kong, where he served from 1879-1885. Mosby's relationship with former Confederate Brigadier General Eppa Hunton had improved, and Mosby sold his Warrenton house to Hunton, who was very pleased to be buying "for eight thousand dollars a very fine residence on Main Street in Warrenton." Mosby subsequently worked as an attorney for the Southern Pacific Railroad in San Francisco, and for the U.S. Government in Washington. He died on Memorial Day in 1916, and was buried next to his wife and children in Warrenton. A movement to deny him burial in the town cemetery was thwarted by local authorities.

Mosby's tombstone is simply inscribed:

JOHN S. MOSBY
43$^{RD}$ BATTALION VA. CAVALRY
BORN DEC 6 1833
DIED MAY 30 1916

When Major Frank Myers finally went to Harpers Ferry to get his parole from the Union Army, he called it "the darkest, gloomiest day I ever experienced and I have seen many."Over a year after the war ended, he was still pursued by demons and self-doubt:

> Went to Waterford tonight to the post office. I'm not going into that white mean nigger den any more if I can help it" (undated)...Stayed at [church] but didn't go in. I felt awful wicked. Saw a Yankee officer with all his rigging. Never did the devil tempt me so strongly to do what I would have

been so sorry for. I could have captured and killed him so easy...so I didn't go in to hear the sermon.

When a friend's two children died of diphtheria, he wrote...

> ...all the children have gone to eternity in a week. Death is kind to the children at any rate. How much better off I would be if I had died when I was their age. Don't want to die now though. Saw Frances Ann but didn't hardly speak to her...Saw Frances Ann and was afraid of her...Frances Ann was there. She and I stayed awake all night. I am almost happy...My heart is so pressed down with woe I can't sleep. Saw Frances Ann last night and today. I'm not fit to die now, but oh how I wish I was...Saw one white sad face that is haunting my dreams, when either waking or sleeping. What can I do. I can't go away and I dread to stay. If there is a hell on earth I think I am in it...I can hope some, but oh I have so often been deceived by hope that I am almost afraid. If I had ten thousand worlds I would give them all to know that I am a child of God. I have nothing to sustain me. Oh God, make me fit to die and take me, my heart is crushed. This dull aching pain is killing me. I am trying to pray but the burning tears are scalding and torturing my heart and I can't pray.

Myers was overcome by loss, for which he was blaming himself: the loss of the war; of his closest friends, especially those who died in the Battle of the Wilderness in May 1865; loss of all the early idealism of fighting for a cause; and hatred of all the devastation caused by the war, for which he blamed the Yankees. The publication of his reminiscences in 1871 rekindled old animosities. He did marry Fannie Shawen and opened a store in Waterford. It is hard to imagine Myers happy in Waterford, and the store failed.

In November 1872, Frank Myers's trustee, Nobel B. Peacock, who was a strong supporter of the Confederacy, and who had bribed a Union officer and saved his barn during the "Burning

Raid", and still suffered property losses totaling $4,400, held a three-day auction of Myers's "goods, wares and merchandise." The deed book devotes twelve large pages to recording the thousands of items sold. Auctions were a wonderful place to find bargains. As was the custom, most of the buyers were men, provided with lists by their wives. William Williams purchased three books for 27 cents for himself and wife Rebecca.

The woman buyer who spent the most was Sallie King. For $12.44, she bought 2 plates, Buttons, 10 yards Goods [textiles], paste board, chalk pencils, mace, edging, Shawl, whale bones, 9 yards Trimming, Braid, 15 yards Alpacca, buttons, 6 skeins silk, 12 yards cambril. Total spending by the 163 buyers amounted to $859.02. Nevertheless, Myers's father had to sell 30 acres to cover his son's debts. Frank Myers and Fanny moved to nearby Lincoln, where he eventually became postmaster. He died in 1906.

Some veterans tried to make a profession out of their Civil War experiences. Ed Wright, former sergeant in the 35th Virginia Cavalry, who had been court-martialed in 1865 for stealing horses, was in the business of "requisitioning" horses and cattle again. He was jailed in 1866, escaped, but was tracked down by a posse from the newly formed Loudoun Horse Insurance Association. He was given a ten year sentence, escaped again from prison, and was re-captured. He escaped a third time and was never heard from again.

The Federal Government's attempt to reconstruct governance in the Confederacy by ratifying new state constitutions and holding free elections to establish truly representative state governments was bitterly resented and contested by the vast majority of Southern whites. "Reconstruction" reinforced their belief the Yankees were intent on destroying Southern culture and way of life. Frank Myers, back on his Waterford farm in 1867, complained bitterly in his diary "We must all work for the nigger now."

Such was the hatred of Yankees, especially for those Virginians who had fought for them, that many former Independent Loudoun Rangers felt they had no place in Loudoun. In 1860, Ranger Captain Samuel Means's Waterford Mill was in ruins, and Means was pursued by creditors. It is unlikely hostile neighbors would have allowed him to restore his mill. Means spent his last years in Washington, D.C., where Rock Creek Cemetery contains the graves of Samuel, his wife Rachel and daughter Mary Alice. A simple, flat stone is engraved "Samuel Means, died March2, 1884, aged 57."

Private Briscoe Goodhart was among the Independent Loudoun Rangers who felt strongly he could not live in an unreconstructed Virginia. His granddaughter, Mrs. Rosalie Goodhart, said, "After the war, Briscoe knew that Union veterans would not be too popular in Loudoun County, so he left the homeland he loved, only to return on summers and holidays." Goodhart went west to Ohio, and then moved on to Kansas. He mastered the bookbinding trade, and married Ida Lee Mason from Illinois in 1870. He stayed in the Midwest, never settling in one place for a long time. In 1892, he took a position in the Bindery at the U.S. Government Printing Office, and lived in Washington, D.C. until his death in 1927.

In the conclusion of his book, Goodhart asks the reader to give special consideration to the survivors of Rebel prisons, because they "have suffered and endured what you never can, and I hope your children never may." It seems likely it was the memory of the horrors and near death of his imprisonment at Belle Isle, Virginia, that kept Goddhart from returning to his native state. Former Loudoun Ranger Isaac Hough Jr. left the state because local farmers would not patronize his family's woolen mill as long as he worked there. The mill was burned down by unknown arsonists not long after he left for Maryland.

Former Loudoun Ranger Lieutenant Luther Slater was one of the few who made a successful return to the County. Two months after Lee surrendered, he was appointed Lovettsville postmaster, and served there for two years. In 1867, he moved to Washington, and with high recommendations from two U.S. Army Generals and a U.S. Senator, began a 42-year career in the War Department. He became involved in implementing a new and revolutionary system for handling veteran's affairs using individual index cards, which summarized all relevant information for each veteran. This replaced the ancient time-consuming and costly practice of re-checking original documents every time a request for information was made, and helped preserve original documents from constant handling. Slater died in Washington, D.C. in 1909.

Much southern rage was centered on Abraham Lincoln, even after his death. Local historian John Devine liked to tell the story of his Aunt Dollly, who "hated Lincoln with a passion, and that's all she could talk about…we used to take her to Washington–she would turn her head when we went by the Lincoln Memorial, "Hatred of the Yankees included even ministers of the church. Like all other churches, a new Methodist Church South had split from the national Methodist Episcopal Church over the issue of slavery. After the war ended, the national Methodist Conference sent new ministers down south. They were not welcome, and some congregations refused to let the newcomers conduct services. Others felt stronger action was necessary.

On Sunday, January 14, 1866 the Reverend Joseph A. Ross of the Methodist Episcopal Church (North) had finished a service at Leesburg, and was on his way to preach in Waterford. Three men in Confederate uniforms appeared, "one of whom presented a revolver…stating that I must leave or they would blow me to Hell…[he] demanded my pocketbook, which I at once gave him. He examined it and throwed it down (it was empty)…They then ordered me to leave saying that if I looked back or to the right or left they would blow my brains out." The Rev. Ross was not deterred, and went to nearby Hamilton, where he found the church door locked, and no one who would give him the key. When he was refused a key on the following Sunday, he returned on a third Sunday with Federal soldiers, who forcibly ejected the Southern Methodist minister. Most of the congregation followed the minister, and Ross preached to another group that had assembled in the church. Once Union soldiers left Loudoun County, however, the fate of church property and the issue of control would be decided by local courts and the congregation.

In 1911, former Lieutenant Colonel Elijah White of Leesburg's 35th Battalion Virginia Cavalry presided over the dedication of a statue of a Confederate soldier in front of Leesburg's Loudoun County Courthouse. A large crowd had assembled, and some commented that the soldier's rifle pointed toward Waterford, rather than pointing north.

# Chapter 23
# Refugees and Freedmen

**"Refugees and Freedmen have been summarily excluded from their homes."**
—**Union Major General Oliver Howard**

The most urgent post-Civil War problem facing the Virginia General Assembly was the thousands of freed slaves walking the by-roads of Virginia without food, shelter, or jobs. In Loudoun County alone, 5,501 slaves were freed in June, 1865. Many were separated from their families, and were ill, starving, and unable to travel far.

President Lincoln created the Bureau of Refugees, Freedmen and Abandoned Land in 1865, under the War Department: to protect "the Negroes in their rights as freedmen," with a broad range of responsibilities in re-habilitating and helping ex-slaves to become self-sustaining members of society. A major goal was teaching them to read and write. During its short history (1865-72), the Bureau spent $5 million to educate freed slaves and their families. By 1870, the Bureau had established more than 1,000 schools in the South; half the teachers were Southern whites, one-third was black, and one-sixth was Northern white.

The Freedmens Bureau had ambitious goals, but lacked the financial and human resources to accomplish them. U.S. Army officers under the command of Major General Oliver Howard—known for his piety as the "Christian General"—were responsible for achieving these objectives. Howard did his best (Howard University in Washington, D.C., is a monument to his efforts), but the Army was undergoing a massive post-Civil War down-sizing, and implementing the Bureau's goals became increasingly difficult. Meanwhile, the Quaker network surged into action, providing food, clothing, medical treatment, shelter and schools, in cooperation with federal, state, and local officials working through Freedman's Bureaus.

Quakers understood that education was the most important battleground for achieving Negro rights after the Civil War, and that Americans of color stood little chance of improving their lives or taking their place in the postwar society, unless they were able to become educated. By the end of 1866, the Society of Friends had established ten colored schools in Virginia. Total student enrollment was 355; of which 185 were reading, 250 were writing, and 31 knew the alphabet but were not yet able to read.

In September 1865, Sarah Steer of *Waterford News* fame, and another young Quaker woman, Annie Mathews, began teaching both Negro children and adults in Waterford homes. In 1866, Waterford's Quakers, the local Negro community—which had grown substantially with the return of those who escaped north during the war—and the Freedman's Bureau formed a partnership to establish a school for colored children. With the financial assistance of the Friends Association of Philadelphia, they purchased a half-acre lot on Second Street for $75 from Reuben Schooley, and built a one-room schoolhouse. The deed read "To the Colored people of Waterford and Vicinity."

Henson Young Sr., whose son Henson Young Jr. fought in the 1st U.S. Colored Infantry Regiment during the Civil War, was one of five Negro trustees responsible for school administration and its legal representation. Henson had worked many years for Waterford farmer Henry Virts, until his death in 1890 at the age of 79. Prior to his death, Henson had paid Virtz $15 for a stone tablet to mark his grave in the colored section of Waterford's Union Cemetery, according to Hazel Eleanor Costello, granddaughter of Henry Virts. No new trustee was appointed to succeed Henson Sr. This omission would have important repercussions when the school was closed 67 years later.

Bronwen and John Souders describe what it was like when Sarah Ann Steer became the Waterford Colored School's first teacher, and opened the school door on October 9, 1867. Sixty-three students crowded into the building, 28 of them older than 16.

Philadelphia Friends shipped 175 garments and two boxes of slates and books. During spring planting the boys had to work in the fields, and only 38 students came to class. Students—called scholars in the school's early days—addressed their teachers as miss, ma'am, or sir. Sara Steer never said what her salary was, but teachers who succeeded her were paid $30 a month. The curriculum included writing, arithmetic, grammar, geography and history. Student Mary Sofia Kennedy wrote: "we all ought to try to learn to spell above everything else but I do not like to spell very well I would rather get any other lessons than a spelling lesson it seem so hard to learn when they are long words especially and they are hard to remember." Mary Kennedy's hopes and fears were never to be realized. She died at age 15 of unknown causes.

Lack of capacity to communicate through reading and writing and becoming "literate," was a major barrier to achieving happy productive lives for millions of newly freed Americans of African descent, and achieving literacy for the next generation became the most important goal of the colored schools. By 1867, Loudoun County had 46 schools for white children, and nine for colored children. Quakers operated and administered colored schools in Leesburg, Waterford and Lincoln, and the Freedmens Bureau did the same in Unison, Hillsboro, Hamilton, Aldie, Middleburg and Leesburg.

A February, 1868 monthly report to the Loudoun County School District Superintendent lists three Quaker colored schools in Leesburg, Waterford and Lincoln, with a total of 191 students enrolled, of whom two students were "in alphabet," 89 "read easy lessons," 48 were "advanced readers," and 116 were capable of "writing."

There is no listing indicating how many students could both read and write, but it is impressive that the majority of colored students in the Quaker schools were able to read (61%) or write (71%) to some degree.

Six schools administered by the Freedmens Bureau presented a sharp contrast to the Quaker schools. They had a total enrollment of 174, of which 15 students were "in alphabet," 62 "read easy lessons," 33 were "advanced readers," and 50 could "write." Of these students, only 20% were advanced readers, and just 29% showed writing ability. Teacher training would likely have been an issue. An important Bureau objective was to provide employment for colored teachers, most of whom had received far less education and training than their white counterparts.

A Freedmans Bureau census-taker who visited Leesburg, observed that a federal superintendent was "sadly needed, to rectify some of the acts of oppression done here." He cited Nancy Binns, of a prominent Leesburg family, who "turned off" former slaves who could not care for themselves (a 90 year-old woman, and a crippled old man); owners who allowed destitute former slaves to stay if they worked for no pay; and white citizens who were caring for colored children, whom they "bound out" as servants.

Captain Henry Alvord of the 2nd Massachusetts Cavalry was appointed superintendent of the school district which included Loudoun and ten other counties. He knew northwestern Virginia well after pursuing Colonel John Mosby's Partisans, was energetic and intelligent, and appeared to be an excellent choice. He was mustered out of the Army just one month after his appointment. He tried to be hired as a civilian, but was rejected. Alvord's replacement, Lieutenant Colonel John Marsh, was from the Veteran's Reserve Officer Corps, made up of soldiers who had been wounded and were unfit for active duty. Marsh began his appointment by going on a leave of absence, and then resigning. He appointed a hospital chaplain, James Ferree, as acting superintendent.

Local historian Betty Morefield describes Ferree as "a nervous, fearful man, who realized he was unqualified for the job." Ferree was either unable or incapable of finding serving army officers to fill six of seven vacant assistant superintendent positions. The lack of administrators became so serious the Army ordered local federal provost marshals to assume double-duty as Ferree's assistant superintendents. The marshals had little time or inclination for their additional duties.

Leesburg was a hotbed of anti-Yankee sentiment, and Ferree did not receive a warm welcome. He rarely left his office without the company of a Union soldier, fearing "for his life at the will of a drunken & demoralized ex-rebel Soldiery." Ferree got some help when former captain Henry Alford was finally hired as the assistant superintendent for Loudoun County. Alford found that data was not available to prepare a report on the office's financial affairs, and wrote to Richmond, "I am told to straighten [financial affairs] out in Mr. Ferree's absence, and tho rather a hard and thankless task, am trying to do it."

A major objective of the Freedmens Bureau had been to divide up land confiscated by the Federal Government into 40-acre plots, so that individual freed adult males could receive "40 acres and a mule." In Loudoun County, 81 tracts of land had been confiscated from their Confederate owners. President Andrew Johnson changed all that when he allowed former landowners who signed a loyalty oath to the Union to receive presidential pardons, which would allow them to vote, hold office, and get their land back. Many freed slaves who still lived in houses on their former owners property, found themselves in impossible situations. General Howard received reports that "Refugees and Freedmen have been summarily excluded from their houses by the owners of the land," and ordered all officers and agents to prevent further evictions until "provision is made for resident refugees and freedmen."

Restored landowners wanted those houses back for their new tenants. George Carter at Oatlands Plantation offered to build a house for former slaves Wesley Jenkins and his wife, for their use rent free, for the rest of their lives, if they vacated their present house. Oatlands was the only property Agent Ferree ever visited. He never met with any of the Freedmen who were about to be dispossessed, and in every case, supported the landowners' arguments for eviction.

Seventy-five year-old former slave Paris Champ had lived with his younger wife Sydna in the same house for many years. His former owner, Hugh Smith, had died, and Smith's eldest son Rufus, who had inherited the property, decided to rent the Champ's house to a new tenant. He ordered the Champ family to leave. Paris Champ sought the help of prominent local Quakers, Henry Taylor and Samuel Janney. Taylor wrote an eloquent letter to Union General Winfield S. Hancock: "Paris Champ is nearly blind and seventy five or eighty years old...he is entirely incapable of labor...as they [the Smiths] have had all the benefit of his labor for his whole life, and have sold nearly all of his children as slaves in the South.... they should not be allowed now to turn him out of doors to starve."

Agent Ferree in Leesburg was ordered to provide a full accounting and justification for the eviction. Ferree Smith and "three citizens living in the immediate neighborhood", all asserted Paris and Sydna Champ, their children and "half-idiotic" grandson were perfectly capable of supporting themselves elsewhere. Rufus Smith claimed that 75-year-old Paris Champ "could do almost work enough to support himself," Sydna Champ was "a first rate cook, washer & ironer & able to command the highest wages," son Charles "was one of the best hands in the county," their=16 year-old daughter "could anywhere get 25 or 30 dollars per year over and above food and clothing," and their grandson "though defective in his left hand & half idiotic could still do so much, chopping wood, carrying water, gathering sheaves, going errands, etc."

Although no evidence was provided to support these claims, the agent sent by the Bureau believed them. Paris and Sydna Champ were not allowed to testify on their own behalf by Virginia's antebellum legislation. The Champ family was promised a smaller house at another location, but they insisted on staying in the place they had lived in so long. They had raised a family of 14 children there, 12 of whom had been "sold south" by Hugh Smith. They had given up so much, and now they were "free," they were being forced to give up the only home they ever had. Enough was enough, and the Champs refused to move. Ferree signed the eviction order and it was approved by the Freedmen's Bureau head office.

Ferree's downfall was charging fees, in money or in kind, for his services. This practice was strictly prohibited by the Bureau. Feeree made the mistake of signing a receipt when he charged a local farmer "a small fee for keeping up the office."That receipt was sent to Charles Howard, the Bureau's assistant commissioner in Washington, D.C. Ferree was fired after an investigation revealed how widespread this practice had been. Ferree left Leessburg in a hurry, and did not pay his bill at the Loudoun Hotel. A local newspaper, *The Democratic Mirror,* gleefully reported that Ferree charged all his clients fees, regardless of the color of their skin.

In 1871, Virginia's General Assembly passed legislation adopting public education, and all Waterford schools became part of the local school system. In 1882, Waterford's colored school received its first of many Negro teachers, Harry I. Arnold. On the last day of school, the pupils would put on quite a show of recitations, dialogue and music for the public. A reporter for the *Loudoun Telephone* who was there in 1884, wrote that the pupils spoke and answered questions "with confidence and boldness," and "the singing, with respect to the white folks, was so superior as to compare with the squeaking of a wheelbarrow and the notes of the wood thrush."

The Waterford Colored School was in stark contrast to the rest of the state. Educational reformers in urban communities had begun to turn away from traditional private and church run schools, in favor of "common" schools financed by taxes and subject to local government control and supervision. But three-fourths of Virginians lived in rural communities who were against change. In the 1880s, rural Virginians were no more interested in education reform than they had been during the post-Civil War "Reconstruction", when innovations in education were pursued by an alliance of freed slaves, northern evangelicals and southern Republicans.

According to educator William A. Link, white rural Virginians held on to their deep-seated convictions about individualism, race, family, church, and school proximity, and were overwhelmingly opposed to state or local government "interference" in education. They were also dead set against having their children transported to a centrally located "common" school. It was all about losing community control; and for them "education remained a matter of private choice...in which government had no place."

After the state took over the education of Virginia's colored residents in 1871, keeping former slaves in their place became the main objective of the public education system. Link wrote that from the 1880s on, the curricula for colored schools were limited to meet the primary purpose of "attaching the Negro to the soil and prevent his exodus from the country to the city." In 1893, Loudoun County statistics recorded 1,528 colored students in 29 mostly one-room schools, taught by 32 colored teachers.

By 1926, nothing had really changed: About 1,700 colored students were taught by 28 colored teachers, distributed among 1 multi-room, 2 two-room and 22 one-room schoolhouses. Only 15 of the colored teachers were certified to teach above second grade level. Loudoun County ranked 35th in the state with just 60.72 percent of the total school population attending regularly, and the average length of a school term was only 168 days—138 days for colored schools. Apathy at all levels of government, driven by a lack of funding, ensured that public education for Virginia's Negro population remained a low priority.

After the Civil War, many freed Negroes had become members of the Methodist Episcopal Church of the United States. In an 1875 map of Waterford, the Second Street School building is identified as the "African Church," because Waterford's Methodist Episcopal Congregation held services there on Sundays. In 1889, church members began building their own house of worship. In 1891, the John Wesley Methodist Episcopal Church was completed across from the Old Mill. Male members of the congregation had worked until late at night, while the women held lanterns. Between 1865 and 1900, 30 other churches were established in Loudoun County by Negro communities.

When J. T. Moten, Methodist Episcopal Church Pastor "in charge of the Waterford circuit," concluded his assignment in 1886, he had this to say about the other churches in Waterford: "The Baptists have shown their respect, regardless of color or class. The Presbyterians are kind to the poor everywhere. The Lutherans are quick to do good and help the needy. The Quakers were strange to me at first, but after living in town among them, I found them to be 'Friends' indeed to the poor colored people and thus worthy of their name." Reverend Moten's comment is revealing, because only the Quakers are specifically mentioned as extending a helping hand to the colored people of Waterford.

Before the Civil War, Waterford had supported half-a-dozen schools educating 34 white children. In addition to Elisha Walker's Waterford Academy at Talbot Farm, at least five others were established during the late 18th and 19th centuries. The earliest was probably a small brick building at the rear of the Quaker Meeting House. A restoration in the mid-20th century revealed black-boards painted on the walls. Another Quaker school house can be found on Huntley Farm. Schools were also held in private homes.

In 1872, the school trustees for the Jefferson District held a meeting in Elisha Walker's Waterford Academy to discuss building a new school for white children. The trustees emphasized that public funds would be very limited for the operation of the school, and that private subscriptions would have to fill the gap. They appointed a committee of three Waterford residents to raise money for teachers' salaries, and by the end of the meeting, the new committee had $236 in hand, about one-half the money needed for the school year. This generosity prompted a reporter for T*he Washingtonian,* who was attending the meeting, to write, "It is evident that the people of this ancient town area are alive to the best interest of their children, and are determined to have for them good schools." In 1877, the trustees paid $350 for a one and one-half acre lot along High Street by Butchers Row, and built a new school upon the site.

# Chapter 24
# The Americans Came
# Just as the Blackbirds Do

**"Indians must adopt the habits of civilized life."**
**—Samuel Janney, Superintendent of Nebraska Indians**

In 1803, President Thomas Jefferson overcame his misgivings that a U.S. president did not have the constitutional authority to purchase land from a foreign government, and agreed to pay Napoleon Bonaparte $15 million (about four cents an acre) for 828,000 square miles of the American heartland; ranging north-south from the Canadian border to New Orleans, and east-west from the Mississippi River to the Rocky Mountains. Between the two was a vast plain, broken by a patchwork of rivers and streams. Local Indians called it "Ne-brath-ka," land of flat waters. Nebraska, as it is still known today, was the traditional home to the Omaha, Pawnee, Ponca and Otoe-Missouri Indians. At the stroke of a pen, they became part of the United States.

Jefferson could only afford to pay $3 million in gold, offering to finance the balance with U.S. Government bonds. Napoleon insisted on full payment in gold, and British banker Francis Baring saved the day by agreeing to underwrite the transaction by buying the U.S. bonds at a discount. Since Great Britain was at war with France, Baring sold them to a Dutch intermediary, who made the required gold payment to the French government.

Three decades before becoming president, Jefferson had written in his *Notes on the State of Virginia* of the potential of the Mississippi and Missouri Rivers for furthering commerce and development. He had also compared the lack of productivity of the nomadic Indian with the settled white farmer, eulogizing the latter: "a single farm will shew more of cattle than a whole country of forests can of buffaloes." Although Jefferson admired certain qualities possessed by Native Americans, such as orations the equal of "Demosthenes and Cicero and their "bravery and address in war," he considered them an impediment to achieving a nation of settled agriculturalists. For Jefferson, "those who labor in the earth are the chosen people of God." By 1803, Jefferson was determined to dismantle the Indians' communal hunting-based societies, requiring them to settle and farm individual plots of land, and make available to white settlers the open range the Indians had hunted on for centuries.

As Nebraska's indigenous inhabitants came into ever-more frequent contact with whites, the result was "waves of epidemics–typhoid, influenza, whooping cough, malaria, cholera, and small-pox–which according to Nebraska historian David Wishart,—landed on the Indians "like breakers on the beach." They were also being pressured by eastern tribes that had been "removed west," such as the Shawnee, who had been ejected from their land north of the Ohio River in 1774. These newcomers were being relocated onto lands Nebraska Indians regarded as their own, leading to increasing hostilities and escalating violence.

Beginning in 1830, the tribes had to agree to sign onerous treaties in which they gave up millions of acres of their best land to the U.S Government in exchange for annuity payments and plots of land. The transactions made little financial sense—the Indians received about ten cents an acre—but the Pawnee and Omaha had far more pressing reasons for signing. Large groups of Oglala and Brule Sioux warriors, who were their traditional enemies, were attacking from the north and west. The Sioux vastly outnumbered both Pawnee and Omaha, and although the treaties guaranteed U.S. Army protection, the Army was incapable of providing it.

In 1841, the Sioux managed to drive the Omaha out of their homeland between the Blackbird Hills and the Missouri River flood plain. For the next decade, the Omaha were refugees. They were not allowed to buy guns to challenge the Sioux's firepower, lost most of their horses, and were afraid to venture far in search of the ever-diminishing buffalo herds. They lived on the edge of starvation, eating roots and the occasional muskrat or raccoon. Eventually, they were reduced to eating the thatch off their earth lodges just to stay alive.

Not until 1845, did the U.S Government decide to build a fort on the Platte River to ensure the safety of the immigrants and the tranquility of the Indians. By that time, Nebraska's vast herds of bison were so depleted they could not feed the Indians dependent upon them, who were starving to death. To survive, the Pawnee sold some of their best land—110,000 acres on the Platte River—to the Government so it could build Fort Childs (later Fort Kearney). In return, the Pawnee received $2,000 worth of merchandise. This was the last sale of Indian land before the Nebraska Territory was created and opened to settlement under the Kansas-Nebraska Act in 1854.

During 1854-57, all Nebraska Indians signed a series of treaties agreeing to live on small reservations, and give up most of their land in return for annuity payments. The Indians had no real choice, because they needed the annuity payments just to survive. Living on a reservation provided no protection from their enemies. In 1858, The Pawnee reservation was raided eight times by the Sioux, usually when the men were away hunting. Each time, Indian Agent James Gillis was able to persuade the Sioux to leave, but they promised to return, and did. During one attack, Gillis was able to save women and children from certain death or capture by hiding them in the root cellar of his house. When 500 Sioux warriors showed up late in the year, The U.S. Cavalry had to ride out from Fort Kearney to protect the Pawnee. A long drought and severe winter in 1860-61 reduced the Pawnee to a state of starvation once again.

All treaties with the U.S. Government stipulated that one-half of the annuities Indians received had to be in goods, and the rest in cash. All too often the goods were useless, or they never arrived; and annual cash payments when they were paid—were woefully inadequate. The system for selling reservation land was also deeply flawed. Payments could be deferred if buyers were unable to pay, and there was no enforcement, so arrears and non-payment were built into the system. But the government always deducted moneys due them, and the Indians were the ultimate losers. Even when the annuity system was working, it was plagued by corruption, poor administration, and payments far too small to meet even the basic subsistence needs of individual Indians.

Meanwhile, hopeful settlers had begun swarming across the western borders of Iowa and Missouri into Nebraska, and the Indians were soon surrounded by whites eager to separate them from their land. Nebraska's Indians were in no condition to fight back. The toll from the white man's diseases, the escalation of intertribal warfare over ever-fewer resources, and the stresses created by the total disruption of their way of life, had reduced Nebraska's Indian population by more than one-half. When the Civil War began, the U.S. Army could not spare any troops to protect the Pawnee, and decided to establish a company of Pawnee Scouts, led by white officers. Pawnee young men were delighted at the opportunity to become warriors again, and there were plenty of volunteers.

During the presidential election of 1860, Abraham Lincoln realized his election would depend upon his standing on critical issues besides slavery. He campaigned hard for homestead legislation, knowing it was very popular, especially in the West. The Homestead Act of 1862 provided free homesteads to settlers on the public domain. Settlers were given title to the land if they built a sod house within 6 months of occupancy, and lived on the land for five years.

On January 1, 1863, Union Army Scout Daniel Freeman convinced the local land agent to open his office early, paid a $10 filing fee and staked his claim to 160 acres as the nation's first homesteader in Beatrice, Nebraska. Free land created a settlement frenzy, and thousands more settlers poured into Nebraska. Many came by the Union Pacific Railroad. Addison Sheldon, the pre-eminent Nebraskan historian of the late 19th century, concluded that most of the land sold between the time Nebraska became a territory in 1854 and until the Homestead Act was passed in 1862, was in the hands of speculators, and impatient settlers were demanding access to the land left in the public domain.

Waterford, Virginia's only known Quaker homesteader, Henry Taylor, staked his claim in 1879. Henry had first visited Nebraska in 1852, when he was part of a wagon train heading west to join the California "gold rush." One night he was camped near a Pawnee village, and the next morning found he was missing "a seven pound package of good Virginia Cavendish Tobacco, which was a great loss."

The land was hardly free. Successfully creating a farm required years of labor, plus investments in a house and fields, livestock, a barn, and fencing. Like the Indians, settlers had to endure long freezing winters and hot searing summers and frequent grasshopper plagues, often losing crops and suffering deep social isolation. During 1874-76, clouds of grasshoppers ate their crops three years straight. As one homesteader put it, "The government bets you a quarter-section that you can't survive on the land for five years." According to Richard Edwards, Director, Center of Great Plains Studies at the University of Nebraska, almost two million Americans became homesteaders, but roughly one- half who tried it failed.

When Ulysses Grant assumed the presidency in 1869, he decided to do something about the deplorable conditions on Indian reservations. Grant placed the reservations under military control, and put General William Tecumseh Sherman in charge. Both men were in complete agreement about Grant's "Peace Policy," which General Sherman described as "a double process of peace *within* their reservation, and war *without.*" Nebraska historian, Clyde Milner, writes that the U.S. Army undertook over two hundred military actions against American Indians while trying to enforce the government's "Peace Policy."

President Grant also wanted to reform the often corrupt administration of the Indian agencies, and he appointed Brigadier General Ely Parker, a Seneca Indian from New York and one of his top aides from Civil War days, as his Commissioner of Indian Affairs. Parker had a high opinion of Quakers, and urged the President to appoint them as Indian agents. In his 1869 message to Congress, Grant emphasized the need for reform in Indian affairs and the Quakers' reputation for "strict integrity and fair dealings," calling them uniquely qualified to work among Indians, and citing their peaceful settlement in Pennsylvania, as compared to the Indian wars that had plagued the other American colonies.

The Quakers' reputation for good relationships with American Indians and their "Long Peace" in Pennsylvania, had become widely disseminated through two famous paintings: Benjamin West's *William Penn's Treaty with the Indians* (1775),and Quaker Elias Hicks's *Peaceable Kingdom* (1820). Both paintings were reproduced for popular consumption as engraved prints, and as decorative motifs on glass, china, textiles and other consumer products. Meanwhile, the Society of Friends had been suffering its own inner turmoil. It had been profoundly affected by the Evangelical Movement,  and when "Orthodox" Friends adopted a worship service which commemorated and celebrated Christ's death and resurrection, traditional "Hicksite" Friends continued to reject  any formal creed, and retained their simple service focusing on individual "revelation from within."

The Baltimore Yearly Meeting, which represented Hicksite Quakers, and was trying to organize a Quaker-wide response to President Grant's request, sent a letter to Orthodox leaders on March 25, 1869, asking whether "some measure cannot be devised in the wisdom of truth, by which we may be united as a Band of Brothers, to act together to aid the government in this important concern." None of the six Orthodox recipients of the letter responded, such were the "hard feelings" between the two factions.

Loudoun County Quaker Samuel Janney and Benjamin Hallowell, who chaired the Baltimore Committee on Indian Concerns, meet with President Grant on April 29, 1866. Grant agreed that Hicksite Friends should have sole responsibility for Nebraska Indians, and Orthodox Friends for Kansas Indians. Since the 1830s, Samuel Janney had been a prominent educator and abolitionist, who tried to convince Virginia slaveholders on economic grounds to gradually liberate their slaves; arguing that a slave-based economy could never be as profitable as a "free economy." At the age of 69—after several sleepless nights and some friendly persuasion–Samuel Janney accepted President Grant's four-year appointment at a salary of $1,500 as Superintendent of Indian Affairs at the Northern Superintendency (Nebraska), which included five separate Indian agencies: Pawnee, Otoe-Missouri, Omaha, Santee Sioux, and Winnebago.

Janney's daughter Cornelia went with him to run an Indian school. When Janney's chief clerk resigned because of family problems, Janny appointed his daughter-in-law Eliza as his chief clerk. The move became a real family affair when Samuel's brother Asa joined him as agent for the Santee Sioux, along with Asa's daughters Cosmelia (Indian School principal) and Thamsin (dispenser of medicines). Not only was Samuel Janney responsible for the care, resettlement and rehabilitation of 6,000 American Indians, but he also had to deal with rapacious politicians and traders who would try to bribe him or steal from them.

The Janney's left the densely forested mountains and green valleys of the east, and entered a strange and frightening new world: an empty and seemingly endless Great Plain. There were few windbreaks to slow the violent winds which swept in waves through the tall buffalo grass, or to provide shade from the sun. According to author S.C. Gwynne, "In the summer, came brutal heat and blowtorch winds often a hundred degrees...[that] caused the eyes to burn, the lips to crack, and the body to dehydrate at alarming speed...In the fall and winter, there was the 'norther' [with] billowing clouds of blown sand or freezing rain, which could send the temperature plunging fifty degrees in one hour... or snow so dense and temperatures so cold that anyone lost on the shelter less plain was as good as dead."

Author Willa Cather said it best: "the great fact was the land itself, which seemed to overwhelm the little beginnings of human society that struggled in its somber wastes...the land wanted to be let alone, to preserve its own fierce strength, its peculiar, savage kind of beauty, its uninterrupted mournfulness." The Great Plain did support a myriad but dispersed large mammal population of bison, elk and, white-tailed deer, numerous smaller mammals, and about three hundred bird species. When the Spaniards introduced the horse in the 16<sup>th</sup> century, it became an ideal place for American Indians who relied on hunting bison for their subsistence.

The prairie also supported billions of grasshoppers, which descended like a biblical plague every few—sometimes consecutive—years. According to *London Weekly* reporter Edwin Curley, their arrival seemed to be under the direction of a higher power, due to "their habit of selecting the Indian corn, or other [human] food, by its colour while they are high in the air, [helping] to aggregate them in masses denser and more dense...When especially hungry, they will strip the trees of their foliage...gnaw through textile fabric...eagerly contesting for the refuse lemon of a whiskey toddy." Nebraska's 1875 grasshopper swarm was estimated to be 1,800 miles long, 110 miles wide, 1/4-1/2 mile deep, containing 3.5 trillion individuals.

In an article written for the *Friends Intelligencer* of October 19, 1867, Samuel Janney wrote that since restraining white settlement in the West "is probably beyond the powers of any government," Indians must be removed from the path of settlement, give up the hunt, adopt the "habits of civilized life," and probably should "abandon their tribal governments and their mode of holding property in common." By the time Janney arrived in Nebraska in 1869, the government's policy of transforming the Indians' way of life was already failing. Nebraska Indians could no longer follow their age-old subsistence cycle of combining bison hunting by males and small-plot farming by females, and had become wards of the state. They were in a state of deep despair, decline and degradation. Janney's arrival was welcomed by the *Omaha Daily Herald,* which supported President Grant's "Peace Policy".

Samuel Janney could not find a rentable building in Omaha that could house both his office and his family. Janney's chief clerk started a rumor that Janney had no alternative but to cross the Missouri River and find housing in Council Bluffs, Iowa. The Omaha business community became so alarmed about losing the flow of federal dollars that would accompany Janney's residence that they built him a nine-room house and charged him $50 monthly rent. Since Janney's U.S. Government monthly allowance for office rent was $35, it cost him only $15 a month to house his family in the residential part of the house. Janney hung a copy of Benjamin West's painting *William Penn's Treaty with the Indians*, in his new Omaha office. One of his first visitors was entrepreneur "Buffalo Bill," who had become world famous for his "Wild West Show." Janney adamantly refused to allow "Buffalo Bill" to hire any Pawnee as a participant in the show, which, in his view, simply reinforced the perception among whites that the Indians were depraved savages. Samuel Janney and his fellow Quakers believed, that living on individual allotments, was "the Indians only remaining opportunity to hold onto any land at all."

After visiting each of the Indian tribes under his supervision, Janney submitted a report to the Commissioner on Indian affairs "On the General Condition Among the Indian Tribes" He described the Winnebago (who had been "removed" from Wisconsin) as being in poor condition physically and morally, living uncleanly in ill-ventilated lodges, suffering from diseases of a scrofulous nature [this term signified physical as well as moral corruption and degeneration] and being addicted to vices. The Pawnee were the most warlike and generally backward in their civilization, living in miserable, ill-ventilated lodges and consequently suffering much from disease. The Otoe and Missouri were extremely ignorant and superstitious, lived in damp, squalid lodges and were great sufferers from scrofula and other diseases.

Janney did not have a negative word to say about two tribes that were adopting the white man's ways: the Omaha were orderly, progressive and provident, and realized the need of turning to the pursuit of agriculture and in general to the ways of civilized life. Janney was also pleased that many of the Santee Sioux (removed from Minnesota) were professing Christians who lived in much more comfortable log houses than the lodges and wigwams of other Indians. Janney's opinions were shared by most other whites.

Edwin Curley described the Pawnee "as peaceable and inoffensive as dirty, lazy vagabonds and vagrants can well supposed to be...[who] live principally by begging, gathering the refuse of slaughtered cattle and other waste of the whites." The Pawnee, who believed they were descended from the stars, would have been extremely reluctant to leave their large earth-lodges, whose circular structure both reflected and connected them with the supernatural world above: the floor represented the prairie; the roof, the sky; the smoke hole in the center was the highest point in the heavens, where Ti-ra'-wa, the giver of all life and father of the people dwelt; entwined willow branches on the roof symbolized the stars; the grass mimicked the clouds; and the sod layer was Mother Earth, the final resting place of all beings. The Pawnee, like other Native Americans, believed natural and supernatural phenomena were simply different aspects of the same reality.

The conflicts and misunderstandings between white Americans and American Indians represented the collision of two incompatible belief systems, which were based upon different conceptualizations of how the universe was created, and how mankind's role had been defined. Most whites believed in the God of the Christian Bible, creator of heaven and earth and of man and woman in his own image, whom God gave "dominium over every living thing that moveth upon the eart." Unlike this linear, predictable, morally-defined universe, the cyclical Indian cosmos in which birth-life-death was endlessly repeated, was governed by a powerful, creative, but unpredictable force, responsible for establishing the "order and rhythms" of nature. Indians believed humans were but transient beings attempting to survive in a capricious world. Good and Evil, in the Christian sense, did not exist, because the Indian world was neither moral nor amoral. It simply WAS.

Quakers and Nebraska Indians did share a belief in the inherent spirituality of every individual and in the importance of community in binding each individual into a greater whole. But they shared little else. For Quakers and other whites, the natural world was to be tamed rather than respected and worshipped; and its inhabitants were cultural inferiors who required "civilizing" through the acceptance of Christian values. In 1869, the Quaker Yearly Meetings in eastern cities each sent delegates to visit the

Nebraskan Indian agencies. The delegates were most impressed when they visited the wild Pawnee:

> The evening was beautiful, and hundreds of Indians, with their bright red blankets, could be seen wandering or riding over the broad prairie in all directions, giving a life and picturesqueness to the scene, and awakening much thought, which would be tinctured with sadness! What is to be the result? How can we get hold of them so as to give beneficial direction to their wanderings?

Getting the Pawnee to adopt Quaker pacifism became Janney's main strategy in dealing with the Sioux attacks. Jacob Troth, a Quaker farmer from Fairfax County, Virginia, who had been appointed as agent for the Pawnee, fully agreed with Janney. They both believed–naively, as it turned out–that this would be a first big step toward negotiations with the Sioux. They never asked the U.S. Army to protect the Pawnee against Sioux attacks, successfully pressured the Pawnee to return stolen horses, were able to disband the Pawnee Scouts—despite the vigorous protests of Brigadier General Christopher Augur at Fort Kearney—and attempted to begin peace negotiations with the Sioux. The Pawnee were furious.

Meanwhile, the Sioux kept on raiding, killing and stealing, and the Pawnee were the losers. They could not convince either Janney or Troth that the pacification effort was simply weakening them further, and desperately tried to ignore or by-pass their Quaker advisers. Janney visited Red Cloud, Chief of the Oglala Sioux, but Red Cloud refused to negotiate with the Pawnee. Janney was unable to meet with any Brule Sioux chiefs. The Quaker's failed pacification policy had a deep negative impact on their overall goal of "civilizing" the Pawnee, who would no longer even consider settling on dispersed individual allotments, which left them even more open to attack.

In 1871, Samuel Janney testified before Nebraska's state legislature against Indian removal, but both houses passed resolutions calling for the federal government to remove all Nebraska

Indians to Indian Territory. The federal government refused to do it. Janney was sick with the ague (most likely malarial fever), frustrated and worn out by his efforts to improve the quality of life of once proud tribes reduced to poverty and desperation. He resigned in October 1871. One newspaper editor, who knew Janney well, was convinced he had made a difference, and had this to say In the August 18, 1871 issue of the Omaha Daily Herald:

> **INDIANS: BEWARE.** Lt. General Phillip Sheridan says it has been his belief that it is necessary to kill the Indians in order to secure peace on the frontier. This is no news. Nothing but a general slaughter of these long-suffering and outraged red men will suit the bloody-minded Sheridan. And yet every white man of ordinary intelligence in this country knows that all that is required to secure the peace of other days on these frontiers is that the government shall place men like Samuel M. Janney in absolute control of the Sioux agencies.

Concurrently with Samuel Janney's resignation, non-Quaker Elvira G. Platt, who was Principal of the Pawnee Manual-Labor School, sent her annual report to Major J.M. Toth, U.S. Army Agent for the Pawnee. Her Quaker staff consisted of "one gentleman and eight ladies," including Ann Gover from Waterford, Virginia, who was one of two women responsible for teaching sewing and maintaining the sewing room. Ann Gover was a good example of the commitment that Quaker women made to bring the light of Christ to those living in darkness. She was 50 years old, single, part of a large, closely-knit Quaker family in Waterford, and an active member of the Fairfax, Virginia Women's Meeting. Yet she left all that behind, and was willing to live on the wild prairie to help the Pawnee adapt to the white man's world.

Principal Platt reported that "after varied experiences during the past year...we are today in prosperous condition. Of the 80 scholars connected with us...one day scholar has been discontinued, five have been married...two have been killed by the Sioux, two died of chronic diseases, and one of an epidemic. Of the 69 remaining, one is apprenticed as blacksmith, one as tinsmith, and four are farm laborers, leaving 63 in daily attendance." What the report did not say was that the Brule Sioux taunted the Pawnee by bragging to their agent they had killed the two school boys.

In addition to their studies, the students were required to perform a certain amount of labor every day. The boys had converted several acres of prairie into a vegetable patch, while the girls cooked, "supplying us with an abundance of vegetables for the table, a luxury we have never before enjoyed." The girls were also required to become skilled "laundresses, housekeepers and seamstresses, under the watchful direction of those who instruct them."

Miss Platt had a gift for irony as she pleaded for the Army to provide "fresh recruits" to fill the empty places in her school; "two capacious cisterns, that we may have an abundant supply of soft water for the cleansing of the outer man;" and an enclosure for cows and draught animals, who were "presently fenced by the stooping sky." What she really wanted most was a barn, but dared not ask directly; simply referring to her "oft-expressed wish to hear again the familiar voice of the barn-yard fowl." Whatever its deficiencies, the Quaker school had become one safe haven for Pawnee children in a very dangerous world.

Principal Platt did not discuss academic performance in her report, simply stating that "the progress of the children in their studies...has been encouraging to us, though it is a work which requires an unlimited amount of patience and perseverance." Her report stressed the farming and domestic skills her students were developing, and is clearly targeted to her audience. Major Toth's main interest would have been whether or not the students were acquiring those skills which would enable them to become self-sustaining members of Christian society.

Nine months after Principal Platt sent in her report, she was visited by members of the Baltimore Friends Committee for Indian Concern, and was dismissed because she was "not efficient and did not promote harmony." What the committee's letter of dismissal left out was that the visitors had found out several of her female pupils were sexually active, and her Quaker visitors were deeply shocked Platt had "allowed this immorality to continue un-checked."

By 1872, the Pawnee realized they could no longer survive the relentless attacks of their better armed and more numerous Sioux enemies, and the demands of settlers; who were not only oc-cupying all the land "with timber, water and easily worked soils" on the reservation's perimeter, but also stealing vast amounts of timber from the Pawnee reservation. Wood was not plentiful on the prairie, and was expensive to import. Pine lumber from Canada could be exported to England at a cheaper price than it would cost to export it to Nebraska. White settlers knew they would never be prosecuted because a U.S. district court judge had ruled in 1872 that crimes committed on Indian reservations were under the juris-diction of local courts which favored the settlers. So many Ne-braskan settlers were stealing Pawnee timber they created a road for easy access to-and-from the reservation. The Union Pacific trains that crossed the prairie also had a great appetite for wood–by 1870, the fireboxes of America's locomotives were consuming eight million cords of wood annually.

The turning point for the Pawnee came in the winter bison hunt of 1872-73, when 400 Pawnee men, women and children with the skins and meat of 800 buffalo, were trapped in a canyon by 600 Sioux. Estimates of Pawnee killed varied from 70 to 100. Many more were wounded. They lost everything, including 100 horses. Despite many promises, the government had again failed to protect them, while still refusing to sell them arms. Dispersing the Pawnee on individual allotments and making them even more vulnerable to attack, had become impossible, and the Shawnee agreed to leave Nebraska for the "rough terrain covered by thin soils and scrub timber" of Indian Territory. They left behind "their sacred sites, their ancestors, and memories of hundreds of years of living in that land."

In 1876, the Pawnee reservation was sold in 160 acre tracts to the highest bidder for a total of $750,000. After the government subtracted its costs, the Pawnee were left with $280,000, about $1 an acre for their homeland, "as good a land, perhaps, as there is in Nebraska," according to historian Wishart. Epidemic diseases and warfare with the Sioux had reduced the total number of Pawnee by two-thirds. On their new Indian Territory reservation, disease and starvation would kill many more.

Joseph La Flesche was born in 1818, the son of a French fur trader and an Omaha woman. In 1853, he became a chief after he was adopted by Big Elk, one of two principal Omaha chiefs. La Flesche tenaciously pursued enforcement of the Omaha treaty rights during the 1854 treaty negotiations. He got the help of a Presbyterian minister to audit the agency's accounts and insisted the Omaha be paid what they were due in coin rather than paper money. He made sure annuity funds were used to buy agricultural implements, medicines and other critical supplies. He helped families construct their own homes, take up agriculture and send their children to school. His initiative was not unique. The Omaha Sacred Legend of Creation emphasized the role of humans in developing the basic elements of society through an interactive question-and-answer process, rather than relying on the intervention of spiritual intermediaries.

This was "the kind of success story [the Indian Office] wanted," and La Flesche was praised for his "sagacity, integrity, intelligence, excellent example, and untiring efforts to advance the conditions of his people." But La Flesche did not speak for all the Omaha, many of whom continued to adhere to their traditions and beliefs, and called La Flesche and his followers "make believe white men". After a deeply disappointing visit to Washington, D. C. with the other principal chiefs, La Flesche became increasingly pessimistic about the Omaha's ability to influence the U.S. Government.

Both Omaha men and women did become farmers, and by the mid-1860s were harvesting annually 20,000 bushels of corn, smaller crops of wheat, sorghum, potatoes, and hay for their horses. By 1874, their annual corn output had increased to nearly 35,000 bushels, besides beans, potatoes and other vegetables. They owned 700 horses, 200 hogs and 175 cattle; cut 200,000 feet of timber, and built seven frame and eight log houses. In 1871, three schools (single room, single teacher) were teaching 144 out of about 160 school age children. Samuel Janney marveled that the Omahas "do an astonishing amount of work."

The "Financial Panic of 1873" caused the Federal Government to close down all Indian superintendencies except those run by Orthodox Quakers in Kansas, and Hicksite Quakers in Nebraska, as part of government cost-cutting measures. The Quaker-run superintendencies were saved because Samuel Janney's replacement, Barclay White, kept $60,000 of Quaker money on deposit at the First National Bank of Omaha; enabling the bank to pay off hundreds of panicked depositors, and to stay open. A grateful First National president, Augustus Kountze, called his personal friend, General Phillip Sheridan, who interceded with President Grant to keep the superintendencies open. However, times were even harder in 1876, and Grant ordered the Quaker superintendencies closed. Thereafter, all field agents reported directly to the Department of the Interior. For the Indians, cash-crop farming was no longer a viable option, as agricultural prices continued to fall in a long-lasting decline in which the price of corn became so low by the late 1880s farmers were burning it for fuel. Many Omaha who had received title to their land, sold it just to survive.

President Grant's successor, Rutherford B. Hayes, abandoned Grant's "Peace Policy "in the aftermath of the killing of Lieutenant Colonel George Armstrong Custer and 265 U.S. Army cavalrymen by Sioux warriors at Wyoming's Little Big Horn River in 1876. In 1877, Hayes 'new Secretary of the Interior, Carl Schurz, dedicated himself to purging Grant's religious appointees, and instituting "bureaucratic efficiency "as the sole criteria for managing Indian affairs. Schurz used a system of informants to undermine the Quakers. This led to numerous investigations and forced resignations of all but one of the remaining Quaker agents by 1882. None were ever indicted for fraud or any other crime. It is a wonder that anything was achieved in such an atmosphere of "bureaucratic efficiency."

President Grant's reputation has not stood the test of historical time well, but his contemporaries knew better. For Frederick Douglass, Grant was "a man too broad for prejudice, too humane to despise the humblest, too great to be small at any point. In him, the Negro found a protector, the Indian a friend, a vanquished foe a brother, an imperiled nation a savior."

Meanwhile, the Omaha gained an influential friend in Alice Fletcher; an ethnologist at Harvard University's Peabody Museum, who successfully lobbied Congress to pass The Dawes Act of 1887, which allowed Indians to become U.S. citizens and obtain 80 acre allotments. To keep the Indians from selling the land, the government held title to these allotments in trust for 25 years.

The Omaha believed that Wakon'da, the mysterious, all-encompassing life force, created the universe through the sexual union of the male sky and female earth Like Samuel Janney, Fletcher became convinced the Omaha had to give up thinking of themselves as a part of nature, and therefore not capable of owning land. Fletcher convinced the hereditary keepers of the three sacred tents of the Omaha to send their treasured possessions to the Peabody Museum in Cambridge, Massachusetts for safekeeping. The rituals which bound the Omaha to these objects were what held the tribe together, because they both manifested and connected the Omaha to the supernatural world. The contents of the last tent were stolen a few days before they were to be shipped east. The lost items included one of the Omaha's most sacred relics. A white buffalo hide, "symbol of Omaha survival, which presided over the seasonal buffalo hunts on which the tribe depended, and a sacred pipe, which had a red stone bowl shaped like a buffalo's hoof."

Two sacred pipes representing this dual yet indivisible cosmos were all that was left of their sacred objects. Although Fletcher eventually managed to locate the stolen hide and one pipe in Chicago, the collector would not sell. In 1976, the Omaha robe and pipe were identified by a sharp-eyed custodian during an inventory of the million Native American artifacts collected by New York's Heye Foundation. Yet nothing happened until the Heye collection became part of the new National Museum of the American

Indian. In 1991, the Omaha were able to regain possession of the robe, pipe, and other sacred artifacts.

During the decade of 1869-1879, all of the $60,000 and more Quaker money in the First National bank of Omaha was used to help Nebraska's Indians. Quakers continued to believe the money had been well spent. In 1921, the Quaker Executive Committee on Indian Affairs in Philadelphia took a retrospective look, and concluded that Quaker implementation of President Grant's "Peace Policy" had brought peace. "There were faults in the whole Indian system that militated against it. There were faults in the work done by Friends. Yet on the whole, the effort was crowned with a fine success. The Indians, many of them wild and warlike, or filthy and debased, made remarkable progress toward civilization, especially in the early years when Friends were unhampered by adverse political circumstances [President Hayes overturning President Grant's 'Peace Policy'] as evidenced by the school systems, the training in agriculture and domestic arts, and teaching by precept and example the benign principles of Christianity."

The Quakers failed to understand that the allotment system was a total failure. The purpose of the Dawes Act was to break up the communal society of the Indians by converting individuals into private property holders, which would enable them to be eventually assimilated into civilized society. Private ownership would stimulate them to be more industrious; and therefore more prosperous and self- sufficient, or so the Act's sponsors believed. Forcing the Indians to adapt to a monetized cyclical economy at the best of times was difficult enough, but with recurring financial panics and deeply depressed agricultural prices, allotment was a recipe for disaster.

In 1882, Joseph La Flesche was looking back on all the changes he had seen during his life. What saddened him the most was the "emptiness" of a fully-settled landscape. Before the Americans came, the Indians were the only people, but the prairie was full of living creatures. Then the Americans came "just as the blackbirds do, and spread over the country." As the land filled with Americans, it was emptied out of animals, and Indians felt an "unspeakable sadness–a loneliness so heavy [they] would suffocate under its weight".

Many of the Omaha were so deeply in debt or so poor (or both) they sold the land they had received title to. By the 1930s, two-thirds of the land allotted to the Omaha had been sold to outsiders, and much of the rest was leased. By 1970, not a single Omaha farmed full-time. In spite of all they had suffered, the Omaha remaining in Nebraska managed to maintain their cultural unity by preserving the central core of their beliefs founded on a deeply held tradition of cooperation and sharing during hard times ("uki'te,").

Whether the Nebraska Indians were at the very least complicit, if not active participants in the sale of their land, rather than being forced to do so at the point of a gun, has been a much debated issue since the earliest colonial times. Historically, land only began to have value when nomadic hunters-gatherers-seasonal-plot farmers became settled agriculturalists, and had to develop urban-based value systems. The nomadic Native Americas who first came in contact with European explorers-settlers believed that natural and supernatural worlds were inseparable, and the idea that land could be owned or sold by human beings was inconceivable. Professor of law Stuart Banner also argues persuasively that their land transactions were largely voluntary. Indians were only forced to sell their land when the U.S. Constitution of 1787 gave Congress sole power "to regulate Commerce (which included land purchase)....with the Indian tribes."

Unfortunately for America's Indians, they were also facing one of history's juggernauts: militant Christianity united with balance-of-power politics. Historian Fred Anderson argues that the French and Indian War (1755-1763) "undermined any semblance of authority the Native American nations had over their own land." Attaining America's "manifest destiny "coupled with a rapidly rising tide of settlers demanding land, pushed the government to purchase the entire western half of the United States from its native inhabitants in less than 40 years. This was only achieved by compelling the Indians to leave the land of their forefathers and live on reservations where the land was often unproductive.

# Chapter 25
# Two Fair Crops out of Three

**"Hurrah for Nebraska, and an extra cheer for old Furnas County."**
**—Henry Taylor, Waterford Homesteader**

On August 12, 1879, Waterford native Henry Taylor and his family claimed a Nebraska homestead on Section 27, Town I, Range 23. While writing his (unpublished) autobiography at the age of 104, he remembered the exact date because there had been a total eclipse of the sun that day. Taylor worked for another homesteader to feed his family, and managed to finish his sod house just one week before the six-month deadline for building it. He wrote: "I have been in the old sod ever since. While I have seen some sorrowful days, I have enjoyed many happy ones...give me two fair crops out of three, and I can have a good living and enjoy: Then, Hurrah for Nebraska and an extra cheer for Furnas County."

Henry Taylor was born in 1819 on the family farm near Waterford, Virginia. Taylor's family left Virginia in 1832, after a fire destroyed their grist mill, and a family friend failed to pay back $10,000 he had borrowed from Taylor's grandfather, who was forced to sell one-half of the family's farm. As a devout Quaker, "these losses so discouraged him that he grew despondent and feeble, then sickened and died." Henry's father decided to move the family to Ohio. When Henry crossed the Shenandoah River, he had no idea that he, like the composer of the song "Oh Shenandoah," would not stay long in Ohio, and was "bound away, across the wide Missouri."

Ohio had become "the great El Dorado of the West, "and after selling the rest of their assets, the family moved to Wellsville, Ohio on the banks of the Ohio River, where they lived and worked as "watermen" on the river. The first time they saw a steamboat, "it seemed to me to be some monster living beast…the furnaces were all aglow with flames. The stalwart darkies were liberally replenishing the fires by shoving in wood, while myrads [sic] of sparks were flying from the smoke stacks. All the time they were singing merrily:

> I will fire this trip, I will fire no more,
> Then to see Miss Dinah I will go,
> For I never 'see'd' a yellow gal in all my life,
> But what she'd be some fireman's wife.

The Taylors learned to handle all kinds of river vessels, and stayed in Wellsville until 1841. Their goal was to save twelve to fifteen thousand dollars, enough "to buy a good bottom farm in Ohio." They were not able to save that much, and decided to move to Iowa Territory, where land was cheaper, and they settled near Iowa City. With winter came bilious fever: "I have shook every day, and every other day, and every third day, then gone back to every day. The only way to get a vacation from this was to buy fifty grains of quinine to mix with flour, knead into dough, roll into long strips, then cut it into fifty little cakes, each with a grain of quinine. After weeks of high fever and sweating, you was so weak as to be almost unconscious." Two such winters were enough to convince the family to move to Wisconsin, where a friend told them there was plenty of money to be made at the lead mines. Henry's father bought a lead mine, and hired an experienced miner from Cornwall, England. The boys helped father build a house and worked the mine. Henry fell in love with a pretty but shy young woman, whom he escorted to various parties and dances. He was also quite shy, and was desperately searching for a way to tell her how much he loved her. One night, when he was walking her home, she told him how much she liked his mother. He thought "now or never," and responded "How would you like that nice old lady for your Mother-in-Law?" She replied, "How would you like to have the right to call my mother, your Mother?" They were married by a "minister of the Gospel" at her father's home on New Year's Day, 1851.

During his courtship, Henry referred to his future wife as "Miss E," and after his marriage as "my wife." Other women are only mentioned by their married names. That custom reflects the formality of the times. After all, Abraham Lincoln always called his wife "Mrs. Lincoln, and he was "Mr. Lincoln."

Henry planned to make Wisconsin his family's permanent home, but his wife became seriously ill. Henry sought the help of three different doctors before the third one was able to restore her to health. They had been in Wisconsin almost five years, but had saved only 100 dollars, and there was nothing left after the doctors and medicines were paid for. Henry decided he had to join the gold rush to California to improve the family finances. His tearful wife agreed, on condition he stayed away no more than two years. He assured her that on his return "we'd build a nice little cottage with a white paling fence all around it, enclosing the yard with beautiful shade trees with gravel walks from the porch to the gate."

He sold his almost new wagon and harness for "80 ten dollar gold coins", and bought three cattle. He was given an old wagon by his father, and repaired it. To complete his "outfit," he bought 350 pounds of hardtack, 300 pounds of bacon, 150 pounds of sugar, 50 pounds of rice, 50 pounds of dried fruit, 75 pounds of beans, 150 pounds of flour, 25 pounds of coffee, 20 pounds of tobacco, 5 pounds of tea, and 5 gallons of vinegar–to be given to the cattle as an antidote to alkali poisoning. His two brothers joined him, and It was time to go. His wife gave him a gold dollar, with instructions to remember who gave it to him, and for it to be the last dollar he would ever spend. With 66 dollars in his pocket, Henry "took one last lingering look" at his "dear ones," knowing he would "see them no more for nearly two years."

The Taylor brother's first big test was crossing the Missouri River at Council Bluffs, Iowa, which they reached on May 15, 1852. The river was running high and still rising, and could not be crossed for two weeks. Wagons were camped "from the bluffs to the river, as far as I could see." The boys could not afford to eat up two weeks of provisions. Henry convinced the owner of a trading post to lend them his skiff, arguing that they had grown up on the Ohio River, and were skillful at handling "all kinds of river craft from canoe to steam boats." The people on the shore called them foolhardy idiots and worse. One fellow traveler who had lived near them in Wisconsin, said he would watch them cross so he could report their deaths to their family.

The wagon bows and wheels were removed and placed in the wagon body, which was put in the forward part of the skiff. Their goods were wrapped in the wagon cover. The loaded skiff's gunwale (side) was only six inches above the running river, so any movement to rock the boat would have been disastrous. The boys were not afraid: "I suppose to one inexperienced it looked dangerous, but to we three brothers it was real fun." They needed a second trip to get all their goods across. By this time, it was growing dark, and others had gained the courage to cross. The brothers spent the entire night helping other teams cross the wide Missouri. Then they swam the cattle across using a rented skiff. The next day, the Missouri rose so high it could not be crossed.

While waiting to cross into Nebraska Territory, the brothers had heard many stories about Indians raiding wagon trains: " Killing and scalping the men, and carrying off the women and children to the mountains...Most of the imagrants [sic] gave no credit to those reports, but about one-half the men had colts, navy revolvers, buoy [sic] knives, and the best rifles and shotguns. We had an old shotgun I used for killing birds and squirrels. All this was useless. I never saw a hostile Indian the whole trip". Perhaps because of his Quaker background, Henry did not carry a gun. They joined many other wagons camped near the Elkhorn River, with a Pawnee Indian village close by. More than a hundred Indians came strolling by, peeping into the wagons. "We thought we were keeping a close watch, but they got a seven pound package of good Virginia Cavendish Tobacco, which was a great loss."

The brothers joined a wagon train camped on the banks of the Platte River, near Grand Island. It was headed for Fort Laramie, and at the end of the first day, men from a nearby wagon were digging a hole in the ground. One of the boys went over to see what was going on. He returned with the news that the men were digging a grave for a member of their family who had died of cholera. From there to Fort Laramie, the wagon train "was more like a funeral procession rather than men going after wealth. There was not a day went by that you could not look forward or backward without seeing three or four teams turned out of the road digging graves in which to bury their dead companions."

Their next objective was crossing the Loop [sic] River. They drove all night to be first in line, arriving at their destination at three o'clock in the morning. The ferry men were all asleep, so the boys borrowed their flat boat, and in less than an hour had their wagon and cattle across the river. When the ferry men got up, Henry gave them four dollars for the use of the boat. The men didn't understand, and when Henry explained, one of them took the money and remarked "Well that beats all H—!

At Fort Laramie they rested, cleaned their "outfit" and repacked their supplies. Brother Edward felt sick and was too weak to walk - he had cholera. Ed became weaker and weaker and soon could not talk above a whisper. Meanwhile, Henry desperately searched for a doctor, hailing every team that went by. He finally recognized a fellow traveler, Dr. Van Blake, who confirmed the disease was cholera, but said that to treat it, he needed his "injection pipe,' which was back in his wagon at a camp nine miles away. He told Henry if he ran to the camp he could ride the doctor's horseback.

Henry ran all the way and found Mrs. Van Blake sitting in front of a tent. She gave him the injection pipe, but declined to lend him a horse, saying "The doctor has ridden down almost all our horses, and we will not have enough left to haul us to our journey's end." Henry was greatly disappointed, looked her in the face and asked her if the young man standing there was her son. "He is." She said. "Madam," he said, "that sick boy has a mother one thousand miles east, she will count the days when he will return to her arms, but alas, he died for want of timely remedies. Can't you imagine yourself and your son in a similar condition?" She looked at Henry hard in the face. Tears filled her eyes. All she said was "John, saddle your Father's horse for this man," and walked into her tent. Dr. Van Blake's injection pipe worked wonders, and soon Ed was on the road to recovery.

The train climbed the Rocky Mountains to escape the cholera; but, brother Tom was attacked by mountain fever "in the most malignant form attended by bilious diarrhea." They reached the summit of the Rockies, "with the waters of one spring flowing off to the southwest to find its way to the Gulf of California, while the other bore off to the southeast to loose [sic] its waters in the Gulf of Mexico" The brothers camped and kept a fire going all night to keep Tom warm. The men from the other wagons reluctantly stopped, held a meeting, and then informed Henry they were moving on early the next morning. Henry felt "grieved, hurt and angry at those selfish men leaving us there, and with the excuse that they had started for California to make money enough to get homes for their families, and every day they lost on the trip was a loss of five dollars. I reminded them that we had saved them two weeks' time in getting them over the Mississippi, and three or four days at the Loop [sic] forks."

That evening, Henry had a visitor, a man who wanted to borrow a candle. His wife had died on the Platte, and left him with a two-year-old boy who had the mountain fever. He needed the candle so he could care for his son during the night. Henry gave him six candles. The next day, a doctor arrived, and turned out to be Dr. Kirby, the first of the three doctors whom Henry had sought to help his wife during her illness in Wisconsin. Dr. Kirby also visited the man with the sick child. He told them all "to get off that cold snowy mountain" and drive slowly down to a camp on the Little Sandy River and join his train of twelve wagons. Under the doctor's treatment and food prepared by the ladies of the wagon train, Tom improved rapidly. Henry and his brothers completely changed their opinion of women as companions on their great adventure: "we thought they would be encumbrance and a drawback, supposing they would be to tender and delecate [sic] for a trip and be sick and helpless most of the time. After eating a delicious meal prepared by one of the ladies, Henry asked Tom how he thought now about travelling with women. "Well," said Tom, "if I was going to the Devil, I think I would be selfish enough to want a woman to go with me."

To reach the Green River, their next crossing point, they had a choice of saving two days travel by crossing a desert, or going around it. Most of the men voted for going around the desert. The women in this wagon train had the right to vote, and they voted as a group to go through the desert. They won, and when the wagons reached the Green River, the women all gathered together and gave three cheers.

It cost three dollars to cross the Green River on the ferry, and Henry only had the gold dollar left his wife had given him. When it came time to cross, Dr. Kirby told Henry to get in line behind their wagons, "drive on, say nothing, and it will be all right." And so he did. He asked brother Tom if he thought the good doctor has paid their way across. "No, said Tom, I am a good Odd Fellow, the doctor is a good Odd Fellow, and so is the ferryman."

In the next train, a quarrelsome man whose name Henry forgot, got into a fight with a man named Charlie, who gave him "a severe drubbing and would cease only by his promising to be a better and more peaceable man in the Future." The next day, the man shook Charlie's hand; apologized again, promising once more to be a better man. That evening antelope were spotted, and the man invited Charlie to go hunting with him so they could have venison for breakfast. After it became dark, they heard a shot. The man came back alone, and said that Charlie had met a distant cousin who was also out hunting, and had gone back to the cousin's camp for a visit, and said not to wait for him and he would catch the train by the end of the week. The men of the train said nothing, but agreed among themselves to wait for Charlie.

The next morning, the man said, "If you fellows want to stay and wait for him, alright. I am going on." A dozen men went and got their guns, and forced the man to go with them. They found Charlie's body concealed in some bushes. The man said Charlie had attacked him, but poor Charlie had been shot in the back of the head and almost his entire face had been torn off. A jury of twelve men was selected from other wagon trains. After the prosecution made its case, the prisoner broke down and admitted his guilt, begging for mercy on account of his wife and children. The jury took less than ten minutes to decide he was guilty of willful and premeditated murder, and he was sentenced to be hung. The women had been shielding the man's wife, but when she saw the rope being attached to one of the wagon bows, she shrieked, and fell prostrate to the ground. Henry had also seen enough, and he, some men, and most of the women drove their wagons out of sight. The condemned man's last words were, "Well boys, all I ask you to is get my wife and children through to California."

After days of travel over mountains and beautiful little valleys, crossing streams that emptied into the Snake River, they reached the Bear River Valley. The boys had been acutely feeling the loss of their Virginia tobacco. Henry took a fishing pole, put a grasshopper on the hook, and almost immediately pulled out a three-pound trout. A one-pound trout soon followed, but that was the end of Henry's luck.   He put the fish up for auction, and Mrs. Turner, the wife of the wagon train leader, got the fish for one pound of tobacco. By this time, the travelers were so tired of hardtack and salt pork beans; that three wagons left the train to take a two-day detour to buy vegetables in Salt Lake City. They agreed to meet again at the Humboldt River, in what is now Nevada.

When the wagon train reached Humboldt Springs, they stopped to rest. Henry was guarding the cattle one night, when the animals became restless and started to move about. He fired a shot to raise the camp. It turned out that digger Indians had been trying to lure the animals into a canyon. "Some of the boys proposed to fire a few shots into them, but they were soon shamed out of their cruel intentions, as it was agreed that the poor untutored Indians were hungry." When the wagon train left, Indian women and children "went swarming through the camp picking up the odd and ends that might be left." To Henry, the digger Indians seemed to be a dwarf species, void of all shame, and "many of them both sexes were in the condition of Adam and Eve before they made aprons out of fig leaves. They were good shots with their bows and arrows and seldom missed their game which is a small animal between a squirrel and a rat, and good eating and very fat."

Grasshoppers were also an important part of the digger Indians diet. They would dig a hole about three feet in diameter and place a finely woven grass basket of the same size in the hole. Then, the women and children formed a circle fifty yards wide around the hole, driving the grasshoppers into the center. The basket would hold water, and when it was full of grasshoppers, water was poured into it with a heated rock to boil the water. When fully cooked, the grasshoppers were put on a grass mat to dry, then pulverized and stirred into water, creating a mush, "and eaten as though it was the most delicious food in the world."

The wagon train had to cross another desert, where they came upon a man lying almost unconscious. Like many others, he had set out to walk across the desert, and had run out of water and food. He completed his crossing in the wagon. According to Henry, "the long trip was hard, and many lived to cross the desert, only to die at the end." Early next morning they reached a beautiful river called the Truckee, and realized they were in California. There, they found a depot with provisions donated by a candidate for the office of governor. Every American citizen arriving in California was entitled to vote for governor. Travelers who had no money were given food for free; those who were sick were treated, and those who were beyond any aid were given a final resting place. That candidate won the election.

Having run out of supplies, they headed for Beckwith Ranch, whose owner was a friend of Mr. Turner, leader of the wagon train. But Beckwith was out of food and awaiting his supply train. The next morning, the three brothers divided the last food they had—one piece of hard tack soaked in water and vinegar seasoned with sugar. They decided to go all out for the American Ranch which they heard was well supplied, and was in gold country. At the ranch, they were provided with "an abundance of bread, meat and vegetables."

The brothers sold their three cows for $350 and their wagon for $200. They split the money and each chose to go to a different place where gold had been discovered. Henry chose to walk forty miles to Downieville, where his brother-in-law and uncle-in-law had put up a large tent as a trading post. Henry worked mornings, evenings and Sundays at the trading post to pay his seven dollars weekly room and board, and prospected during the day. The brothers agreed to meet in one month's time at Nelson Creek, where brother Tom would be doing his prospecting.

On his first day as a "gold digger," Henry pulled away a root of a fallen pine tree, and found wedged in the roots a piece of gold weighing one and one-fourth ounces. A few minutes later, he found a second piece weighing one-fourth ounce. Together they were worth twenty five dollars. He was sure he had struck "his pile," and worked there three more days but never found another grain. He explored other potential "piles" with his pick and pan, but never made more than three dollars' worth of gold a day, often ending up with nothing. Brothers Tom and Ed came to Downiville before the month was over, because neither had had any luck. At Nelson Creek, the only unclaimed ground was on a flat (terrace) 300 feet above the creek, and "the only way to get the dirt to water was to build a rail road." The topography was "one of the most rugged and mountainous a man ever travelled over," and with winter coming, the brothers decided to delay their project until Spring.

Henry sent home two hundred of the five hundred dollars he had received from the sale of the cattle and wagon, and decided to buy three hundred pounds of pork, beans, and flour, "which was to be kept as a reserve, and proved to be a most lucky investment." The boys spent the Fall working the crevasses on the creek, and they averaged four dollars in gold per day per man. The flat in front of their cabin had been rich in gold, and was completely worked over—except for some large tree stumps which had been left alone because they would have required "some timbering to get access to them." The boys had learned all about "timbering" when they were mining lead in Wisconsin, and they managed to extract four hundred dollars' worth of gold from under the stumps. That money would get them through a terrible winter.

On the first of December, it started snowing and did not stop until the 27<sup>th</sup>. Henry made his way through 10-15 feet of snow drifts to Downieville, which was one mile away. He was one among some four thousand miners all searching for food, and managed to buy 14 pounds of beans for twenty dollars. He remembered having passed a local farm before the storm, and seeing that when the farmer cut his cabbages, he left the stocks on the ground. Henry and Tom visited the farmer and asked if they could have the stocks."How are you going to get them," replied the farmer. "They are four to five feet under the snow." The brothers went out and each came back with a gunny sack filled with cabbage stocks. The farmer charged them an ounce of gold ($16.00). The farmer seemed to Henry to have a tender heart, because he asked him, "have you a family?" Henry had no hesitation in answering "yes, I have a wife and child." The farmer sold Henry thirty pounds of potatoes for $24, after Henry promised not to tell anyone else.

Fifteen hundred miners left the area after it stopped snowing. "Many of them were weak and feeble from want of proper food, and gave out on the way and laid down, never to rise again. Passing friends wrapped them in their blankets where they lay until Spring." The Downieville post office hired digger Indians on snow shoes to deliver the mail, escorted by government guards. At last the time came when the boys had to leave or starve. The next morning they pulled out with blankets strapped to their shoulders, and about six pounds of food between them. Late in the second day they reached Sleighville House, where they found three pack trains unloading. That night they finally had a square meal of pork and beans. The brothers decided to buy food and return to their cabin. Each carried fifty pounds of food on his back. It began to rain hard, and they reached a stream which had become a raging torrent. They cut down a large fir tree to serve as a bridge. To fall in was certain death, and they crawled across on their hands and knees. When the rain stopped and the waters receded, they could see thousands of dollars worth of gold resting on the bedrock under the water. The brothers picked up four hundred dollars' worth in two days, "but then all of Downieville came swarming up the river like suckers rushing for a spawning place in the Spring of the year."

The boys said goodbye to Downieville, reaching Nelson Creek in four days. They went back to the "flat" that had interested them before, and decided to build a "railroad" of wooden cars to carry the dirt down to the creek. The loaded cars going down would lift the empty cars going up. They also built a water wheel to wash the dirt. "The first day's work panned out five hundred dollars. You know, we felt rich!!" After that day, the yields got less and less, and settled at fifty dollars a day. The boys continued to work until Fall, when they were offered $1,800 for their claim. Henry's share (one fourth) was $450. That evening he weighed his gold dust and decided the dust plus the $450 would enable him to buy the home he had come to California to get.

It was extremely dangerous to leave the mountains, because the gold rush had attracted almost as many outlaws as miners. Many men who left with their gold were never heard from again. Henry wore a belt with eighteen buckskin purses attached, each of which held four ounces of gold dust, all totaling seventy-two ounces (worth $1,300 on the New York market). He also carried over three hundred dollars in coins. The three brothers (who did not carry guns) joined three well-armed "Wisconsin boys." They left at midnight, avoiding all roads and trails, climbing rapidly through the woods. The group was carrying $30,000 in gold. They camped the next night and dined on cheese and crackers. At four o'clock in the morning, they were awakened by rain and began their journey down the western slope of the mountains. They found a hotel an hour before sundown. "We were about the roughest looking outfit that went into Marysville that day. We had beards and hair two years old, with nothing but worn out pants and coats to cover our bodies. My right foot was clear of sock and boot, with one big toe exposed to the gaze of an ideal world."

The next morning they breakfasted, bought new clothes, and went to a barbershop which also had a bathtub. "We looked like birds of another color. I tell you, it was with difficulty we recognized each other." That evening, they boarded a steamer for Sacramento City, where they bought carpet bags, and filled them with tobacco, cigars, clothing and many books devoted to romances, which were passed around and exchanged while aboard another steamer bound for San Francisco. Passage to New York was $75. The brothers decided to go home by way of Nicaragua rather than Panama. That decision saved their lives.

They booked passage in Cornelius Vanderbilt's ship *Sierra Nevada* from Sacramento to Nicaragua. The days and nights aboard ship were delightful. In Nicaragua, the *Sierra Nevada* disembarked at the town of Sandulcet, where the Wisconsin boys crossed from the Atlantic to the Pacific side of Nicaragua in a small steamer. They marveled at the coconut, orange, lemon, pineapple, and banana trees, all bearing fruit, woods full of birds of the richest plumage, and monkeys of all sizes, and at night seeing great streaks of lightening leaping hundreds of feet from the mouth of a nearby volcano, causing the earth to tremble and the ship to vibrate.

At Gray Town, on Nicaragua's Atlantic coast, they boarded Vanderbilt's *Northern Light,* one of the largest passenger steamers afloat. After several days of smooth sailing, and while approaching Cape Hatteras, North Carolina, the wind began to blow much harder and the sea rose higher and higher. Henry noticed the sailors taking in all the sail, and that the ship was running under steam power with "bare poles." The boys were in steerage class—the cheapest accommodation below the waterline and near the rudder—with about three hundred other men. A crew member brought down life preservers, which Henry interpreted as a good omen. "It was after midnight that the vessel received a shock as though she had run on to a reef: she seemed to rebound and quiver, as if settling beneath the ocean wave. All the lanterns broke or were extinguished. It was then I heard an awful wailing cry from three hundred throats, imploring the almighty to save them from a watery grave (I never want to hear it again)." Henry smoked cigars all night, and was, like the others, "sitting in a death chamber waiting for the last rites to be performed over some departed friend."

The next morning the hatches were thrown open and Henry and other passengers swarmed up on deck. The sea was still running high but the *Northern Light* was holding her own. The captain spoke to the passengers, saying "Boys, I will have you in New York for dinner." Not until he read a newspaper the next day, did Henry realize the magnitude of the storm. Hurricane force winds had sunk Vanderbilt's steamship *Central America* about 160 miles east of Cape Hatteras. That ship was enroute from Panama to New York with many "forty-niners" as passengers. From its position, Henry estimated that the *Northern Light* could not have been more than 30 miles from the *Central America.*

During the height of the storm, the *Central America's* boilers lost steam, and her water pumps and paddle wheels shut down. A bucket brigade of all available men could do little to stem the rising waters, and the ship was at the mercy of gigantic waves. Neighboring ships had time to rescue all the women and children, but not the men. About 425 were lost, along with 30,000 pounds of gold valued at about $2 million. The ship's captain, retired U.S. Navy Commander William Herndon, refused to leave on the last boat. A town not far from Henry's home town of Waterford was named after him.

During 1852-57, the *Central America* had carried to New York about $150 million in gold, roughly equal to one-third of the entire California gold rush output. With the *Central America* at the bottom of the sea, New York banks did not have the gold they needed to meet their financial commitments, and began to close their doors, thus initiating the "Panic of 1857." (Author's note: In the 1980s, much of the gold was salvaged from the wreck of the *Central America.* The biggest find was an 80-pound bar of gold, which today is considered to be the single most valuable monetary unit in the world).

In New York, the boys exchanged each ounce of gold dust for eighteen dollars. Henry believed the storm at sea was still pursuing them, because it took 14 snowy days to get to Wisconsin by train, stagecoach, and cutter (a larger version of the horse and buggy). He must have been confused about dates, because the hurricane occurred in September 1857. Perhaps the boys stayed in New York longer than he remembered. Anyway, Henry remembered it was still snowing as he approached his father-in-law's farm driving the cutter wrapped in a buffalo robe. The wind carrying the tinkling of the cutter's bells announced his arrival, and everyone came to the door. Henry heard a faint little scream, and saw his wife leaping through deep snow drifts. They embraced over the rail fence in snow three feet deep. Henry carried her back to the house, and gave her back the gold dollar he had carried throughout all his adventures.

Henry's wife had picked out a pretty house on a beautiful 100-acre farm. He bought it and reminisced, "Oh! How happy I was!" Alas, ambition soon caused him to sell the property and to obtain a bank loan to buy a larger farm. The farm was not a success, and Henry complained that "we had enough bugs in Wisconsin to eat up every bit of corn, oats and wheat we raised;" and of the awful weather: "four feet of snow, the thermometer 30 below zero, and not a drop of moisture for 40 days." The Civil War added to his problems when agricultural prices plummeted, the bank called his loan, and he had to sell the farm at a $500 loss.

After the war, Henry became a businessman in Boscabel, Wisconsin. He did not discuss what he did there. With the economy still suffering from the Panic of 1873, it is likely Henry was having great difficulty finding employment. Yet Henry never forgot his dream of becoming a successful farmer, and in 1878 he and his wife "pulled out for Nebraska, with two good teams and but little cash." After all his failures to become a success in Ohio, Iowa, and Wisconsin, Henry finally found success and happiness in his middle age on the wild prairie of Nebraska.

Henry's experience was not unique. Distinguished historian Daniel Walker Howe has pointed out that a study of American frontier settlement patterns has revealed that settlers who did not prosper "often simply moved on. Sixty to 80 percent of frontier residents moved within a decade of their arrival. Many would fail repeatedly, drifting ever further westward in the hope that their luck would change."

# Chapter 26
# A White Gentleman in Jacket, Tie, and Hat

**"We are going to sing 'America the Beautiful.'"**
**—Mildred T. Boyde, teacher, Waterford Colored School A**

More than half a century after Virginia adopted public education in 1871, nothing had really changed in Loudoun County: 1,700 colored students distributed among 1 multi-room, 2 two-room and 22 one-room schoolhouses, were taught by 28 colored teachers—but only half of them were certified to teach above second grade. Loudoun County ranked 35th in the state with just 60.72 percent of the total school population attending regularly, and the average length of a school term was only 168 days—138 days for colored schools. Apathy at all levels of Government driven by a lack of funding, ensured that public education for Virginia's colored population remained a low priority, which persisted until the 1950s.

Waterford's Colored School A (known today as the Second Street School) continued to provide a basic primary school education for local children of African descent. Local historian Eugene Scheel describes a typical early 20th century day in the school. The teacher would arrive about eight in the morning. In winter, she would first light the kindling the boys had placed in the black iron stove the afternoon before. Then she would go to the coal shed, fill the coal bucket, and feed the fire. Two buckets were enough coal to last the whole day. Promptly at nine, the teacher rang a hand bell to begin the day. School would start with prayer, songs, and bible verses. Favorite songs were "America the Beautiful," the "Star Spangled Banner," and spirituals like "Swing Low Sweet Chariot," and "We Are Climbing Jacob's Ladder." During World War II, the pledge of allegiance to the flag was added.

Water was kept in a galvanized bucket, and everyone drank from the one dipper. At that time there was no typhoid epidemic, but that disease had been the scourge of Waterford in the past, and a metal cooler with individual cups was installed in the 1920s. Most children went home for lunch, which lasted an hour. On very cold days, the teacher would place cocoa or soup, provided by the parent-teacher association, on the stove. By the 1930s, most children were bringing lunch to school, and in the 1950s, milk was delivered to the school from Leesburg, and each child paid one cent (later two cents) for a half-pint.

Like all buildings in Waterford, the greatest danger to the school was fire. On October 12, 1933 embers from the cast iron stove were carried out of the building, setting fire to the roof. The school bell was rung, and townspeople rushed to help, climbing the ladders and chopping holes in the roof, while the school children formed a bucket brigade from nearby wells. The fire was put out before it spread. Four days later the school was re-opened with a flue lining enclosing the naked stovepipe, and a patched roof.

On November 23, 1979, Eugene Scheel interviewed Mildred Boyde at her home in Harpers Ferry. She was a graduate of Dunbar High School in Washington and Minor Normal School (today's Federal City College). She taught at Waterford's Colored School A from 1934 to 1937. She had always wanted to be a teacher, and as a youngster in Washington, D.C. would cut out paper dolls and make believe she was teaching them.

Miss Boyde told Scheel that one day in 1934 a white gentleman in a jacket, tie, and hat walked into the schoolhouse and introduced himself as Mr. Gresham from the State School Superintendents office. "My, what a cozy little school room," he said. "Can these children sing? Ask them to sing Old Black Joe." Now if there were any song Miss Boyde hated, it was "Old Black Joe." Not this time, she thought. "We are going to sing 'America the Beautiful,' " she countered. Mr. Gresham's face grew flushed. She followed "America" with "Give Me that Old Time Religion," and "Battle Hymn of the Republic." "Well they can sing," said a more composed Mr. Gresham. "I don't know why it is that this little school has never had an attendance of below ninety-two percent and an average of ninety-six percent." "The children even come when they're sick, and I have to send them home," replied Miss Boyde. She did not mention the "perfect attendance pins" she gave out. Some pleasantries ensued, and thus ended the one visit to the Waterford School from the Virginia State Superintendent's Office.

Miss Boyde recalled that, "Waterford children had a reputation for being a rough bunch," but she acted firm in the beginning, and the children were well behaved. "I stressed good manners all the time," she said; "I always taught my girls to be ladies and my boys to be gentlemen." Miss Boyde was also a talented musician, and taught piano at 50 cents a lesson. She often took the school children to the John Wesley Church so they could sing accompanied by a piano and Sears Roebuck organ. Every year there was a choral concert involving all the colored schools in Loudoun at Leesburg's Providence Baptist Church, and every year Miss Boyde's class won the coveted cup.

Meanwhile, the Waterford Elementary School for white children burned down in 1909, when the janitor with the unlikely name of Hector Tecumseh Calhoun Hough, accidentally left a bucket of hot ashes on the oiled wooden floor. The school was rebuilt the next year, and included all 12 grades, but was subsequently reduced to seven grades when the county school board took control, and began its experiment in "consolidation" of the higher grades into larger, more centrally located schools. In 1928 an auditorium was built adjacent to the school, and in 1948 a kitchen was constructed, joining the two buildings together. After a new Waterford Elementary School on the north side of town was dedicated in 1965, the Loudoun County School Board decided to sell the "Old School" at auction. The Waterford Foundation board of directors authorized its treasurer to bid up to $18,000. A developer wanted to build apartments on the site, and when the bidding reached $20,000, Waterford resident Florence Ebling said "she would see we get the building," and she did.

The coming of the railroad did spell the end of Waterford's small-scale manufacturing, which could not compete with mass produced manufactured goods arriving from the cities. It also enabled the Midwest's vast grain producing states to more economically ship their flour to eastern markets, thus undercutting the price of locally produced flour. Nevertheless, what was true in some parts of Loudoun County was not so in others and the fine soils of the Catoctin foothills enabled Waterford farmers to continue profiting from wheat production.

Waterford's reputation as a hard drinking town developed after Quakers were no longer a majority and the town had become an important regional economic center. By 1835, its citizens and visitors to the town were supporting four taverns. The "Waterford Waifs" gossip column in the February 24, 1888 issue of the *Loudoun Telephone* had this to say about the state of Waterford: "Socially, there is nothing brilliant; the men attend the Farmer's Club, the ladies go to their Household, both take a hand in an occasional quilting and the young folks hang over the front gate in the moonlight. The several stores seem to be doing a fairly good business and the Mills seem to be quite busy but ready cash is not abundant. Religiously, the Town is experiencing no sensation at this time. Morally, there is occasion for the remark that Waterford is too near "The Point" [Point of Rocks], for its own good. In other towns of the county I hear the charge that there is a good deal of drinking in Waterford–and I am afraid the town is not in position to bring suit for slander on this score. Stop the jug tavern business." The town's reputation persisted until 1920, when the eighteenth amendment to the Constitution banned the sale, production, and transportation of alcohol. After the amendment was repealed in 1933, Waterford's thirst was again evident.

# Chapter 27
# Together and Apart

**"Hell, we were all poverty stricken."**
**—John Devine Jr., Waterford Historian**

In the early 20th century, the divide between rural and urban America was greater than ever. The automobile had the potential to change that disparity. In 1916, Congress passed the Federal Road Aid Act, authorizing federal participation in state road construction, but lobbying by industrial and financial interests and their political allies, insured most of this assistance improved urban transportation networks. Since rural roads made up over four-fifths of all Virginia roads, Waterford and many other small towns were "left behind."

The Washington Ohio and Western Railroad, which had reached Leesburg in 1860, was extended south of Waterford in 1870 to Paeonian Springs at Clarke's Gap, and on to Hamilton, which became the area's principal market town. Some people say Waterford was by-passed by the railroad, as a causal factor in the town's further decline after the Civil War. However, Waterford's location deep in the foothills of the Catoctin Mountains made it a wholly unlikely destination for a railroad line. Waterford is just three miles from Paeonian Springs, the nearest railroad stop, and the road there had been used by Waterford farmers to bring their crops to market since the 18th century. The railroad line simply followed the only economical route, which was through Clarke's Gap to Paeonian Springs.

Historians Bronwen and John Souders describe the uniqueness of Waterford as a place where the races lived "together—and apart." There was no black section of town. The mutual readiness of both races in Waterford to help each other in time of need is remarkable considering the social inequality between them. Part of the reason was their long familiarity with one another. For generations they had lived side by side, often in the same households." Another part of the reason was their mutual dependency on one another. Still another was the Quaker belief that all humans shared the inner presence of God. Nevertheless, few black people had the skills to advance economically, and some whites were not inclined to see them as doing so. A few became known for a particular talent, such as stone mason, post-and-rail fencer, whitewasher, wagoneer. Even as recently as the 1930 census, all but three of Waterford's black males were working "odd Jobs" or "general farm labor."

Wheat farmers were still a special breed in northwest Loudoun County. In 1914, there were only 200 gasoline-powered tractors in the entire state of Virginia. By 1918, there were 1,500, but gasoline tractors were not generally accepted by Loudoun farmers as superior to the horse until the 1930s. Acreage under wheat for the county as a whole was 33,518 in 1909, but only 3,100 acres in 1990; although yields rose from 13.3 bushels per acre to 38.3, mostly in northwestern Loudoun County. Douglas Myers, President of the Waterford Foundation in 1966, remembered the old wheat steam thresher very well. The thresher separated the wheat from the chaff. Six to eight men were required to stoke the engine with wood, keep the boiler filled with water, fork the wheat into a hopper and bag it in sacks. It had a very loud and shrill whistle that could be heard over long distances, and was used to signal the farmer next in line to get ready for its arrival. When the boys in town heard it, they ran to meet the engine, and the best runner would, hopefully, win the honor of riding the engine or water wagon all through Waterford. They were often disappointed because "the engineer was in a bad mood and would let us walk home." One time, sparks from the engine set a house on fire. The townspeople saved the house, but the town council passed an ordinance that prohibited the engines from coming through town unless they had installed a spark arrester. "Boys like myself," reminisced Myers, "will forever remember the old threshing engine."

Francis Peacock was a sixth generation farmer, of good Confederate stock, and would not take his wheat or

corn to be processed at Waterford's Old Mill. He told in-
terviewer Sara Huntington: "I've farmed this land ever
since I could walk. We had 132 acres and an 18-acre wood
lot. We ran cattle, and we had sheep and hogs, and we had
crops in wheat, hay, alfalfa, corn and orchard grass. The
Farmer's Almanac was our bible...wouldn't sow a seed until the time was right. When I was growing up, we farmed
the land with horses. We thrashed wheat and we had four
teams of horses...we'd be sure to stop every once in a
while and walk around each horse to make sure it was
breathing right. We'd take so many bushels of wheat to the
mill down the road, and we'd get so many pounds of flour
back; the same with corn...I don't believe there is a farmer
living who would sell his farm if he was making a half de-
cent living. And I never thought it would happen to me."

John Divine Jr. and William B. Virts have written accounts of
growing up in Waterford during the 1920s-30s. Both describe a
largely self-sufficient village in which little money circulated, most
people raised or grew their own food, and nothing was wasted.
During spring plowing or fall harvesting and slaughtering, people
helped each other. The lack of modern conveniences did not seem
to bother either Virts, or Divine who reflected, "Hell, we were all
poverty stricken, we just didn't know it." Virts describes "a cold
December evening when a trip to the privy was required. There
was no tarrying then when a brisk north wind whipped up through
our standard one-holer." Times were better in spring, when an
enormous lilac bush which shielded the privy, burst into bloom.
"The fragrance from that bush is with me to this day," Virts reminisced. The same bitter north wind attacked the privy at the Samuel
Hough House. The path to it was lined by peonies, which today
still envelop the garden with their beauty and sweet aroma.

Virts did admit to racial and class differences: "Waterford
had a population of 350 in my youth. Half were Negroes, who
were definitely second-tier citizens in that community. They were
not treated with disrespect by the whites, merely with difference. I

can't recall hearing the word nigger until I went to New Hampshire at age seventeen. The primary word used when I was a child was colored. The issue then, as today was access to economic opportunity and precedent, with precedent coming first. In our community, one was either in or out of the economic opportunity arena. Entrance into that select group was usually by birth, but could be forced by an aggressive few: Everyone in their place and no boat rocking."

Virts and Devine also made the point that most people who had lived their whole lives in Waterford, regardless of their economic situation, liked or accepted things just the way they were. Change, however, was inevitable. When Waterford's Fairfax Quaker Meeting was "laid down" in 1929, It was simply the final act in a long running drama. The number of Quakers in Waterford had declined from 50 percent of its adult population in 1810 to just 5 percent in 1910.

Eleanor Elliot James (no relation to W.C. James) reminisced about coming to Waterford in 1926, when she was a young bride: "To a young city girl it was like stepping into a completely new world. The little lamp posts up and down the streets with their flickering kerosene lights looked like fireflies in the dark. The lamps had been shortened to accommodate the lamplighter, who was a very short man. Very early on summer mornings I would often awaken to the tinkling of bells coming from the bell around the neck of a fat cow being led up the street by a small barefoot boy, who whistled and sang as he went. The cow was taken home each morning and evening to be milked...The mail was brought on the Washington and Old Dominion Railroad to Paeonian Springs twice a day, along with passengers and their baggage. The mailman in his Model T Ford would bring them all to Waterford and people came to the Post Office just to see who had arrived in town. Few people had automobiles of their own and many still drove a horse and buggy. Many children living in the country rode their own horses to school. When lunchtime came each student fed and watered his horse as well as himself...My husband and I owned the first radio in Waterford. It was a cathedral shaped job we thought was simply wonderful. It is hard for this generation to imagine the thrill of getting up in the dead of night to fix the baby's bottle, turning on that little knob and hearing lovely music from, oh, so far away."

Although expanding urbanization was very slow in reaching Waterford, it became evident in the decline of front porches as a socializing force. An unidentified lifelong resident of the town interviewed in 1971 emphasized that "Porches were **lived** on. Around 1920, the short walk from the Corner Store to the end of Second Street might consume about two hours on a fair day. Among the inhabitants of the street were many widows and maiden ladies. Weather permitting, they sat on their porches while they sewed, snapped beans or hulled strawberries, while chatting with anyone handy. A resident, walking the street, did not pass by anyone without a neighborly 'howdy,' and perchance, a bit of gossip. These little calls took time. Sincerely interested in one another, we were a **community.** Our porches were an essential part of that community." Veranda porches had become quite the fashion, and there were seven veranda porches on Second Street alone. The porches on the Samuel Hough House and nearby Mahlon Schooley House were dismantled in 1968-69 during renovation of both houses.

In 1932, the Virginia General Assembly passed the Byrd Road Act, which transferred 35,000 miles of Virginia's 40,000 miles of rural roads to the state road system, permitting counties to turn over responsibility for these roads to the state highway commission. County roads connecting Waterford to neighboring towns and highways were among the roads paved in the mid-1930s. Waterford did not have the funds to pave its own streets. In 1936, the County Board of Supervisors insisted that Waterford find the money to do so, and, according to town council member Douglas Myers, the town council borrowed $2,800, but could not repay the loan. Facing default, council members voted to give up Waterford's 100-year-old charter of incorporation. The loan was eventually repaid out of a fund established by the Loudoun County Board of Supervisors. Waterford had become a ward of the county.

According to John Souders, Waterford's economic vitality was already draining away as the nation faced its greatest economic crisis: "Increasingly, opportunity lay beyond the old village, and its outmoded, contracting economy...the town was no longer the commercial center of the surrounding farms, and the Great Depression squeezed much of the remaining life out of its farms."

# Chapter 28
# Whose House Is It?

**"[Lawsuits] construing a vested remainder in an estate are almost as countless as grains of sand on the seashore."**
**—Justice Edward W. Hudgins, Virginia Supreme Court**

William James's father Elijah died in 1880 at the age of 96, and his will instructed his executors to divide the estate equally among his nine children. Four of his six sons were named executors. Son William was not named because he owed 98 percent ($ 7,094.70) of all the debts due the estate at the time of Elijah's death. Son Mahlon, the black sheep of the family, was also not named, and his share in the estate, after payment of his debts, was placed in a trust for his wife and children. Henry Virts witnessed the will, and served as appraiser of the estate after Elijah's death.

William James's debts became due and payable to the estate, and he spent the next five years attempting to meet these obligations, while desperately trying to maintain his ownership of the store, residence, and stable he built in 1856-57 at the juncture of Waterford's Main, Second and Water Streets. He was unsuccessful, and on October 15, 1880, he deeded to a trustee, Chas. Janney, all his rights and interest in the estate.

His troubles had just begun. James was also indebted to others, and in 1882, a suit was brought against him in Chancery Court. On January 23 1883, the Court decided that "all the real estate of W. James, in the bill & proceedings mentioned, be sold at public auction." James's trustee agreed to deed the property to Charles William Rinker for $1,616. Rinker sold the property to Lemuel P. Smith in 1897.

"Lem" Smith was one of Waterford's great characters and entrepreneurs. He became a fixture at the center of town after he and his brother-in-law purchased the James property. Smith won a contract to provide the oil for street lamps, and Waterford became the first town in northern Loudoun County to have coal-oil lamps in 1897. Smith later joined another brother-in-law in taking over Waterford's mortician business. A neighbor remembered him "as a nice man who always whistled as he worked," preparing his clients for their eternal rest. When business was brisk, neighbors remembered being kept awake by the sound of nails being hammered into coffins. "Lem" was the third person in Waterford to buy an automobile (a Model T Ford). He sold the former James property in 1930, and was on the town council that voted to de-incorporate Waterford in 1936.

William Carlyle (W.C.) James was born in 1859 in his father's house at the juncture of Main and Second Streets. He married Emma Cecilia Brown in 1881. In 1884, James purchased the Samuel Hough House and the ¾ acre lot across the street from Jacob Scott for $1,800. In its May 9, 1891 edition, The *Brunswick Herald* commented that "W.C. James is building an addition to his residence which will be a decided improvement." The Herald was referring to a three-sided brick bay window in the dining room of the Samuel Hough House, whose protruding cornice with patterned interlocking bricks at angled corners is characteristic of the 1890s.

W.C. James was a dedicated member of Waterford's town council, on which he served from 1895 to 1911. He was said to have been "a merchant, farmer and livestock dealer," which spans the most important businesses in Waterford. His will indicate that–unlike his father–he was a highly successful businessman. He bought a 100-acre farm near Waterford in 1891 from the B.W. Paxson estate for $5,000, and B.W. Paxson & Sons general merchandise store in 1903. James's pre-independence day sale advertisement for his store in the July 3, 1903 issue of the Leesburg newspaper *The Record* provides an insight into "soft-sell" turn-of-the-century advertising techniques:

We naturally desire that our business relations shall be satisfactory both to our customers and to ourselves. In order that they may be so, we will extend a credit of thirty (30) days...so kindly come and confer with us before opening an account elsewhere...if you would save money watch the columns of this paper for our bargains. We have a lot of off-style and slightly shop-worn Shoes, Hats, and other goods which we will sell, while they last, at hair raising prices. Come and look them over.

A photograph of the Samuel Hough House, taken about 1910, shows a girl, probably James' daughter Imogene, who was born in 1892, standing on the front porch. Her father removed the front porch and built a wrap-around veranda porch on the house in 1913.

W.C. James died of a heart attack in 1929, having lived in the Samuel Hough House for 45 years. His property passed to his wife Emma, who lived there with her daughter Imogene (Gene) and her husband J. Reid Mays. Emma also received $50,000 "for her sole benefit and use during her natural life." Upon her death, the estate was to be divided equally among their children: Arthur A. James, Frederick C. James and Gene James Mays.

Arthur James and his wife, Edna Carr James, lived in a stone farmhouse, Moxley Hall, on Water Street. Arthur hung himself in his barn on November 22, 1938. According to long time Loudoun resident Wilbur Dobbs, Edna had gone shopping, and when she returned, she could not find Arthur. She asked a hired hand who worked on the farm, where Arthur was. "Oh, he's out in the barn," was the reply. Edna had Arthur cremated and his ashes placed in an urn, which she kept on the living room mantel. On Sundays, she would go out for a drive with Arthur's ashes in the passenger seat. A memorial stone in the path to the garden at the Samuel Hough House is inscribed simply, "A. J."

After Emma James died in 1940, Arthur's premature death created a doubt as to who would inherit the portion of the W.C. James estate bequeathed to him. Edna Carr James maintained that on the death of Emma James, the right to one-third of the property passed to her under Arthur's will, entitling her to a "vested remainder" under W.C. James's will. The other James heirs contended that since Arthur died before his mother, the beneficiary of his will (Edna) had no vested interest in the property. They brought suit against the will's beneficiaries in the Circuit Court of Loudoun County to construe the intent of W.C. James's will.

The Circuit Court ruled Edna Carr James was entitled to one-third of the James estate. The Circuit Court's decision was appealed to the Virginia Supreme Court by Gene Mays and Frederick James. On November 24, 1941, with all justices present, the Supreme Court upheld the decree of the Circuit Court. In his opinion, Supreme Court Justice Edward W. Hudgins complained that law suits construing a vested remainder in an estate "are almost as countless as grains of sand on the seashore," and intent to postpone vesting must be clearly indicated by James' will, which it did not.

Only Imogene Mays was interested in living in the house. A hearing was held on March 18, 1942 in Chancery Court to determine the value of the real estate and ascertain "a fair charge" for Gene James Mays's use of the real estate. Counsel for Edna Carr James cross-examined prominent Waterfordians Douglas Myers, Secretary, Loudoun Mutual Fire Insurance Co.; Arthur Peacock, farmer; Edgar H. Beans, livestock broker; and Leslie Myers, stinmith; whether they had colluded with Imogene Mays about what to say at the hearing. All denied it.

The defining issues in determining the sale price of the Samuel Hough House were whether it had indoor plumbing, a bathroom with hot water, and a furnace for central heating. The house had none of these amenities. The Court decided that Edna James should "make a price," and on March 26, 1942 Edna agreed to sell the house to Imogene for $6,500, minus $475 back rent.

Electricity was not an issue, indicating that–like other Waterford houses–a single electric line had reached the house in the 1930s. Although two steam-driven electricity plants—serving Leesburg, Purcellville, Hamilton and Round Hill, had brought electric power to western Loudoun by the early 1900s, Waterford was left power-less until President Roosevelt created the Rural Electrification Administration in 1935. Totts Edwards and George Bentley, who grew up in Waterford in the 1920s-30s, recalled the individual light fixtures located at every intersection, and in a "roundabout" in front of the Corner Store.

In 1936, Waterford became a ward of the County. Yet, the very issue, that caused the loss of Waterford's corporate identity, provided the basis for its revival and renewal. With the paving of Waterford's streets completed by the County in 1937, the village became readily accessible to automobiles and trucks from the out-side world. The automobile and the radio changed a way of life. Waterford was no longer an isolated self-contained community.

Nevertheless, significant urbanization creeping west from the Washington area did not reach Loudoun County until after 1950, and it took 15 more years to reach Waterford. Between 1950 and 1960, Loudoun County's population increased 16 percent, while the number of people living on farms declined by 46 percent. Such a sharp decline was due to the construction of Dulles International Airport in 1958, which involved acquiring 5,000 acres of agricultural land, and forcing 500 people to give up their homes.

# Chapter 29
# In the Nick of Time

**"Remnants of history which have casually escaped the ship-wreck of time"**
**—Sir Francis Bacon, English Philosopher**

Sir Francis Bacon, the great English philosopher, statesman, and natural scientist, who in 1605 said antiquities are "remnants of history which have casually escaped the shipwreck of time," perfectly defined Waterford's dilemma three hundred-fifty years later, according to Philip Ehrenkranz, Board member of the Waterford Foundation during the 1960-70s. Prior to, and during World War II, Washington DC had become a magnet for a newly affluent generation, who owned automobiles and were searching for a place to raise a family or have a vacation home in the country. Some were drawn to a rural small town lifestyle, and found Waterford.

Others were disappointed. In 1940, U. S. Secretary of War, Harry R. Woodring, bought the beautiful Pink House in the center of town, intending to move there. President Franklin Roosevelt would have none of it, so Woodring decided to move the house brick-by-brick to Georgetown. The word got out; gossip columnist Drew Pearson spoke about it on the radio, and *The New York Times, Baltimore Sun,* and *The Christian Science Monitor* picked up the story. After all the fuss, the brick proved to be too soft for removal and re-use.

In the aftermath of the Great Depression, it seemed Waterford's charm would soon disappear anyway. Many of Waterford's pre-Civil War commercial structures had disappeared. Comparing a modern map of Waterford with an 1874 map indicates about fifty structures had been abandoned, consumed by fire, removed or replaced with newer structures. There were also some near misses. After the Second World War, the roofs of two of Waterford's grandest houses, the Hague-Hough House and The Dormers, had fallen in, and the buildings were in danger of total collapse. They were saved "in the nick of time" by new owners. There are many stories in Waterford about the trials and tribulations of fixing up these houses. Some of them are quite amusing, especially one involving the house next to the Samuel Hough House (south side).

"They's someone a startin to fix up this old house. Taint no good but ter tear down!" Two passersby made these remarks in 1950 shortly after Lucy MacCallum bought her little house on Second Street next to the Samuel Hough House. "In the three years since, she has been tempted to think sometimes that they were right; but not for long...She and her son Spencer find themselves very much in the process of restoring and remodeling...Spencer offered to re-glaze the windows. After he had taken out all the window frames he refused to put any back until he had old glass for all of them. This necessitated three weeks of sorties through the countryside. Fortunately, this was through a summer drought, however, many interesting visitors, including all the dogs in town, came in through the open windows." Lucy named her house "Catoctin Creek," and operated a boy's school and camp there.

Longtime residents Leroy and Edward Chamberlin realized that Waterford's new accessibility would ignite new interest in its historic houses. They began restoring Waterford to its former elegance. Edward, who was blind, and had married an heiress, Vera Moses, provided the financing, while Leroy, who was an architect and a builder, carried out the restoration and the renovation. From the 1937-40, they were responsible for restoring 19 properties in and around Waterford. These included *Fairfax Meeting House*, which was converted into a residence, three houses in *Arch House Row, Huntley* and *Talbott* farmhouses, *Bank House* which had housed Waterford's only bank, and *Mill End*—the miller's house across from the Old Mill. They also enabled Waterford's first indoor plumbing by installing a septic system across the street from *Arch House Row*, to serve those three houses.

In 1937, Polly and Paul Rogers purchased a farm near Waterford. Many years later, Polly described her introduction to Waterford: "I rode around the countryside making the acquaintance of the world in which we planned to live...I happened upon Waterford and lost my heart...Most every  building looked as though it was about to fall apart...Waterford haunted me–it was like finding an abandoned child. You wanted to take it home, love it and try to save it from complete disintegration." Soon, America was at war, and Polly started rolling bandages at the Red Cross, where she met Mary Phillips Stabler, who was the local Red Cross Executive Secretary. Mary lived in Waterford at the Phillips Farm, which she had inherited from her father. She and Polly became great friends and decided they wanted "to do something to save Waterford for posterity–but where to begin?"

They had no money, but finally got a loan. "We were off and running. Such planning and scheming and groping for direction! And such a fever of excitement and high hopes...We decided to ask town residents of long standing as Board members thinking they would share our enthusiasm...this was not always the case...we were 'new people,' of course, and deeply suspect therefore."

Help arrived when new arrivals Allen McDaniel and his wife joined the Board. The Waterford Foundation was established in 1943, with McDaniel as its first president. He held that office for 12 years. The board's first major act was to acquire the Old Mill in 1944 from Fenton and Dolores Fadeley, who bought it and donated it to the Foundation. Polly had "only one burning passion–to restore the Mill to running condition, and sell the ground meal...but others had other ideas."

Having an influx of strangers coming to live in Waterford frightened many of the long-term residents of this small, isolated town, especially when it involved a collision of urban and rural cultural values. Like any small town, rumors circulated much faster than facts (they still do), and it was all too easy for misunderstandings to arise. In 1971, Eleanor James wrote: "With the movement of the urban into the rural, we wonder what will be the result in years to come. Will there be no more nice peaceful little villages and lovely pastoral scenes. I have seen throughout the years 'newcomers' arrive, retired career people with pockets bulging, city people with a rural yen, etc. all ready to reform the whole place." But the newcomers had precisely the same goal she had–to preserve the peaceful little village of Waterford and its lovely pastoral scenes. Older residents were resistant to change because they feared loss of personal or group identity and control over their future. Waterford's history tells us that change was a fact of life. The real issue was how to manage change.

Mary Stabler and Allen McDaniel suggested having a traditional handicraft exhibition and sales. The first Waterford Craft Exhibit was held in the old Quaker Meeting House in October 1944. Mary Stabler recalled that "the weather was perfect–we sold $90 worth of merchandise and 500 people signed the guest register. Everyone was ecstatic!"Plans were made to hold a similar event every year. After a month studying weather records, Allen McDaniel announced that "its least likely to rain in the first week in October."

Waterfordians began studying 18th and 19th century decorative techniques. Mrs. Paul Rogers launched an experimental class in lamp-base and shade making. Five Waterford women went to Gatlinburg, Tennessee to learn weaving skills from the Southern Highlanders Craft Guild, and returned to teach others all about color, design, and fretwork. Mrs. Anna Hutchison gave spinning wheel lessons. Leroy Chamberlin and George Hughes taught wood carving. Others held classes in pottery making, illustration, and illumination.

In 1950, the Waterford Foundation took a retrospective view on its first seven years of existence. It had raised $25,677.71 from the sale of crafts, membership fees and Crafts Exhibit ticket sales. The Foundation was run by a board of directors made up of eight married couples. But new members were by invitation only, and the annual Crafts Exhibit did not welcome people of color. Something had to be done!

Historian and Board member John Devine told the rest of the Board that the Foundation needed to create goodwill among *all* the inhabitants of Waterford. He proposed giving free Waterford

Exhibit tickets to them all. This would require establishing a specific time in which colored people could visit. The Board decided
that "Exhibits would be open to the Colored people of Waterford
on Thursday afternoon."

The Waterford Fair, as it is commonly known, has been
held the first three-day weekend in October ever since—except
when a storm intervened in 2015. The big attractions were the 18th
and 19th century village itself, private homes open to the public, the
expertise and beauty of hand-made crafts, and the Waterford A
Capella Chorus under the direction of Helen Cooley, which sere-
naded visitors with "Negro Spirituals, English Folksongs, and Rus-
sian Airs."

The Waterford Foundation received its first national recognition when *Good Housekeeping* magazine sent two reporters to
research a story for its "Town of the Month "series. The story appeared in the October 1950 issue, but the Foundation must have
received an advance copy, because it was discussed at the September 1950 Board meeting. Mrs. Douglas Myers, who was in charge
of publicity, regretted that "the article was written in the fanciful
way it was," and that her name appeared in it. Chairman Faveley
commended Mrs. Myers on the magnificent job she had done, and
told her "not to be disturbed by any of the petty unfavorable com-
ments."

Mrs. Myers was particularly upset because the *Good
Housekeeping* article quoted her as saying: "It was heartbreaking
to see our town slump, during the depression, from a charming
self-reliant little community to a cluster of houses indifferently
cared for or actually caving in; a community with no civic interests, no inspiration in the dull monotony of its existence, almost no
life. Waterford's resurrection began one chill evening in November
1940, in the living room of the Allen McDaniel home [formerly the
Fairfax Quaker Meeting house]. Five families were gathered before the crackling fire—the McDaniel's, the Fadeleys, the Myers,
the Stablers, the Rogers–all old Waterford residents who had
watched with mounting dismay the spiritual and physical deteriora-
tion of their town."

Mrs. Myers had good reason to be upset. Television was still very new, and monthly magazines like *Good Housekeeping* were widely read and very influential. A "Good Housekeeping seal of approval" is still today an important recognition of excellence. After its woeful beginning, however, the article fairly burst with good cheer: "Waterford was renowned for its artisans—makers of the finest furniture, cloth, blankets, brooms, baskets, leather goods, wrought-iron and silver work to be found in the new world. These old time skills, long lost in the machine age, were to be refound and relearned by twentieth-century Waterfordians. A percentage of the profits from the sale of these articles plus sponsor fees and donations coming to the Foundation were to be used to restore old Waterford buildings. Turning a civic somersault, the unhappy little town became, almost overnight, as bouncing and earnest as a freshman class pledged to do or die."

Some long-time residents were even more upset than Mrs. Myers. Charlton (Mrs. Leroy) Chamberlin wrote to Herbert Mayes, Editor of *Good Housekeeping,* suggesting that: "in writing future articles, your representatives are required to obtain the facts, and avoid publishing such mis-statements as this article contains. The truth about the saving and reconstruction of the old town of Waterford is so much more interesting than the untruth written by Katherine Best and Katherine Hillyer. In the very row of houses shown in the illustration in the article, the first reconstruction was begun. This was 1937! Two brothers, Leroy and Edward Chamberlin, 4th generation residents of the Waterford neighborhood, worried by the unemployment of many Waterford men and by the falling into ruin of the houses shown in the picture, undertook the work–this row and many other houses–thirteen in number were finished by 1940, when in the article it is stated the Waterford Foundation saved and restored the town. This particular untruth referred to above, is only one of the many misstatements, many of which are resented by Waterford residents. I don't know who in our neighborhood could be responsible for these errors but I should think that you and they–and the authors using the Good Housekeeping seal of integrity, would sincerely regret such an article and be very certain it didn't occur again"

Margaret Cousins, Managing Editor of *Good Housekeeping,* responded that: "We are sorry that our reporters, who have always been extremely reliable, were mis-informed by residents of Waterford, Va., about the town. If their article contains untruths, we do not believe they derive from misquotation but from misinformation...We are naturally unhappy to have offended any of the citizens of Waterford and we apologize for including Waterford in our series."

Charlton Chamberlin became very angry at Margaret Cousins; not only because she dismissed Chamberlin's complaints, but because of Cousin' disavowal of Waterford as a community worthy of *Good Housekeeping's* attention. Her fury is evident in her terse reply: "Your letter to me of October 16 shows that you have a number of other things to apologize for, besides including Waterford in your series. Your housekeeping may be good but your lack of courtesy is deplorable." Years later, Charlton Chamberlin's daughter-in-law, Ann Carter Chamberlin Smith confessed to a friend that "her full name was Rose Charlton, but she was no Rose!"

For the next 25 years, the Waterford Foundation focused on demonstrating and teaching traditional crafts by inviting crafters from outside the village to participate in the Fair, and continued buying and preserving the town's historic buildings, such as the Old Mill (1944), Red Barn (1948), Weavers Cottage (1958), and Old School (1966). Building restoration and maintenance costs were high, and money was in short supply. Yet when the Board decided to increase the Fair entrance fee from $1 to $1.50, Board member John deCourcy recalls that Douglas Myers objected, insisting that "no one will come!"

The Board felt strongly it should support local recreational activities. At the February, 1964 Board meeting, President William Nickels told Board members that the Waterford colored baseball team was trying to raise money to purchase uniforms. "Mr. Bentley moved we contribute to the cause. Mr. deCourcey seconded the motion and it was passed [unanimously]." Five months later, however, the Board felt quite differently about the granting of a beer license for a private club sponsored by the Leesburg Colored American Legion, to be housed in the old church and school building on [blank] and Janney sts." The Alcoholic Beverage Control (ABC) Board in Richmond was informed "the Foundation has gone on record opposing granting the license."

The Waterford Foundation Board realized it needed to be more opportunistic in finding ways to raise or save money. When local C & P Telephone Company manager Frank Caldwell telephoned Board President Nickels and asked "for permission to let his workmen use the Red Barn privies while working in Waterford," Nickels got Board agreement to grant permission if C & P gave the Foundation "a free listing with information and long-distance operators at the time of the Fair."

The Foundation did not decide to actively pursue new members among Waterford's black community until the 1970s. In March, 1972, the Board sent "the black community a letter of invitation"...but "there was no response". Board president William Baine asked Board members to "talk to leaders of the black community and plan to set up a meeting." Five months later, nothing had happened, and Baine urged "individual members of the Board to make a direct request to individuals in the community to become members of the Foundation." Three months later, the Foundation did have three black members. However, since they only amounted to one percent of total membership of 309, Baine insisted that the Board still needed to do "a more thorough job in getting more [black] members."

Waterford was saved from Sir Francis Bacon's metaphorically watery grave by the National Historic Preservation Act of 1966. The U. S. Government had concluded that preservation efforts were inadequate to save America's rich heritage "in the face of ever-increasing urban centers, highways and residential, commercial and industrial developments."

A major effort was begun to gain national recognition of the importance of Waterford as a pre-industrial farming community which uniquely included not only many of its original 18<sup>th</sup> and 19<sup>th</sup> century buildings, but also the farms surrounding it. Saving the farmland around Waterford therefore became essential for preserving the character of the village. Virginia's legislature also provided Waterford with an important preservation tool when it passed the Open Space Land Act of 1966, which allowed designated state agencies to accept "open space easements," which would limit development on the property to specific economic activities (i.e. agriculture, viticulture, animal husbandry) while providing the owners with significant tax benefits for relinquishing some of their "development rights."

According to W. Brown Morton III, who developed the boundaries for what was to become the Waterford National Historic Landmark District, "it is Waterford's setting which gives the startling quality to the landscape. Every historic building in town backs away to an unspoiled natural view." In 1967, Morton moved to Waterford and joined the National Park Service as Principal Architect, Historic American Buildings Survey. When asked by the Virginia State Historic Preservation Office to help develop a state boundary for the Waterford Historic District, he agreed, knowing it would have to be acceptable (and legally defensible) at the federal level.

Morton was convinced the farmland surrounding Waterford provided the economic justification for the mill and the commercial activities which developed around it. He therefore conceived "a landmark boundary proposal that had entirely visual criteria, was not based on historical or present day property lines, and drew the boundary far enough beyond visible ridge lines to protect the view shed." Waterford—with Morton's boundaries—was listed on the Virginia Landmark Register and National Register of Historic Places in 1969, and in 1970, and was granted the nation's highest designation for historic property, when the US Department of the Interior created the 1,420 acre Waterford National Historic Landmark District.

Waterford had achieved the status of Mount Vernon, the Alamo, and many other historic sites, but being a national landmark provided no protection against encroaching development. In a letter sent to the Waterford Foundation many years later, the National Park Service emphasized that "We can identify a problem, call attention to the threat, and engage in persuasion, but there our ability to protect ceases. But if Waterford is unable to prevent undesirable development, the National Park Service retains the right to withdraw its designation if Waterford's historical integrity has been greatly compromised." The U.S. government's message was clear: although it had provided the justification for historic preservation, it was up to private individuals to actually do it. If the private sector failed in its task, then the government could revoke Waterford's national landmark status.

Purchase and restoration of important buildings in the village had always been a primary goal of the Waterford Foundation. But to respond to the government's challenge, the Waterford Foundation had to greatly expand its efforts. Beginning in the 1970s, it acquired the Corner Store and nearby commercial buildings in the center of town, the John Wesley Church, the Bond Street Meadow, and several residences on Main and Bond streets. In 1971, the Foundation achieved a major goal, when all the landowners bordering Water Street agreed to place similar open space easements on their respective properties, thus preserving the beauty of the northern entrance to the village in perpetuity. According to the National Park Service:

"Waterford is one of the few places in the country where the historic relationship of a common human settlement to the land can still be so clearly seen and understood. In its own way, Waterford's National Historic Landmark is a living museum."

# Chapter 30
# Education Consolidation

**"The insidious 'feeding'...that took our high school."**
**—Douglas Myers, President, Waterford Community Citizens Association**

On February 12, 1947 many people from the Waterford community attended a Waterford School Parent-Teachers Association meeting to discuss matters relating to Waterford's school for white children. In the ensuing debate, a group of those present who felt the PTA was "not fully qualified" to deal with school issues and problems, formed a separate Waterford Community Citizens Association.

Prominent Waterford citizen Douglas Myers was elected president. Two days later, Myers sent a letter to the Division Superintendent of the Loudoun County School Board, asking him to clarify what were the specific objectives to be achieved by consolidation of the schools in Loudoun County, because "we have been hearing about [consolidation] now for nearly twenty years, and still have only a vague idea about what it means."

Myers and others had developed a very negative view of the consolidation process, which involved "the insidious 'feeding' [taking students from one school to another] process that took our high school, thereby killing something very vital to the life of our community, we are suspicious and resentful to learn the same 'feeding' is now being considered by you or your board in connection with all we have left, our grade school."

Superintendent D. L. Emerick's answering letter, to Myers's angry one, was polite and explanatory. He admitted the county was "very much on the spot in a sort of squeeze between the broad views of the state educational authorities and the specific views of patrons," when a school closing was involved. He referred to the Loudoun County School Board Resolution of February 28, 1940, which listed "four permanent" high schools: Aldie, Lincoln, Leesburg and Lovettsville; and 16 permanent elementary schools, including Waterford."

Emerick also mentioned that beginning in the 1949 school year, high schools would include five grades, and elementary schools seven grades. Regarding the possibility of closing Waterford Elementary in the foreseeable future, he wrote: "Where we already have an elementary school located in a definite community and where there is a reasonable certainty that it would justify itself as a four teacher school there should be no thought of discontinuing the school." More pointedly, he wrote: "I do not know where the suggestion arises that we are planning to feed some pupils away from Waterford Elementary School to some other point in the county." But he also maintained that "a great deal of effort has been made in this county to explain the advantages of consolidation to our people,"

Neither letter raised the issue of segregation; or, was concerned with the schooling of students in Waterford Colored School A. Nor did the letters consider the broader impact of school closings on small towns and villages. The loss of a school through consolidation represented the loss of the only place beside the local church that served as a community center where parents could readily participate in school activities, and really get to know their children's teachers. The availability of school auditoriums and sports fields also provided most small towns with the only venues they had for staging major community events. Closing a school meant a tragic loss of those events and relationships that brought communities together. Consolidation, with all its social and political implications, had only became possible statewide following the introduction of paved roads and bus transport after World War I. Even then, it moved at a glacial pace, hindered by meager funding, lack of state initiative in paving local roads, and because it was bitterly resisted by most small towns.

The Waterford Citizens Association shared with the Foundation the goal of preserving Waterford's heritage and character while focusing on developing community-based programs and activities in the village. It also attracted Waterford residents who felt the Foundation did not represent their points-of-view, or who wished for a smaller, more informal and locally focused organization. A major goal of the Association was preservation and beautification of the village; centered on restoration and maintenance of the Friends and Union cemeteries, and tree planting along Waterford's streets. Its most important community activity still is the annual 4th of July celebration. For many years, it began with a morning parade led by Waterford's "Uncle Sam," Paul Rose. Everyone gathered in the Bond Street Meadow to sit on hay bales, sing patriotic songs and hear a speech from a local politician or distinguished visitor. Prizes were awarded to youngsters who decorated their bicycles for the parade. A mid-day picnic of hot dogs, watermelon and lemonade preceded an afternoon softball game, followed by a potluck dinner. After the sun set villagers and visitors watched a truly spectacular fireworks display.

For almost a century after the Civil War, white and black children attended segregated schools, based on the rationale of "separate but equal" schooling for both races. Their education was separate but hardly equal. In 1954, The U. S. Supreme Court unanimously ruled in the case of Brown versus Board of Education of Topeka, that "separate educational facilities are inherently unequal." Laws, under which such facilities were mandated, were therefore unconstitutional, and states were required to integrate black and white schools. The name of the Waterford Colored School A was changed to The Waterford School (now called the Second Street School). In May 1957, teacher Violet Archer locked the school doors for the last time, and Waterford's black children were bused to a larger facility in Leesburg.

In 1966, the Loudoun County School Board sold the school at auction. There was no one to object, because the five original trustees selected in 1868 and still listed by name as owners in the school's deed, had all died. According to a 1950 state law, in cases where buildings had been in continual use as public schools and there were no surviving trustees, the property reverted to the county school board. The school board sold the property to Robert Milam Jr. for $4,000 dollars. The "colored community of Waterford and vicinity" received no compensation for their ownership of the property for ninety years! In 1977, Milam benefited from the land rush in Waterford, and sold the school to the Waterford Foundation for $28,000.

The purchase of the Second Street School was a step in a new direction by the Waterford Foundation. In the early 1970s, the Internal Revenue Service was scrutinizing organizations that claimed to qualify as "charitable." The Foundation's classes in weaving, pottery, and painting, to qualify as a tax-free educational entity under the IRS code, had been only moderately successful. The Foundation had to consider better ways of using education as an outreach tool to inform the general public about Waterford.

The idea of using the school as a living history program for Loudoun County school children, originated among Waterford Foundation Education Committee members Abbie Cutter, Nancy Felton, and Margaret Morton. Abbie suggested applying for a grant from the National Endowment of the Humanities, where she worked, to help develop the educational program. A $3,000 grant was awarded in 1980, and educator Suzanne Schell was hired to produce a curriculum and teacher's manual. In 1982, Waterford Foundation Executive Director Connie Chamberlin handed the finished manual to the Education Committee and said: "Make this happen." With the help of many others, they did.

To reflect a classroom of the 1880s, a team tasked with refurbishing the building scoured antique stores and auctions for period desks, a teacher's table, maps, and pictures from the 1880 era. Committee member Betsy Schrenk designed a 1880s style skirt and petticoat for volunteers playing the part of the teacher, Miss Aura Nickens, as well as a dunce cap for children who misbehaved. Census data from 1870 and 1880 were analyzed to help other volunteers write biographies of the students who had attended the school. This enabled local school children to assume the identity of actual pupils and experience a school day in the 1880s. The program received the blessing of the county's Superintendent of Schools.

Today, everything in the classroom is from the period, including an 1880 map of the United States; texts providing lessons in arithmetic, penmanship, reading and geography. "Miss NIckens" also uses $19^{th}$ century pedagogical methods in her teaching. The living history program has been a great success, and over 35,000 Loudoun County fourth graders have spent a day as black children learning their ABC's, and playing skip-rope and roll-the-hoop at recess. It was all made possible by dedicated volunteers of the Waterford Foundation, who, over the years have had the pleasure of introducing local school children to their black historical counterparts of 137 years ago.

# Chapter 31
# Best of Friends

**"The only thing we didn't do together was go to school."**
**—Karen "Sister" Mallory Spriggs**

In the mid-1950s, U.S. Navy Captain (retired) Clarence Winekoff, an ex-submariner, taught sixth grade at the Waterford Elementary School for white children. The Captain was known as "Uncle Chink" by his students, and he lived close to the school on Patrick Street, in a 1906 Queen Ann-style house, he had painted battleship-grey. Today, it is remembered as the Captain's House. Pinky Pierce had many other happy memories of "Uncle Chink" and Waterford's Old School. Years later she came to know Kitty and Paul Rose who bought the Captain's House, and in a series of emails and letters, she described her life in Waterford and the school:

> ...the grand old lady atop her Waterford Hill, imperious with her white columns and glorious high windows over-looking the surrounding village. How wonderful to be a pupil there in the 50's—the private French lessons by a lovely lady from Belgium, arranged by Uncle Chink; the art classes; our feisty intramural girls' softball games.

"Uncle Chink "was a great favorite of his students. Pinky Pierce reminisced:

> I adored him, and after moving to Alexandria, I returned to visit him and his wife many, many times, where he and I would adjourn to sit together in his lovely side garden for his evening glass of Scotch whiskey...Capt. Winekoff was such a fine example of what I later thought retired military

men should be...like my father, a Marine officer in WWI and WWII.

Her younger brother "Winky," who was two grades behind her, was the star pupil in French, because the kind lady said he had the perfect mouth for it. Her best friend was "Sister" (Karen Mallory Sprigs). After seeing Sister, years later, she recalled:

> She is just as I remember her, still a miraculous gift of friendship and kindness...Sister is indeed, "living history." Together, we brought back the Waterford of old—with all of its quirky characters, family secrets—and sadness.

In 1957, Pinky was art editor of *The Chatterbox,* the school newspaper. Uncle Chink gave her "free reign," and she won the *Washington Star* newspaper's student art competition with one of her original cartoons. In the Christmas, 1957 issue she wrote a short story entitled "Timothy's Lesson," based upon a stuffed mouse one of her sixth grade classmates brought to school every day in his pocket. Pinky's "Timothy" lived alone, one of a brood of eighteen mice kicked out of a nest in an old clock. Timothy was poor, and spending a sad, hungry Christmas, when a knock on his door announced the arrival of a little bird, "with his arms full of goodies and his eyes full of tears." The bird had also been forced to fly from his nest to make his own way in the world. But his family was rich, and so the lonely little bird was looking for someone to share Christmas with.

    Pinky concluded her story: "Always remember that you may have all the troubles in the county, but someone else might have all the troubles in the world. Never feel sorry for yourself... Always keep in mind that you're not the only pebble on the beach of life."

    These words would define Pinky Pierce for the rest of her life. Pinky and seven others (four boys and four girls) graduated from seventh grade in 1958. The Old School's total enrollment for all seven grades was 125. Many years later, Pinky reminisced "through all the years, Waterford and the Old School and all of the 'characters' have never left my heart." Pinky's mother, Lucille, "came from an Irish immigrant background, and had a terrible time growing up in the tenements of New York City in the early 1900s. All her life, Lucille pretended to be of English descent." She married a prominent New Yorker, William Wilson, who owned hotels in New York and Paris. When she met Pinky's father, Walter B. Pierce, they had an affair, and she divorced her first husband. After she married Pinky's father, "she went through a wrenching relocation from her glamorous life in Manhattan to mothering two small children in Shepherdstown, West Virginia, where she remained long hours alone with two babies, while my father was away all day at his stock brokerage office in Hagerstown, Maryland." Walter Pierce died when Pinky was very young. Pinky remembered him for "imbuing us with a real love and curiosity about the Revolutionary War."

Lucille married soon after for the third time to Pinky's stepfather, Harold Cahn. Pinky credited him for "a wonderful introduction to all the accoutrements of the Federal Period," and for '"apprenticing" her in his architectural interior design firm at 50 cents an hour from the age of nine—which she said was responsible for "anything I was able to accomplish later on, career wise." She grew up fascinated with history, especially historic architecture, and archaeology, which she called "like digging up old histories."

By the late 1950s, her mother had divorced Cahn, and had "deteriorated into alcoholism and mental illness, and was quite delusional the remainder of her life." Her mother and her friends liked a good glass of whiskey, and her stepfather used to say, "Waterford is the only place I know of where women drive down to pick up the mail at 11 o'clock in the morning with a glass of bourbon in one hand."

Pinky Pierce never finished at the University of Virginia, and many years later confessed: "My dream has always been to go back to school, study American history and civilization and complete my degree." She did get engaged in college, but her fiancé... "married someone else during our engagement, and I never managed to get back on the horse, as they say. I did not follow in my mother's footsteps...divorced; widowed; divorced ...or my dad's, divorced; divorced; died during his third...Never thought I was any kind of candidate for a good marriage so have remained single (and have lived the monk's life) since college...many, many male friends...lucky there was never any involvement other than friendship as now can count on some real guy friends for life."

Pinky Pierce was haunted her whole life by a terrible tragedy that occurred in her sixth grade year. One day, while her mother and stepfather were away and she and her brother were at school, a classmate entered her house..."found my stepfather's service revolver and hid, watching for my brother and me to come home...he watched my brother and me cut across...the back of our yard, up on to the side porch, he fired the pistol thru the downstairs window, narrowly missing my brother's face...Later that day, having tried to set several fires around the house using whiskey he found after breaking the lock on my stepfather's liquor cabinet, found a full five gallon can of gasoline for the lawn mower...and lighting a fire [with leaves] outside our kitchen porch, tried to upend the full can onto the fire to further ignite the flames. The fire from the leaves travelled right up into the gasoline can and imploded, engulfing him in a seventy foot tower of flame...A neighbor wrapped him in a rug to try to extinguish the flames, but he had already run burning all around the far side of our house, up on our porch, then down the steps to Second Street, fully ablaze from all the gasoline."The arsonist was taken to Loudoun Hospital by ambulance and died early the next morning from second and third degree burns over 90 percent of his body.

Many years later, while visiting the Winekoffs, the subject of the fire came up, and Mrs. Winekoff said she was one of the very few survivors of the horrible Coconut Grove nightclub fire in Boston in the 1940s. Mrs. Winekoff "opened the top of her dress and showed me the red scars on her chest and on her throat and arms. Even then, she suffered from breathing and lung troubles as a result of the fire."

By the 1980s, Pinky seemed to be following in her father's footsteps: "I was Vice President-Director of Marketing, Partnership Investment—'heavy lies the head that wears the crown,' ho-hum—for many years for Legg Mason Wood Walker Inc. Members New York Stock Exchange, in Baltimore. My late father had owned his own brokerage firm on Wall Street between World Wars, so, to my brother and mother, who both had high hopes for my aggressive social achievement, this was a 'natural fit' career-wise. I got over THAT as soon as I was able; pissed away all my brokerage money and drifted, sort of consciously, into selling."

Now, I live as I'd always intended, totally unencumbered by "things" and "stuff" having driven (lost one cat, pre my dear Mini) cross-country and back alone twice, landing in odd, small places, meeting ordinary people everywhere. I WORKED three jobs in one place, to overcome the local minimum wage. Best of times! Being a sales person of some achievement (skills, not $$$), since 1987, I've sold Ford trucks; men's suits; appliances...but always keep reading and writing, given any spare time. When I was in the brokerage business, I published over a dozen articles on selling and sales management. Even published a book in 1983 called *Dancing Down Deep With the Blues* about the vanishing road houses in the South. Sadly, all 1,500 copies have vanished into a black hole."

Pinky always loved cats. "Well over forty, I could name thirteen at one time in Waterford alone!" In her final years, she lived with her feral male cat Mini (short for "Minnow"), and with "Marbles," a 20-year-old neutered female cat, whose owner wanted to "put her to sleep." Marbles was in bad shape: down from 16 to just 4 pounds; with severe arthritis of her back, failing kidneys, and a broken front leg which her owner, who had tripped over her, never re-set. Pinky took her home and set about bringing her back to health with the same determination she tackled all of her projects. Marbles was given three meals and plenty of fresh water each day beginning at 4:30am, before Pinky left for work. Marbles got along well with Mini, who regarded her as "a very curious critter, indeed, bump-bump-bumping along...cooing and chirp-chirping (as cats do) to get him to pay attention to her."

Pinky loved and enjoyed Marbles's company for a wonderful fifteen months, before she had to put her down when Marbles' kidneys failed and she could no longer walk or climb.

Feral Mini was the man in Pinky's life: "He dances all over when I come home, chittering and chattering about his 'day.' He is really quite a companion, so handsome, soft and snugly. We watch a little TV or do our reading, then off to bed and another day. Mini gets me up at 6:20 a.m. every morning."

After she discovered a lump in her groin while playing with the cats, Pinky was diagnosed with Stage 3 lymphoma. Three weeks later, Pinky lost her Mini the day she moved from her apartment. The cat carrier opened unexpectedly, Mini jumped out and "bolted so fast no one could see him fly by." An operation revealed that Pinky's cancer had spread to lymph nodes throughout her body. She started intensive chemotherapy and visited the animal shelter twice a week, but there was no sign of Mini. Although Pinky grew very tired, she still worked a full work week at Macy's, and never lost her upbeat attitude: "I am soldiering on as only a Waterford School grad can, slathering on my bronzer, soaping up and shampooing  my shorter summer 'do with expensive roots' nourishing shampoo from Trader Joe's."

She drove around most nights missing Mini terribly and looking for him. She lost 20 pounds and "am clinging for dear life to every gram of fat left on thighs, upper arms, anywhere." She fell in love with two pet brown and white brother rats at the animal shelter, "one very social; the other very shy." She sent her Waterford friend, Kitty, a humorous note and a portrait of the rats, who signed themselves "Bold and Shy Ratatouille." Despite very aggressive chemotherapy, the cancer continued to spread. On September 14, 2009, six months after first being diagnosed with cancer, Pinky Pierce died.

"The only thing we didn't do together was go to school," Karen "Sister" Mallory Spriggs said, reminiscing about her friendship with Pinky Pierce." Skating, bicycle riding, climbing trees, fishing and picking wild berries...this friendship took Pinky away from home, where the environment was chaotic. If, what a lot of things grown-ups do is 'off the wall,' then it is really hard on their children." Sister regrets losing track of Pinky Pierce in later years, but Pinky called her during her last days, and they happily talked about growing up in Waterford.

Although Sister had to attend Waterford's Colored School A for black children, like Pinky, she knew and admired Captain Winekopf, who had also captured the heart of her twin brother Charles. "Brother was always with the Captain. Mother would tell him 'I'll just pack your bag and you can move in with the Winekopfs.' Brother loved the Captain's stories about all his adventures. The Captain was very proud of his last car, a Buick Riviera. The dashboard had a plaque inscribed 'This car was made for Captain Winekopf.' When he was unable to drive it anymore, James Mallory, a cousin of Sister's, became the Captain's driver. When the Captain died, he left the Buick to James.

Sister's first memories are living in the tenant house at Huntley Farm at Waterford's south end. She lived there with her grandparents, Towney and Annie Ferrell. Towney was a carpenter, and had attended the school for black children at Hillsboro through the seventh grade. Annie was a housekeeper and school teacher. Sister's mother, Louise Mallory, had five children while living at Huntley Farm: Teresa; Patricia; Karen (Sister); Sister's twin Charles, whom everyone called "Brother"; and Wesley, the youngest. Sister remembers watching chickens in a huge vegetable garden, and "on a summer's day, everyone would sit on the big front porch after dinner and I would try to catch lightening bugs."

Sometime before Sister was old enough to go to school, Towney bought a house on Main Street, known today as the Goodwin Sappington House (number 40155/40157). Sister said the house had electricity, but no other modern comforts, and that "not one black person that lived in Waterford in the late 1940s–early

1950s had a bathroom, or plumbing or central heating!" Neither did some white folks. One of the unintended consequences of the re-gentrification of Waterford was a widening gap between whites and blacks: in the latter's access to modern services.

Sister says, "I have always been family-oriented, and you greet family members with a hug and a kiss, and then when leaving, you do the same...in my Bible it says, 'enjoy the fruits of your labor,' and that's family. Now, Dad and all the brothers are gone— no uncles left on father's side. On mother's side, two aunts in their 80's are left. We keep in close touch. I talk to my aunt in D.C. three times a week, and call my aunt in Leesburg daily."

Sister's dad died of a heart attack at age 59. Sister and Brother were just seventeen years old. Sister's "baby brother" Wesley was a marine in Vietnam, who was burned over 90 percent of his body by an exploding mortar round. He died of septicemia (blood poisoning) in a Veteran's Hospital. "Baby Brother looked like Bill Cosby...he would imitate Cosby talking. He was *so* funny. Losing him was so quick, it affected us all, especially Brother. He wouldn't talk about it much."

Her own son, Timothy Kevin, is a staff sergeant in the U.S. Army, who has completed five tours in Iraq and Afghanistan. "I never realized how much it affected my mom," Sister said, "until I went through it with my own son." Although the great anxieties and tragedies in Sister's life are related to family members serving in the military, Sister is proud to be part of a military family. Religion has been a big part of her life, and has been a great comfort to her in times of trouble. She is an active member of the Mount Olive Baptist Church in Leesburg, Virginia, and says "the more prayers go up, the more blessings come down."

Dogs were also part of the family. One day, Sister's son Kevin brought a dog home and said "Mom, can I have this dog?" Sister said, "No. We live in an apartment. Wouldn't it be fair to the dog to be confined in an apartment?" He's just a little dog, replied Kevin."No, Kevin," Sister said. "He's going to be a big dog. After the dog came and sat down beside me and kept rubbing his head on my leg, I thought 'oh lord'; we ended up keeping him." "Dunstan" was part of the family for 17 years. Dunstan even had his own real bed. Kevin had a double bunk bed, and Dunstan would sleep on the bottom bunk. Sister says, "Dogs are very smart. They listen to you, and love you unconditionally. They are God's creatures put on earth to heal us."

Sister's education really began at home. "Grandmother was the smartest lady I ever knew. As a young lady, she went to Store College in Harper's Ferry, W.Va. Because she was a school teacher, our education was very important to her. She taught us, and we knew the alphabet, reading, numbers, addition and subtraction. All before we went to school."

Sister attended Waterford's segregated one-room Colored School A from first grade through sixth grade. Her teacher, V.E. Arter, "was a good teacher and disciplinarian; a remarkable lady. She had so many activities for us—music lessons and recitals, and square dancing. Those were good days." Sister's grandmother was a substitute teacher at the school when Miss Archer was not able to be there.

When Sister entered the seventh grade she rode a bus to Leesburg to attend Douglass Elementary School, and later Douglass High School. "Leesburg was a new experience. It was 'city' and I was a country girl. It was a very big adjustment–rushing from one class to another with a different teacher each time. My teachers were all black. I adjusted pretty well. My grades were average." Sister is so proud of her youngest grandson, Carlton, who graduated from Old Dominion University, with a 4.0 grade average. She says, "Grandmother and mother would be overjoyed."Sister says: "I love Waterford. I really do. The things that I did growing up here will always be fond memories for me. I met so many people and experienced the things they did. I would not trade a single year of the 40 I lived here for anywhere else."

# Chapter 32
# Where History Ends Up

**"I understand them enamel tubs can be slippery and are quite dangerous."**
**—Anonymous Waterford Storekeeper**

During 1960-70, the urbanization of Loudoun County began in earnest. Its population increased 54.7 percent (to 37,150), while its farm acreage decreased 16.7 percent (to 216,574). Per acre real estate values soared 199 percent (to $840). A new wave of urban immigrants seeking the country life had arrived, and many Waterford houses were being modernized. New and much deeper wells were being drilled to supply flush toilets, bathtubs, showers, sinks, and machines to wash dishes and clothes. Waterford's septic tanks and drain fields were overwhelmed and overflowing; contaminating the water supply. In 1966, the Loudoun County Health Department declared Waterford a serious health hazard, and the county's governing body, the Board of Supervisors, authorized construction of a sewage treatment plant, which commenced operating in 1980.

Although a small plant was designed, its capacity far exceeded the needs of the village population. Waterford became deeply divided between preservationists who feared the plant would attract further development to the village, which would destroy its historic character, and those whose primary concern was resolving the sanitation issue and preserving their property values. The latter argued against linking construction of the plant to the issue of controlling growth. The preservationists felt the opposite was true, and discussions became heated and emotional. Eventually, a majority agreed the sanitation issue had to be dealt with, and voted in favor of locating the plant as close to the village as possible to prevent development between the two. Construction began in 1976, and the Waterford sewage treatment plant began operating in 1980. It was not unusual for emotions to run high and for feelings to be hurt over proposed changes affecting the village. As in most small towns, issues, which represented a change in Waterford's *status quo*, were perceived by some as a welcome and necessary change, and by others as a threat to their way of life.

The Samuel Hough House provides a case history of one family's resistance to change. In 1966, the house was still heated by fireplaces with coal-fired cast iron stoves, and there was only a cold water "bathroom" next to the well on the side porch, which was unusable in winter. An outhouse was located 40 feet behind the main house juxtaposed to a bed of peonies. Gene and Reid Mays felt very comfortable in the house they had lived in for so long. They did not want electrification, indoor plumbing or bathrooms, because they feared the disruption these changes would bring.

Others felt the same way. On viewing two new indoor bathrooms in a house a few doors down Second Street from the Samuel Hough House, an anonymous local storekeeper said…"I started to put one of these in my house, but the Second World War came around and with the boy being drafted, I never got around to finishing it. Besides, I understand them enamel tubs can be slippery and are dangerous." Other Waterford citizens–including most black residents—did not have the funds to install modern systems and appliances in their houses.

Gene Mays's husband Reid died in 1967 of pneumonia. Gene sold the house for $13,600 to a developer, who constructed a sewer line, septic tank and drain field. Just 18 months later, the developer sold the house for $46,000. To command such a price, the developer drilled a 340 foot deep well in the driveway, installed an electrified well pumping system, a 500-gallon septic tank and sewer line–convincing evidence that the house had no indoor or exterior plumbing before that time—indoor plumbing and bathrooms, central heating, a modern kitchen, and completely electrified the entire house. The National Trust presently holds a total of ten historic easements on buildings in Waterford, and the Samuel Hough House is one of only two houses with an interior easement.

By 1986, the Waterford Homes Tour and Crafts Exhibit had evolved into a handicraft and culinary display spread out all over town. The "Waterford Fair," as it was commonly known, was attracting as many as 25,000 visitors over a three-day weekend. The modest 1946 booklet had grown into a 35=page handbook describing the skills of 215 craft demonstrators clustered around 14 major locations in the village. An art exhibit and mart had been added, with prizes for the best artists. The art exhibit awarded the $2,000 Florence Kiley Fellowship to the best high school senior class artist, to further his or her studies in the fine arts.

Encampments of Civil War re-enactors and Revolutionary War soldiers enticed history buffs. The Iron Men of Loudoun showed off their steam tractors and other machines. Entertainment was provided by a fife & drum corps, dulcimer band, string bands, Morris dancers, fiddlers, cloggers, and various singing groups. A dozen historic houses were open to visitors, including the Samuel Hough House (it still is today). A large easy-to-read map helped visitors find their way. Executive Director Constance Chamberlain urged readers to help save the land around Waterford "which has been farmed for 250 years... there is no place like it anywhere else in the United States."

During 1981-84, the market value of rural land in Loudoun County increased by just 13 percent. During 1985-88, it increased 81 percent as residential construction consumed thousands of rural Loudoun acres. The housing bubble burst in 1989, sending prices skidding downward 10-20 percent. The decline was only temporary, however, and land prices began to climb again, as suburban development moved ever closer to Waterford. An even bigger, far more dangerous housing bubble was in the making, one that would eventually burst with disastrous consequences two decades later.

Since the 1970s, Waterford has been very busy defending the Waterford National Landmark against encroaching development. This meant the Foundation had to defend the Landmark boundaries by buying and preserving land. The largest individual purchase, with a price tag of $3.9 million, was a 144-acre parcel of the Phillips Farm overlooking the entire village. The village rose to the challenge, with the *Journey Through Hallowed Ground Partnership* joining the Waterford Foundation in playing key leadership roles in the acquisition of the Phillips Farm in 2003. The full story of how the village and its supporters managed to accomplish this feat, provides an inside look into historic preservation, initiated and primarily financed by private individuals and organizations, with the strong support of local, state, and federal governments.

But that's another story. For almost three centuries, Waterford has been home to people of different races and religious beliefs pursuing the American Dream. What they have in common is a shared history. Today, Waterford's history is helping other Americans to reconnect with their own past. No matter how brief, a visit to Waterford can be like coming home. Two hundred years from now–barring some apocalyptic natural disaster–Waterford will still be here, "where history ends up."

## About the Author:

Neil C. Hughes has lived with history all his life. In 1989, after a long career in ternational finance, he bought an old house in Waterford, Virginia, built by Quaker Samuel Hough in 1819. Hoping to learn about the village, he joined the Waterford Foundation, a non-profit corporation dedicated to preserving the Waterford National Historic Landmark, and served as board member, president, and an active volunteer in the Lanmark's preservation. During these years, he has devoted himself to the study of the history that surrounds him.

Hughes received his B.A. in history from The College of Wooster in 1959. After a year studying British colonial history at Edinburgh University, he served three years aboard the USS Mills in the U.S. Navy Atlantic Fleet Destroyer Force. After the Navy, Hughes decided on a career in finance, and graduated in 1965 from The Fletcher School of Law and Diplomacy at Tufts University, with an M.A. in international finance and public policy. He joined Bankers Trust Co. in New York, but moved to the World Bank in 1968, and spent the next 33 years working in 25 countries as an industrial and financial development specialist.

Hughes's last World Bank assignment was in China. From 1992 to 2001, he helped state-owned industry in China's largest municipality make the difficult transition from a planned economy to a more market-based one. In 2003, M.E. Sharpe published his book *China's Economic Challenge: Smashing the Iron Rice Bowl*. His articles about China's rise have been published in *Foreign Affairs* (1998, 2005), *Asian Wall Street Journal* (2003), and *The American Interest* (2008).

Photo: Schulyer Richardson

## Acknowledgments

I could not have written this book without the help and support of my wife Kathleen, The Waterford Foundation, The Thomas Balch Library, The Loudoun Mutual Insurance Company, The Loudoun County Circuit Court Archives, John and Bronwen Souders, Richard Edwards and Phillip Ehrenkranz. Many thanks also to Taylor and Cordelia Chamberlin, David and Carolee Chamberlin, Abbie Cutter, John and Mary Fishback, Richard Gillespie, Margaret Good, Calder Loth, Timothy McGinn, Brown and Margaret Morton, Katherine Ratcliffe, Paul and Kitty Rose, Eugene Scheel, Christopher Shipe, Sandy Smart, Edward Spannaus, and Daniel Wallace.

# BIBLIOGRAPHY
## Published & Unpublished Sources

*A Citizen's Guide to Loudoun and the Civil War*. Civil War Sesquicentennial Committee of the American Civil War. Loudoun County, Virginia. Leesburg. 2009

*American Heritage Dictionary of the English Language*. American Heritage Publishing Co. Inc. New York. 1969

Anderson, Fred. *The War That Made America: A Short History of the French and Indian War*. Viking, New York. 2005.

Anonymous. *Abrams Delight*. Nancy Melton Collection. ACC#24. MMF. WFCHS. The Stewart Bell Jr. Archives Room. The Handley Regional Library. Winchester VA.

Anonymous. *History of the Catoctin Presbyterian Church*. Catoctin Presbyterian Church. Unpublished. MS.

Anonymous. *The Waterford Baptist Church*. Unpublished MS. Research by Walter M. Everhart.

Anonymous. *A History of Waterford*. Waterford Fair Booklet. 1948. The Waterford Foundation. Waterford, VA.

Anonymous. The MacCallum House. Waterford Homes Tour and Crafts Fair Booklet. 1953. The Waterford Foundation. Waterford, VA.

Anonymous. *Untitled.* Waterford Fair Booklet 1971. Waterford Foundation Inc. Waterford, VA.

Anonymous. *Houses on Tour*. Waterford Fair Booklet 1987. Waterford Foundation Inc. Waterford, VA.

Anonymous. *Milling in Waterford Virginia, 1740s-1930s*. Waterford Fair Booklet. 1998. Waterford Foundation, Inc. Waterford, VA.

Anonymous. *Easement Program*. Waterford Fair Booklet 2006. Waterford Foundation Inc. Waterford, VA.

Anonymous. *A Blind Man, an Heiress and a Builder: The Remarkable Origins of Waterford's Resurrection*. Waterford Fair Booklet. 2013. Waterford Foundation Inc.. Waterford, VA.

Bacon, Sir Francis. *The Essays: On Seditions and Troubles.* 1601.

*Baltimore American.* June 22, 1864.

*Baltimore Sun.* July 16, 1861.

Bessen, James. *What Looms Tell Us About Workers, Wages.* The Washington Post. January 20, 2014.

*Blue Ridge Herald.* February 14, 1957.

Black History Committee of the Friends of the Thomas Balch Library, Leesburg, VA. *The Essence of a People: Portraits of African Americans Who Made a Difference in Loudoun County, Virginia.* Thomas Balch Library. 2001.

Brown, Stuart F. Jr. *Virginia Baron: The Story of Lord Fairfax.* Chesapeake Book Co. 1965

*Brunswick Herald.* 9 Brunswick, MD, May, 1891.

*Brunswick Herald.*" Waterford Whispers" column, Brunswick, MD, 26 June, 1891.

Cash, W. J. *The Mind of the South.* Alfred Knopf. New York. 1941.

Cather, Willa. *O Pioneers!* Barnes & Noble Books. New York, NY. 1993.

Catton, Bruce. *Grant and the Politicians.* American Heriage. October 1968.

Cave, Alfred. A. *The French and Indian War.* Greenwood Press. Westport, Conn. 2004.

Chamberlain, Joshua Lawrence. *BAYONET! FORWARD! My Civil War Reminiscences.* Stan Clark Military books. Gettysburg, Pennsylvania. 1994.

Chamberlin, Constance. *Waterford: the Challenge.* Waterford Foundation. 1980. Waterford, VA.

Chamberlin, Charlton. Letter to Herbert Mayes, Editor. *Good Housekeeping.* 30 Sept. 1950.

Chamberlin, Charlton. Letter to Margaret Cousins. Managing Editor. *Good Housekeeping.* 31 Oct. 1950.

Chamberlin, Leroy. *Advertisement: Restorations in and adjoining Waterford.* Waterford Fair Booklet. Waterford Foundation Inc. Waterford, VA.

Chamberlin, Taylor, M. and James D. Peshek. *Crossing the Line: Civilian Trade and Travel Between Loudoun County, Virginia, and Maryland During the Civil War.* Waterford Foundation Inc. Waterford, Virginia. 2002.

Chamberlin, Taylor. *Captain Samuel Means and the Loudoun Rangers, Part 2.* The Bulletiin of the Loudoun County Historical Society. 2011 Edition. GAM Graphics and Marketing. Sterling, Virginia.

Chamberlin, Taylor M. and Souders, John M. *Between Reb and Yank: A Civil War History of Northern Loudoun County, Virginia.* McFarland &Company, Inc. Jefferson, NC. 2011.

Chambers, Doug and Bronwen Sounders. *African-Americans in Waterford's History.* Waterford Fair Booklet 1991. Waterford Foundation, Inc. Waterford, VA.

Churchill, Winston S. *The Age of Revolution: A history of the English-Speaking Peoples, Volume III.* Barnes & Noble. New York. 2003.

Conroy, Emma H. "Girls Publish Civil War Newspaper," *Baltimore American*, February 5, 1922.

Constantino, Roberto. *Colonial Catoctin: Colonial Development and Dynamics on or About the Potomac River at Catoctin Creek up to Waterford 1728-1829.* Vol. 2. Heritage Books. Westminster, MD. 2006.

Cousins, Margaret. Managing Editor. *Good Housekeeping.* Letter to Charlton Chamberlin. October 16, 1950.

Crook. Edward L. *Notes of Edward L. Crook.* Waterford Foundation Archives.

Crawford, J. Marshal. *Mosby and his Men.* G.W. Carleton & Co. New York. 1867. Reprint by Bibliolife LLC. Undated.

Cresswell, Nicholas. *The Journal of Nicholas Crestwell 1774-1777.* L. MacVeagh. Editor. The Dial press. New York. 1924.

Crothers, A. Glenn. *Quakers Living in the Lion's Mouth: The Society of Friends in Northern Virginia, 1730-1865.* University of Florida Press. Gainsville. 2012.

Crouch, Richard. *Rough-Riding Scout: The Story of John W. Mobberly, Loudoun's Own Civil War Hero.* Arlington, VA. Elden Editions. 1994.

deCourcey, John. *Personal Communication.* February 27, 2014.

Divine, John E. Undated. Hand Written Real estate transactions for the Samuel Hough House. Waterford Foundation Archives.

Divine, John E. Speech at the Dedication of the Waterford Elementary School. December 6, 1965. Waterford Foundation Archives.

Emerick, O.L. Letter to Douglas Myers. February 19, 1947.

Deck, Patrick and Heaton, Henry. *An Economic and Social Survey of Loudoun County.* University of Virginia. Charlottesville, Va. 1926.

*Democratic Mirror.* Leesburg, VA. 14 March, 1866.

Devine, John. *Waterford in 1863.* Waterford Fair Booklet 1963. Waterford Foundation Inc. Waterford, VA.

Divine, John. *A Bridge is Built.* Waterford Fair Booklet 1966. Waterford Foundation Inc. Waterford, VA.

Divine, John. *Waterford 1864. Waterford Perspectives.* Waterford Foundation Inc. Waterford, VA. 1983.

Divine, John. Preface to Goodhart, Briscoe. *History of the Independent Loudoun Virginia Rangers: 1862-65.* McGill & Wallace. Washington, D.C. 1896. Reprint by Olde Soldier Books, Inc. Gaithersburg, MD. Undated.

Divine, John E. with Bronwen & John Souders. *When Waterford and I Were Young.* Waterford Foundation. Waterford, VA. 1997.

Duncan, Patricia B. and Elizabeth R. Frain. *Loudoun County Marriages After 1850: Volume 1, 1851-1880.* Willow Bend Books. Westminster, MD. 2000.

Duncan, Patricia B. *Loudoun County Virginia Birth Register: 1889-1896.* Willow Bend Books. Westminster, MD. 2002.

Ehrenkranz, Philip. *Open Space Easements in Waterford: Avoiding the Shipwreck.* Waterford Fair Booklet. 1972. Waterford Foundation Inc. Waterford, VA.

Ellers, Joseph J.. *His Excellency George Washington.* Alfred A. Knoff. New York. 2004.

Fairfax, Harrison. *Landmarks of Old Prince William: A Study of the Origins of Northern Virginia.* Vol. I &II. Gateway Press, Inc. Baltimore. MD. 1987.

Finkelman, Paul. *Defending Slavery, Proslavery Thought in the Old South: A Brief History With Documents.* Bedford /St. Martin's. New York. 2003.

Fletcher, Alice C. "Lands in Severalty to Indians: Illustrated by Experiences with the Omaha Tribe." *Proceedings of the American Association for the Advancement of Science* 33. 1884.

Fram, Elizabeth R. and Marty Hiatt. *Loudoun County, Virginia, Death Register, 1853-1896.* Willow Bend Books. Westminster, MD. 1998.

Frederick County Historical Society Website. 2011.

Gamerman, Amy. *Lost and Found: The Saga if the Sacred Buffalo Hide.* The Wall    Street Journal. August 27, 1991.

*Genius of Liberty.* 8 September, 1827; 30May, 1829; 9 May, 1835; 5 September, 1835; and 15 October, 1836.

*Gettysburg National Military Museum and Visitor Center. Official Guide Book.* Beacon Books, Nashville, Tennessee. Undated.

Gillespie, Rich.ard T. Director of Education. *The Civil War Comes Home to Roost.* The Mosby Heritage Area Association.2014.

Gillespie, Richard T. Director of Education. *John Divine's Civil War: A Closing Civil War Interview with Loudoun's Famed Historian.* The Mosby Heritage Areea Association. 2015.

Goodhart, Briscoe. *History of the Independent Loudoun Virginia Rangers: 1862-65.* McGill & Wallace. Washington D.C. 1896. Reprint. Olde Soldier Books, Inc. Gaithersburg, MD.

Grantham, Dewey W. *The Life and Death of the Solid South: A Political History.* The University Press of Kentucky. Lexington, Ky. 1988.

Gray, Lewis C. *The History of Agriculture in the Southern United States to 1860.* 2 Vols. Reprint. Gloucester, Mass. Peter Smith.

Gray, Thomas R. *The Confessions of Nat Turner, the Leader of the Late Insurrection in Southampton, VA, As Fully and Voluntarily Made to Thomas R. Gray.* Published by Thomas R. Gray. Lucas and Deaver, Printers. Baltimore. 1831.

Grey, Gertrude. *Virginia Northern Neck Land Grants: 1694-1742.*

Griffith, Richard. *Abram's Delight.* Newspaper article. MMF 69 W7 CHS. Stewart Bell Archives Room. Stewart Bell Jr. Archives Room. Handley Regional Library. Winchester VA.

Guild, Jane Purcell, ed. *Black laws of Virginia, A Summary of the Legislative Acts of Virginia Concerning Negroes from the Earliest Times to the Present.* Willow Bend Books. Westminster, MD. 1996.

Gwynne, S.C. *Empire of the Summer Moon.* Scribner. New York. 2010.

Hall, Wilbur C. *John Janney of Loudoun.* Civil War Centennial Commission of Loudoun County, Commonwealth of Virginia. Potomac Press. Leesburg, VA. 1961.

Hardin, Terry. Editor. *Legends & Lore of the American Indians.* Barnes and Noble Books. New York. 1993.

Hayes, Kevin J., *The Road to Monticello: The Life and Mind of Thomas Jefferson.* Oxford University Press, Inc. Oxford. 2008.

Hazel, Eleanor Costello, granddaughter of Henry Virts. Bills from William James Store, and, receipt for gravestone tablet in her possession.

Henriques, Peter R. *Realistic Visionary: A Portrait of George Washington.* University of Virginia Press. Charlottesville, VA. 2006.

Hirst, Helen. *Some Early Loudoun Water Mills.* Bulletin of the Historical Society of Loudoun County, Virginia. Vol. 10. 1958.

*Holy Bible. To The Most High & Mighty Prince James, King of Great Britain, France & Ireland, Defender of the Faith.* 1611. Meridian Books. Harrisonburg, VA. 1974.

Holzer, Harold. "Lincoln, Man of Surprises." *The Washington Post.* April, 28. 2013.

Hough, Samuel. Letters to John Hough James dated 10 December 1816; 14 February, 1818; 13 September, 1818; 27 July, 1819; 2 November, 1821. Walter Havighurst Special Collections, Miami University Libraries. Oxford, Ohio.

Howe, Daniel Walker. *What God Hath Wrought :The Transformation of America, 1815-1848.* Oxford. Oxford University Press. 2007.

Hughes Neil C. *Why Preserve Waterford?* Speech to the Rappahannock League for Environmental Protection. June 16, 2000.

Huntington, Sara, and Gale Waldron. *In Their Own Words: Recollections of an Earlier Loudoun.* Meeting House Press. Lincoln, VA. 2002.

Hunton, Eppa. *Autobiography of Eppa Hunton.* The William Byrd Press. Richmond, VA. 1933.

Hutchison, Lloyd. *Corby Hall, John Hough's 'Mansion House,' Circa 1744.* Brochure.

James, John Hough. Letter to Samuel Hough dated April 12, 1820. Walter Havighurst Special Collections, Miami University Libraries. Oxford, Ohio.

Janney, Asa Moore and Werner Janney. *Ye Meetg Hous Small: A Short Account of Friends in Loudoun County, Virginia 1732-1980.* Self Published in Lincoln, VA. 1980.

Janney, Samuel M. *Memoirs of Samuel M. Janney.* Friends Book Assoc.. Philadelphia. 1881.

Janney, Samuel. *Friends Intelligencer.* October 19, 1867.

Johnson, George W. *The Fairfax Correspondence: Memoirs of the Reign of Charles the First.* 2 vols. London. 1848.

Joint Committee of Hopewell Friends. *Hopewell Friends History 1734-1934, Frederick County, Virginia.* Genealogical Publishing Co., Inc. Baltimore, MD. 1975.

Kelsey, Rayner Wickersham, PhD. *Friends and the Indians 1655-1921.* The Associated Executive Committee of Friends on Indian Affairs. Philadelphia. 1927.

Kenworthy, Leonard S. *Quakerism: A Study Guide on the Religious Society of Friends.*

Larson, Rebecca. *Daughters of Light: Quaker Women Preaching and Prophesying in the Colonies and Abroad 1700-1775.* Alfred A. Knopf. New York. 1999.

*Leesburg Record.* Leesburg, VA. July 3, 1903.

*Leesburg Times-Mirror.* Leesburg, VA. 16 May 1929.

Lewis, Thomas A. *For King and Country: The Maturing of George Washington 1748-1760.* Harper Collins. New York. 1993.

Light, Mary Jane Jollif. "The Hollingsworth Family." *Winchester-Frederick County Historical Society Journal.* Vol. II. 1987. Commercial Press. Stephens City, VA.

Link, William A. *A Hard and Lonely Place: Schooling, Society, and Reform in Rural Virginia, 1870-1920.*

Loth, Calder. Email response to Neil Hughes. *"Quaker Interior Decoration in My Waterford House."* September 21, 2009.

Malone, Dumas. *Jefferson the Virginian.* Eyre and Spotswoode. London. 1948.

Marsh, Helen Hirst. *Some Early Loudoun Water Mills.* Vol. I. 1958. The Bulletin of the Historical Society of Loudoun County, Virginia, 1957-1976.

Martin, Joseph. *The 1835 Gazetteer of Virginia and the District of Columbia.* Mosley & Thompkins. Charlottesville. 1835. Reprinted by Willow Bend Books. 2000.

McGavack, J.T. *An Abridged History of the Mutual Fire Insurance Company of Loudoun County, 1849-1940.* Presented to the Board of Directors May 6, 1940.

McGinn, Timothy, H. *How the Evolution of Paved Road Systems Impacted Rural Historic Districts. Waterford, Virginia: Case Study.* Goucher College. Master of Arts Thesis. 2004.

McIntosh, Bruce. Personal Communication. September 22, 2011.

McPherson, James. *Battle Cry of Freedom: The Civil War Era.* Oxford University Press. 1988.

Meserve, Stevan F. *The Civil War in Loudoun County Virginia: A History of Hard Times.* Charleston, SC. The History Press. 2008.

Miller, Virginia Lindsay, and Lewis, John G. *Interior Woodwork of Winchester, Virginia 1750-1850: With Some History and Tales.* Stephens City, VA. Commercial Press, Inc. 1994.

Milner, Clyde A, II. *With Good Intentions: Quaker Work Among the Pawnees, Otos, and Omahas in the 1870s.* University of Nebraska Press. Lincoln, NE. 1982.

Morefield, Betty. *The Freedman's Bureau in Loudoun County, Virginia: Getting Started, June 1865-March 1866.* Bulletin of the Loudoun County Historical Society. Round Hill, VA. 2007.

Morton, Margaret. *Civil War Sesquicentennial: Remembering Sheridan's Devastating Burning Raid on Loudoun.* Leesburg Today. November 20, 2014.

Myers, Douglas. Letter to D. L. Emerick. February 14, 1947.

Myers. Douglas N. *The Old Threshing Engine.* Waterford Fair Booklet 1966. Waterford Foundation Inc. Waterford, VA.

Myers, Douglas N. *I Remember.* Waterford Fair Booklet. Waterford Foundation Inc. Waterford, VA.

National Park Service. Letter to Constance K. Chamberlin, Executive Director, Waterford Foundation. 1986

Patchan, Scott C. *Shenandoah Summer: The 1864 Valley Campaign.* University of Nebraska Press. Lincoln & London. 2007.

Penn Warren, Robert. *The Legacy of the Civil War: Meditations on the Centennial.* Random House. New York. 1961.

Rawls, Wait. *Civil War 150.* The Washington Post. October 9, 2011.

Rhodes, Harriet Bruce. *Abram's Delight.* Hollingsworth Family Papers. Box 2. WFCHS. The Stewart Bell Jr. Archives Room. The Handley Regional Library. Winchester, VA.

Rhodes-Pitts, Sharifa. *Extra Men: The Struggle to Assert Black Humanity.* The New York Times Magazine. October 12, 2014.

Rogers, Polly. *Beginnings.* Waterford Fair Booklet 1981. Waterford Foundation Inc. Waterford, VA.

Ruane, Nihael,Wshington Post. June 30, 2017

Salmon, Marilyn. *Women and the Law of Property in Early America.* The University of North Carolina press. Chapel Hill. 1986.

Sargent, Winthrop. *The History of An Expedition against Fort Du Quesne in 1755 Under Major-General Edward Braddock.* Lippincott, Grambo & Co. Edited from original manuscripts. 1855.

Scheel, Eugene. Letter to Waterford Foundation Board members. May 30, 1972.

Scheel, Eugene. *To the Colored People of Waterford and Vicinity: A study of the Architecture and History of Their One-Room School.* Studies in Vernacular Architecture, School of Architecture, University of Virginia. MS. 1979.

Scheel, Eugene. Interview of Mildred Boyde Gray. November 23, 1979. Harpers Ferry, West Virginia.

Scheel, Eugene M. *Loudoun Discovered: Communities, Corners & Crossroads.* The Friends of the Thomas Balch Library. 2002. Volume Five.

Schreiber, Susan P. *Interpreting Waterford: A Microcosm of Change.* Waterford Foundation. Unpublished MS. May 31 and June 31, 1990.

Shipe, Christopher. President, Loudoun Mutual Insurance Co. Email. September 26, 2011.

Smart, Sally. *Notes to James Family Tree.* MS. Purcellville, VA. Undated

Society of Friends. *Friends Intelligencer.* January 5, 1867. Philadelphia. PA, and, October 19, 1867. Philadelphia. PA.

Society of Friends. *With Much Decorum: The Society of Friends in Loudoun County.* Waterford Foundation Inc. 1996.

Souders, Bronwen. *Brief History of the Old School, Waterford.* Waterford Foundation Inc. Unpublished Education Committee Report. November 12, 1996.

Souders, Bronwen. *Homesick for Waterford.* Waterford Fair Booklet. Waterford Foundation Inc. Waterford, VA. 2006.

Souders, Bronwen. Speech. Ground breaking ceremonies for the new Waterford School auditorium. July 1, 2011.

Souders, Bronwen and John. *Descendents of John Hough Jr.* Unpublished MS.

Souders, Bronwen and John. *The African-American Experience in Waterford.* Brochure. Waterford Foundation Inc. Waterford, VA. 2001.

Souders, Bronwen and John. *Share With Us: Waterford, Virginia's African-American Heritage.* Waterford Foundation Inc. Waterford, VA. 2002.

Souders, Bronwen and John. *A Rock in a Weary Land, A Shelter in a Time of Storm: African-American Experience in Waterford, Virginia.* Waterford Foundation Inc. Waterford, VA. 2003.

Souders, Bronwen and John. *Walk With Us Through Waterford, Virginia.* Waterford Foundation, Inc. Waterford, VA. 2005.

Souders, Bronwen and Kathleen Hughes. *Waterford's Agricultural Heritage, 1733-1993.* Waterford Fair Booklet. Waterford Foundation Inc. Waterford, VA. 1993.

Souders, John. Editor& Annotator. *The Burning Cow Question: And Other Tales From The Waterford Town Council.* Waterford Foundation Inc. Waterford, VA.2000.

Souders, John. "Dust to Dust: A Special Exhibit Recalling Vanished Waterford." Waterford Fair Booklet. Waterford Foundation Inc. Waterford, VA. 2005.

Spannaus, Edward. *Life and Times of Lt. Luther W. Slater (1841-1909).* Unpublished MS.

State of Virginia. District Superintendents Monthly School Report for February, 1868. Loudoun Co. 3rd Division. 10th Sub-District.

Steer, Mary Dutton. *Old Memories.*

Taylor, Henry. *Across the Plains: Autobiography of Henry Taylor.* Unpublished MS. 1923

Valiant, John. *The Golden Spruce.* W.W. Norton& Co. New York and London. 2005.

Walker. Elisha Hunt. *Journal.* 16th& 17th July, & 30th November, 1864.

Walker, Eliza. Letter to her husband James. 27 August, 1862. Facsimile copy courtesy of Virginia Friend.

Walker, Eliza. Letter to her Brother. 4 September, 1862.

Walker, James W. Letter to his Brother. 10 January, 1863.

Washington, George. *The Diaries of George Washington 1748-1799.* John C. Fitzpatrick, Editor. Houghton Mifflin Co. Boston and New York. 1925.

*Washingtonian.* Leesburg, VA, August 24, 1872 and November 7, 1874. Waterford Foundation Archives.

*Washington Post.* *"Hardwood, Not Hard Work."* July 28, 2007.

Waterford Foundation. *Transcription of the Diary of Franklin M. Myers.* Local History Collection.

Waterford Foundation. Craft Exhibit Program. Waterford, VA. 1946.

Waterford Foundation. 43rd Annual Homes Tour and Craft Exhibit. Waterford VA.

Waterford Foundation. *With Much Decorum: The Society of Friends in Loudoun County, Virginia.* Waterford, Va. 1996.

Waterford Foundation. *Milling in Waterford Virginia, 1740s-1930s* Waterford, VA. 1998.

Waterford Foundation. Ad-Hoc Water Supply Committee Report. 2011.

*Waterford News.* Loudoun Co., Va., 5[th,] 6th, 10th, 11th, Month, 1864. VOL. 1, No. 1.

Williams. William. *An Account of William Williams Taken Hostage by the Confederates.* 1888. MS donated to the Waterford Foundation by Susan Williams Pidgeon.

William Williams (1816-1892). MS compiled by John Souders.2005.

Wishart, David J. *An Unspeakable Sadness: the Dispossession of the Nebraska Indians.* University of Nebraska Press. Lincoln, NE.1997.

Worrall, Jay Jr. *The Friendly Virginians.* Iberian Publishing Company. Athens, GA. 1994.

Wright, Catherine M. *Lee's Last Casualty: The Life and Letters of Sgt. Robert W. Parker, Second Virginia Cavalry.* University of Tennessee Press. Knoxville.2008.

*Virts, William Benton. The Waterford Years, unpublished M.S*

## U. S. Government Archives

Library of Congress, Manuscript Division, Papers of Ethan A. Hitchcock.

National Archives. Combined Military Service Records. M-1819. Roll 17. Volunteer Soldiers who served with the 1st United States Colored Infantry.

National Archives, Leesburg Oaths of Allegiance, 9Mar1862, M416, Roll 5, Entry 909.

National Archives. Union Provost Marshall's File, M345, Roll 142.

National Archives Record Group. Office of the Adjutant General, Vol. Service Branch, Entry 496, Box 153, File W-463.

United States Census. 1870. Northern District Loudoun County. Family # 707.

## Loudoun County, Virginia, Circuit Court Archives Division

Loudoun County Circuit Court Archives Division. Bargain & Sale. George William Fairfax to Isaac Hollingsworth. Folio 7. Seventeenth Day of July, 1757.

Loudoun County Circuit Court Archives Division. Folio 21. Will of Isaac Hollingsworth. Fifth Day of October, 1758.

Loudoun County Circuit Court Archives Division. 1759. Order Book A Part II, Folio 533-34.

Loudoun County Court Archives Division. Order Book A. Part II, Folio 622, 1762.

Loudoun County Circuit Court Archives Division. Folio 20, Bargain and Sale. Rachel Hollingsworth (widow) to John Hough Jun. Eleventh Day of April 1777.

Loudoun County Circuit Court Archives Division. Folio 299. Court Order to Appraise the Personal Estate of John Hough Junr. Deceased, January 7th, 1793.

Loudoun County Circuit Court Archives Division. Folio 280. Will of John Hough. 21st Day of Second Month, 1797.

Loudoun County Circuit Court Archives Division. Folio 40. Bargain & Sale. Lydia Hough to Samuel Hough 3rd. Tract of land on Beaver Dam Creek. Twenty Third Day of January, 1816.

Loudoun County Circuit Court Archives Division. Folio 41 Bargain & Sale. Samuel Hough to Isaac Steer and Asa Moore, trustees. Tract of Land on Beaverdam Creek. Twenty Fourth Day of January 1816.

Loudoun County Circuit Court Archives Division. Folio 376. Deed. John Palmer to Samuel Hough. Two lots of 8,225 sq. feet and 3216 Sq. feet. $250. 3/4 acre lot with stable across the street. $151. 19th December, 1817.

Loudoun County Circuit Court Archives Division. Folio 294. Grant. Asa Moore to Samuel Hough. Tract of Land on Beaverdam Creek. 1st November, 1820.

Loudoun County Circuit Court Archives Division. Folio 290. Bargain & Sale. Samuel Hough and Jane his wife to Lydia Hough. $3,500. 1st November, 1820.

Loudoun County Circuit Court Archives Division. Folio 429. Bargain & Sale. Lydia Hough to Mary and Sarah Hough. $1. 20th September, 1830.

Loudoun County Circuit Court Archives Division. Certification of Freedom for Milly Winters. Certified by Clerk of Court Charles Binns, Jr. October 14, 1823.

Loudoun County Circuit Court Archives Division. Folio U, Liber 148. Will of Jacob Mock. 27 July, 1831.

Loudoun County Circuit Court Archives Division. Folio 3Z, Liber 3-5. Grant, Bargain and Sell etc. Samuel Hough and Jane Gray his wife to Andrew Graham. Part of "the Beaver Dam Tract" 13 September, 1832.

Loudoun County Circuit Court Archives Division. Folio 4A, Liber 346-350. Deed of Trust. Samuel Hough and Jane Gray his wife to Charles C. Esknage, Trustee. Indebted to Israel Griffith in the Sum of $1,568 as per Three Notes. "29th June, 1833.

Loudoun County Circuit Court Archives Division. Folio V. Liber 323-325. Estate of Jacob Mock, Deceased. 10 November 1834.

Loudoun County Circuit Court Archives Division. Liber 4G. Folio 192. Bargain & Sale. George W. Hough (Power of Attorney for Mary and Sarah Hough) to Israel T. Griffith. $500. 15th September, 1836.

Corporation of Waterford. Inquisition Indenture taken at the house of the late Israel T. Griffith, Deceased, in the Corporation aforesaid, the 9th day of September, 1839.

Loudoun County Circuit Court Archives Division. Liber 4V. Folio 200. Joshua Ashburn, Special Commissioner of the heirs of Israel T. Griffith to Jonathan Cost. 19th May, 1845. $711.

Loudoun County Circuit Court Archives Division. Liber 5H. Folio 97. Mathew Harrison, Commissioner for Myers and Nichols, trustees (Cost was deceased), to Charles L. Hollingsworth. 17th May, 1853. No amount- to settle a debt.

Loudoun County Circuit Court Archives Division. Liber5P. Folio 41. Charles Hollingsworth to Jacob Scott. 6th May, 1857. $1,500.

Loudoun County Circuit Court Archives Division. Liber 6W. Folio 433. Jacob Scott to W. C. James. 1st April, 1884. $1,800.

Loudoun County Circuit Court Archives Division. Register of Free Negroes. Registry No. 1713. 1844-1861.

Loudoun County Circuit Court Archives Division. Liber 3D, Folio 386. Will of Elijah James. April 30, 1869.

Loudoun County Circuit Court Archives Division. Folio 6E, Liber 45-56. Auction Sale of the Goods, Wares, and Merchandise of F.M. Myers. November 9, 1872.

Loudoun County Circuit Court Archives Division. Liber 6P, Folio 298. Deed. Wm James to Estate of Elijah James. 15 October, 1880.

Loudoun County Circuit Court Archives Division. Liber N, Folio 56. Moffet, Mockbee & Hoff vs. James., January 23, 1883.

Loudoun County Circuit Court Archives Division. Liber 6W. Folio 433. Deed. Jacob Scott to W. C. James. 1$^{st}$ April, 1884. $1,800.

Loudoun County Circuit Court Archives Division. Deed. Wm James to Chas Rinker. Liber 6W, Folio 468. 22 January, 1885.

Loudoun County Circuit Court Archives Division. Bargain & Sale. Chas Rinker to L.P. Smith. Liber 7N, Folio 494. 27 March, 1897.

Loudoun County Circuit Court. Opinion by Justice Edward W. Hudgins of the Virginia Supreme Court of Appeals. November 24, 1941.

Commissioners report to the Circuit Court of Loudoun County, March 18, 1942.

Decision of the Circuit Court of Loudoun County, Virginia. F.C. James and Imogene James Mays versus Peoples National Bank of Leesburg, as Trustee for the Estate of W.C. James, deceased. Judge J.R.H. Alexander, presiding. Undated.

Loudoun County Circuit Court Archives Division. Liber 493. Folio 334. Deed. Imogene J. Mays to Armel H. Heilman. Folio 340. Easement. Florence Ebling to Armel Heilman. 8$^{th}$ November 1968.

**Loudoun County Office of Mapping and Geographic Information.** *Map of Original Land Grants and Current Roads of Loudoun County, Virginia,* 7/16/2009, Map Number 2009-125.

**Prince William, Frederick & Fairfax County Archives**

Prince William County Archives. Deed Book C for 1735-38 (missing).

Prince William County Archives. Deeds Abstracts 1740-1764. "Mead to Janney."

Prince William County Archives. Northern Neck Deed Book E.

Frederick County Archives. Abm Hollingsworth. Will. The first day of November 1748. Facsimile copy. Stewart Bell Jr. Archives Room. Handley Regional Library. Winchester, VA.

Fairfax County Archives. Indenture. Capt. John Minor to Amos Janney. Fifth day of March anno Domini one thousand seven hundred and forty three. Bargain & Sale.

Fairfax County Archives. Commission to Examine the Femme. George the Second by the Grace of God of Great Britain France and Ireland King Defender of the Faith to John Colvill, Daniel French, Garrard Alexander and Townend Dade gent of the County of Fairfax. Witness Catesby Cocke Clerk of our said Court the 12th day of March in the 16th year of our reign.

## Quaker Meetings

East Nottingham Maryland Monthly Meeting Minutes 11th Mo 1732/33 thru 10th Mo 1735 Fairfax Meeting of Friends, Waterford, Virginia, Visitor Log: 6 Mo 1761-11 Mo 18 1812

Fairfax Monthly Meeting(Women's) 19th Century. Waterford, Virginia. Minutes.

Fairfax Monthly Meeting (Men's) 19th Century. Waterford Virginia. Minutes.

## Loudon Mutual Fire Insurance Co. Microfilm

The Articles of Incorporation. March 12, 1849.

Constitution. By-Laws. Undated and Unsigned

Annual Meeting. 6 May, 1861. Secretary's Report. Treasurer's Account. Assets of the Company. Directors of the Company. Local Agents.

Report of the Condition of the Mutual Fire Insurance Co. of Loudoun County, Va. 1 April, 1866

Annual Meeting. 1 May 1871. Retirement of Jacob Scott.

**Internet**

Bruce.Peacock@aspire.net

Densmore, Christopher, Email 7-30-12 family treemaker. geneology.com/users/w/e/b/Dave...UHP-0256.html gen.culpeper.com/historical/nneck/5a-leeds.html genealogical gleanings.com/plagues

Loth, Calder. Email response to Neil Hughes 9-21-09. redwards@unl.eduJanuary 8, 2013&April 16, 2014

Shipe, Christopher. President, Loudoun Mutual Insurance Company. Email. 9-26-11.

Souders, Bronwen. bronwen.souders@gmail.com. October 8, 2014.

Wikipedia. Revenue Acts of 1891 and 1862.